Feminism and Sexual Equality

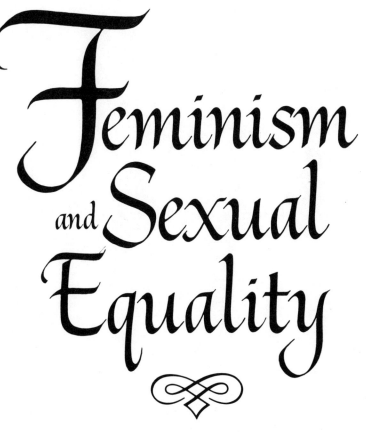

Feminism and Sexual Equality

Crisis in Liberal America

Zillah R. Eisenstein

Monthly Review Press • New York

Copyright © 1984 by Zillah R. Eisenstein
Library of Congress Cataloging in Publication Data
Eisenstein, Zillah R.
   Feminism and sexual equality.
   Includes index.
   1. Feminism—Political aspects—United States.
2. Liberalism—United States.   3. Conservatism—United
States.   5. United States—Politics and government—
1981.   I. Title.
HQ1426.E395   1984   305.4'2'0973   83-4606
ISBN 0-85345-644-5
ISBN 0-85345-645-3 (pbk.)

Monthly Review Press
155 West 23rd Street, New York, N.Y. 10011

Printed in the United States of America
10 9 8 7 6 5 4 3 2 1

for my mother and father,
Fannie Price Eisenstein and Morris Eisenstein

Contents

Acknowledgments

There are several people I very much want to thank for helping me with this book. Miriam Brody, Laura Englestein, Beau Grosscup, Isaac Kramnick, Mary Katzenstein, Susan Buck-Morss, Rosalind Petchesky, Richard Stumbar, Camille Tischler, and Ellen Willis all read sections of the manuscript and provided critical discussion that helped me clarify my argument. I wish to recognize my special appreciation of my friends Ellen Wade, Rebecca Riley, and Mary Ryan for their tireless support; Miriam Brody and Mary Katzenstein for their attentiveness through the summer of 1983, which kept me writing; Rosalind Kenworthy and Elisabeth Bixler for always asking what I was writing about; and Richard Stumbar for the warmth and caring one needs to write. My colleagues Jake Ryan and Bob Kurlander did all they could to help me have time to write. My students at Ithaca College in the tutorials the New Right and the Politics of Sexual Difference kept me from oversimplifying the issues involved.

I also want to thank the various institutions I visited and lectured at while completing this project: Barnard College, Smith College, the University of Michigan, and the University of Wisconsin at Milwaukee and at Madison. Parts of the work, although revised here, appeared as "Antifeminism in the Politics and Election of 1980" (*Feminist Studies* 7, no. 2 [Summer 1981]: 187–205); "The Sexual Politics of the New Right: Understanding the 'Crisis of Liberalism' for the 1980's" (*Signs* 7, no. 3 [Spring 1982]: 567–88); "Some Thoughts on the Patriarchal State and the Defeat of the ERA" (*Journal of Sociology and Social Welfare*, 9, no. 2 [September 1982]: 388–90; "Antifeminism and the New Right," in Amy Swerdlow and Hanna Lessinger, *Class, Race and Sex: The Dynamics of Control* (Boston: G. K. Hall, 1983).

Final thanks to Donna Freedline and Sharon Seymour for all their secretarial skills, to Gert Fitzpatrick for the final typing of the manuscript, and to Karen Judd for her editing.

Introduction

Neoconservatives as well as many leftists and left-liberals argue that today liberalism is in crisis. Neoconservatives believe that the crisis stems from excessive demands for egalitarianism that have created a no-win situation for a liberal democratic society, a society that is supposed to be organized around freedom rather than equality. According to most left-liberals and leftists, liberalism is in crisis because capitalism is in crisis. Markets are not expanding as they once were, third world countries are challenging the hegemony of U.S. world power, and structural changes in the economy have expanded the service sector at the expense of production. None of these critics, however, define the crisis as reflecting a challenge to traditional patriarchal institutions that underpin the relations of capital. New Right groups come the closest to this analysis in their concern with reconstructing the patriarchal, white, heterosexual, nuclear family and the traditional male role as head of household. But even the New Right, which brought family issues and questions of sexuality to the mainstream of politics in the elections of 1980 and 1982, has not systematically articulated why women in the labor force have challenged the system of liberalism so fundamentally, why the notion of equality is as subversive as it is when applied to women, or how feminism's rejection of the public/private split and its recognition that the "personal is political" are central to the crisis of liberalism.

The underlying premise of this book is that liberalism, as an ideology, and capitalism, as its practice, are fundamentally structured by patriarchal social relations and phallocratic ideology. My understanding of the present crisis of liberalism is that its patriarchal foundations—specifically in the family and between the state and family life—are in significant flux and necessitate a reconstitution of patriarchal privilege. Present neoconservative and New Right attempts to restructure sexual inequality represent a major assault against feminism, women's entry into the labor force, and the actual gains made by women *toward* sexual equality.

Not only is feminism—in both its liberal and radical forms—under attack by different factions of the state, but this assault has begun to find its place *within* feminism itself. The basic (mainstream) liberal feminist demands for women's equality before the law (the Equal Rights Amendment), the right to freedom of choice in regard to abortion, and the right to affirmative action are being seriously questioned and attacked by New Right antifeminists such as Phyllis Schlafly, neoconservatives such as Midge Decter, revisionist liberal feminists such as Betty Friedan, and revisionist left feminists such as Jean Elshtain. These developments take place within the wider political context of the Reagan administration's dismantling of the social welfare state. The cutbacks of the social welfare state reflect the state's rejection that it has any role to play in creating greater equality of opportunity for women, whether this means the hiring of professional third world and white women or supplying social services for poor women who are heading families.

One might wonder what has happened to what I have elsewhere termed the "radical future of liberal feminism," given the state's move toward a neoconservative position on feminism and/or right wing antifeminism.[1] Actually, the right wing assault against feminism and the development of what I term revisionist feminism are proof of the continued radical potential of feminism to transform the patriarchal underpinnings of liberalism. If feminism did not have this radical potential the assault on it would not be needed. All feminisms contain aspects of liberal feminism at their core—the demand for equality, freedom of individual choice, and the recognition of woman as an autonomous being. However feminism chooses to define these particular demands, these are its starting points. The demand that woman be treated as equal to (the same as) man, rather than differentiated from him, is a revolutionary demand in terms of the needs of patriarchy. As such, feminism is subversive to liberalism, which is structured by patriarchal relations. Feminism creates a crisis for "the" state and "the" family. It challenges the "male role." Feminism in this sense is somewhat accurately described by the neoconservatives as an excess of liberalism; it takes the promise of individual equality and extends it to women as a sexual class. The negation of feminism is an attempt to restabilize liberalism by rejecting sexual egalitarianism and, with it, equality in general. Liberalism has always had a simultaneous commitment to hierarchy and equality of opportunity. (Liberal) feminism has played a leading role in uncovering the contradictory aspects of liberalism: that equality of opportunity is an unequal system that privileges men by their ascribed status as male. In demanding woman's individual rights for achievement, rather than prescribed ascription, feminism uncovers the "politics of difference" as unequal.

This leads us to the problem of the revisionist feminist rejection of the quest for sexual equality in favor of "sexual difference." Because liberal feminism has implicitly assumed that sexual equality requires that women have the same economic and political rights as men, it has never developed an explicit theory of sexual equality that focuses on sex or the problem of "sexual difference." Feminism in general has not focused on these issues, as revisionist feminists are quick to point out. Revisionist feminism is ultimately reactionary in that it rejects the radical potential of feminism, which is to be found in the liberal feminist demand for sexual equality, and the radical feminist understanding that the personal is political.

In demanding equality—and rejecting the notion that women are different from men (and hence unequal)—feminism has been both subversive to patriarchy and vulnerable to antifeminists and revisionists, who argue that women are simply not the same as men. Clearly this is true on the biological level, in that women have the capacity for childbearing. But this biological fact becomes politically problematic once it is recognized that this capacity has been presented as a liability; thus this "difference" makes a woman less than a man rather than equal to him. As is the case with most political dialogue, one can learn from one's enemies. Feminists need to take the challenge from the right and reactionary feminist forces and begin to delineate a feminist politics that does not deny sexual (biological) difference and is not frightened by sexual equality.

The notion of sexual equality is more problematic than the more general concept of equality, because a simple egalitarianism that assumes sexual sameness will not work. The problems with the view "different but equal" are known. Also bound up with this issue of sexual equality and sexual difference is the concern with sexual freedom. It is on the basis of sexual difference that conservatives have called for the protection of women, rather than their equality. Not until a vision of sexual freedom is defined in relation to sexual equality can feminists hope to move beyond the patriarchal visions of equality that predominate on the left and the right.

However insufficient liberal and radical feminism has been in delineating a notion of sexual equality, it is the demand for sexual equality that has exacerbated the crisis of liberalism, which is a crisis about the meaning of equality. The first part of this book defines the New Right and neoconservative assault against liberalism and the welfare state and explains revisionist liberalism in the 1980s. The second part examines the various revisionist strains within feminism, while distinguishing them from New Right antifeminism, and uses these discussions to move toward a theory of sexual equality that does not reject the radical potential of feminism to move toward egalitarianism.

The political struggles of patriarchal society continue as conservative forces seek to curtail once again the radical aspects of feminism. One cannot predict the outcome. But the purpose of this book is to aid in the process by which women come to a consciousness of themselves as a sexual class, try to take advantage of the gender gap in 1984, and continue to struggle for a radically feminist future.

NOTES

1. Zillah Eisenstein, *The Radical Future of Liberal Feminism* (New York: Longman, 1981).

Part 1
Revisionist Liberalism

The process of reprivatizing the state—the so-called reassertion of the separation between the economy and the state, and redefinition of the relation between family life and the state—has structured American politics through the 1970s. Under the Reagan administration the politics of reprivatization has been fully institutionalized. There are problems, however, with this notion of reprivatization. After all, the state itself defines the realm of what is termed public, and the private realm (of family) is constructed in relation to this initial definition. State and family are therefore not separate realms in actuality but are distinct aspects of a political whole. Nevertheless, the ideological separation of these realms (public and private) is real and has real consequences, as the state takes less responsibility for family life through cutbacks in social services to poor families and less responsibility for certain aspects of the economy, given supply-side economics. It should be noted that reprivatization does not extend to the military or defense departments.

Juxtaposed with this notion of reprivatization is the radical feminist understanding that the personal is political, which rejects the split between public and private life as a tool of patriarchal domination. What appears as private—the realm of sexuality and family life—is recognized as a part of political life, that there is a politics to sex.[1] Family life is defined by the relations of power, which are constructed by and reflected in the state. Radical feminists argue that the so-called private life of the family is political. As such, political solutions are needed for addressing the sexual inequality of power that is structured and maintained in family life.

The division of public and private life as one that differentiates the woman (private) from the man (public) is the overarching ideological tool of patriarchy. The particular historical meaning given to the public and private realms changes, but underlying the distinction between state and family is the universal differentiation of woman from man. The particular division between state and family—which existed in early, competitive, capitalist, patriarchal society—has been challenged by the welfare state in advanced, capitalist, patriarchal society. As the separation of home

16

and market has been subverted by wage-earning women, the state has stepped in to redefine patriarchal relations in the market and in the state in order to protect the distinctness of woman from man, but in partially new form. This need to differentiate woman from man is a basic tenet of patriarchy. Patriarchy is ultimately the politics of transforming females and males (biological sex) into women and men (politicized gender), while differentiating the woman from the man by privileging the man.

As women have entered the market, and as family forms have changed, new forms of patriarchal control are being sought by the state because it can no longer depend on the home/market split as a major political relation to sustain patriarchal control. Women, as they come to occupy both realms, cannot be as easily differentiated from men through an ideology that relegates them to the home or private realm. Woman becomes *less different* from man as she crisscrosses family and market. However, the patriarchal relations of capitalist society necessitate her "difference."

There is a series of alternate approaches concerning what to do about the crisis of the patriarchal foundations of liberal society. Present state politics grows out of these varied attempts to reconstitute male privilege and social order. The New Right and neoconservatives do not agree completely about what to do with the wage-earning woman, or the demands of (liberal) feminists for sexual equality, or family life in general. But they do agree that "sexual difference," rather than an equality that they claim assumes sameness between men and women, should underline the relations between men and women. The rejection of sexual equality in favor of "sexual difference" can be seen as a central part of the reaction to the crisis of liberalism. Patriarchal liberalism, or a commitment to equality of opportunity rather than an equality of conditions, is premised on sexual difference. To the extent that feminism had demanded equality of conditions for women, it has exposed the inadequacy of liberalism to supply equality for women, given its patriarchal priorities, that is, the differentiation of woman from man.

As we shall see, the reformulation of the distinction between equality of opportunity and equality of conditions is central to the neoconservative analysis of the crisis of liberalism. Neoconservatives believe that expectations surrounding one's right to equality have become excessive and detrimental to the political order of society. All one has is a right to an opportunity to achieve, not a guaranteed right to an equal outcome. Interestingly enough, liberal feminism, in arguing for the same equality of opportunity for women that men have, has uncovered the structural constraints that make sexual equality a radical demand. Although liberal feminism has demanded only equality of opportunity, not equality of conditions, the demand for opportunity leads to a demand for greater equality. In this sense, equality of opportunity for women is subversive.

Liberal feminism recognizes the rights of individual women, their autonomy, their right to freedom of choice and legal equality. It also recognizes, however implicitly, that women constitute a sexual class, set apart from men, with different political and economic rights. Affirmative action is an example of how liberal feminists have demanded that individual women be given the rights that have been denied to them as members of a sexual class. Affirmative action begins to uncover how the demands of liberal feminism have gone beyond liberalism. Affirmative action implies a collective identity that must be addressed. As such it puts real demands on individualist-based (patriarchal) liberalism. It is important to note that it has not been as easy for the administration to disregard the tenets of liberal feminism as it has been for them to reject welfare-state liberalism; witness the gender gap as a response to Reagan's antiabortion, anti-ERA stance. Nevertheless, as the United States has moved in the 1970s from a liberal (welfare) state to a neoconservative state, there have been attempts to reject liberal feminism in favor of a revisionist or neoconservative form of it.

NOTES

1. See some of the earliest feminist discussions of the politics of sex in Shulamith Firestone, *The Dialectic of Sex* (New York: Bantam, 1970), and Kate Millett, *Sexual Politics* (New York: Avon, 1971).

1. Antifeminism in the Politics and Presidential Election of 1980

To understand the challenges that feminism faces in the 1980s, we need to clarify the political significance of Ronald Reagan's 1980 presidential election victory. Beyond understanding the election itself, the purpose of this discussion is to examine the systematic attempt by the state to deradicalize the women's movement by trying to dismantle the reproductive rights and pro-abortion forces, because they are the most forceful arm of the feminist movement today. The nonratification of the Equal Rights Amendment (ERA) and the threat to draft women have been used by the state as weapons to limit women's demands for reproductive freedom. Abortion has become the central issue that the state seeks to control because abortion directly relates to the issue of women's reproductive freedom as part of their self-determination. This self-determination is directly at odds with patriarchal control. To the extent that the state is rooted in the patriarchal differentiation of women from men on the basis of women's reproductive capacities, the state fights to directly control this aspect of women's lives.

The 1980 Presidential Election: Was It a "Mandate"?

Some analysts argue that Reagan's "landslide" victory was an overwhelming endorsement of his campaign positions, among them his militaristic and antifeminist policies. I think instead that his victory was not a landslide at all but, rather, reflects a small, highly mobilized and organized section of the electorate alongside a much larger, disorganized, disenfranchised public that did not vote. In other words, although the 1980 election highlighted the shift to the right *within the state itself* (a shift that was initiated under Carter), this is not the same as massive or even majority

19

support for this shift by the public. To understand the so-called Reagan mandate, we need to first delineate the central political issues presented to the public in the 1980 presidential election.[1]

Although Democrats lost the elections of 1938, 1946, 1952, 1968, and 1972 because of right-wing assaults, the 1980 defeat of Jimmy Carter was different in that feminist issues were a central aspect of the right-wing attack.[2] One can argue that this antifeminism is what distinguishes the New Right from the Old Right. This is actually quite different from saying that the defeat of Carter reflects an "antifeminist mandate," because people who rejected the antifeminist assault by the New Right had no significant way of voicing this opinion. Those who wanted an alternative to conservatism and antifeminism did not think they could find it in Carter.[3] And this attitude about the lack of choice for president seems to have carried over to the senatorial races involving other liberals, such as John Culver, Birch Bayh, Frank Church, George McGovern, and Gaylord Nelson, even when there was a significant difference in orientation between the liberal and conservative candidates.[4] As a result, the election mobilized the small but dedicated antifeminist forces and disenfranchised most other elements of the public. This was significant insofar as a small proportion of the eligible electorate votes in American elections today, making it possible to win with a very small but committed bloc of voters. Two things appear to be true. First, the right wing presented a "pro-family," antifeminist politics that was central to Reagan's platform, and therefore the election mobilized this key segment of voters. Second, a majority of the electorate who voted did not vote on these issues but, rather, voted on issues related to the economy. The discontinuity in election politics (what the public is presented and what the public's real choices are) should not be allowed to mask the contradictory reality that antifeminism—on the level of partisan struggle and legitimation within the state—was and is central to the politics of the 1980s; at the same time, the presidential vote itself cannot be read as an endorsement of antifeminism.

Thus it is possible to make sense of the seemingly contradictory analyses of the election by George McGovern on the one hand, and Eleanor Smeal and Karen Mulhauser on the other.[5] McGovern stated in his concession speech that antifeminism was of real significance in the election. "The family issue raised by the right wing was a code word for putting women back in the kitchen, stripping them of any decision on the question of abortion, and forcing them back into the old orthodox roles." Smeal, former president of the National Organization for Women (NOW), argued that the 1980 vote was not a vote on the women's movement but was a protest against inflation, unemployment, and Carter's foreign policy. Mulhauser, then president of the National Abortion Rights Action League, also believed that the 1980 election was not a referendum on the role of women. These statements reflect the contradictory nature of American politics. The party platforms—on the level of election ideology—presented the women's issue as the major difference between the parties. However, it would appear that a majority of the American public recognized these differences as election rhetoric and therefore, if they voted, made their decisions on other issues. A small right-wing element of the electorate embraced the ideology as real policy and elected Reagan to carry it out.

Although Carter presented a pro-ERA platform (which the women delegates of the Democratic party fought for), his record on women's issues had been extremely poor. Therefore, one can begin to understand that although issues relating to the family and women's rights were central to the presidential election in the way they were presented to the public, the public could not and did not turn the election into a referendum on abortion rights, the ERA, and so forth, because there was no appreciable difference in the candidates once Carter's record was compared with Reagan's platform.

The voter turnout in 1980 was approximately 53 percent of the potential electorate.[6] In other words, only slightly more than half of the eligible voting public chose to vote in this past election, or almost one-half of the voting public chose not to vote. Of this 53 percent, Reagan polled 27 percent and Carter polled 22 percent. Ultimately, approximately one-fourth of the potential electorate voted for Reagan and three-fourths did not. This compares with Lyndon Johnson's 38 percent of the vote of the potential electorate in 1964, Richard Nixon's 34 percent in 1972, and Carter's 27 percent in 1976.[7] Reagan was elected with approximately the same percentage of votes that Carter won with in 1976. No one called it a mandate in 1976. Instead, there was great concern about the problem of the shrinking electorate.

What is even more significant to note is that most people who voted for Reagan did not vote for him as a "true conservative." The *New York Times*/CBS News poll reported that only 11 percent of those who voted for Reagan were primarily motivated by his conservative policies and that 38 percent were primarily motivated by dissatisfaction with Carter.[8] In other words, *only 11 percent of adult Americans cast a vote for Reagan that was predominantly motivated by approval for Reagan's conservatism.* Although Reagan's conservatism cannot be equated with his antifeminism, I think it is fair to assume that people voting for him as a conservative were at least partly voting for his antifeminist, "pro-family" platform. Today these policies are central to his identification as a conservative. In any case, this 11 percent cannot accurately be called a popular mandate for conservatism or antifeminism. Interestingly enough, 11 percent recurs as a significant indicator of conservative support in more recent samplings of national public opinion. In reaction to Reagan's 1984 proposed budget, 48 percent of those surveyed believed that the United States was spending too much on new weapons, 25 percent thought spending levels were about right, and 11 percent believed that more money should be spent on new weapons systems. As well, in a January 1983 CBS public opinion poll, 11 percent of those surveyed thought that U.S. aid to El Salvador should be increased.

The people who voted for Reagan reflect the backlash effect of a society in transition. Of the housewives and retired women who voted, 52 percent voted for Reagan and 41 percent voted for Carter. In a society where a majority of married women are in the labor force, it is interesting to note that it is these women who made the significant difference in voting patterns between Reagan and Carter; they split 46 percent to 45 percent. Men backed Reagan by a 56 percent to 36 percent edge.[9] Women who favored the ERA gave Carter 63 percent of their vote; women against the ERA voted for Reagan by a 31 to 69 percent margin.[10]

A February 1981 *Newsday* poll that was conducted nationwide found that approximately 72 percent of those polled were in opposition to a constitutional amendment making abortion illegal.

And although the Moral Majority launched an intense lobbying campaign to defeat a Maryland bill allowing school counselors to give venereal disease (VD) and pregnancy information to students, the bill passed. After Nancy Stevenson, South Carolina's first women Lieutenant Governor, refused to reappoint two anti-ERA senators to a study committee on state employees because she thought that senators serving on the committee should be sensitive to discrimination in hiring and promotion practices, and she assumed their anti-ERA stance would inhibit such sensitivity, she was deluged by mail running three to one in favor of her action.[11]

By pointing out the small number of people who voted for Reagan as a conservative, I do not mean that these small numbers are insignificant. They reflect the well-mobilized New Right, which represents an enormous danger in that it both instigates and endorses the movement of the state to the right. Nevertheless, it is important to put their political clout in the perspective of the American public in general. One must recognize that this "other" (non-voting) public exists, especially because it is this public that must be mobilized against the New Right assault. Although Reagan's election represents a victory for antifeminist forces within the state, the greater part of the American people, I believe, can be described as "feminist," if feminism is defined as the mainstream politics of liberal feminism.

Liberal Feminism and the State

What is interesting about the 1980 election is that Reagan challenged feminist demands emanating from the mainstream of the women's movement, that is, abortion rights and the ERA. This centered the attack on the liberal feminist section of the women's movement, the popular and well-supported part of the movement, which embraces the (liberal) values of freedom of choice, individual self-determination, and equality before the law, specifically for women.[12] The fact that the assault against feminism has taken on the women's movement at its most popularly supported point is due, I think, to the fact that the liberal feminist movement has been radicalizing its demands and by doing so has begun to uncover the real conflicts within the state over how to restabilize family life and, with it, patriarchy.

Liberal feminism is actually a more complicated political phenomenon than it is usually understood to be. It is more than the simple addition of liberalism to feminism because its feminist commitment derives from the recognition that women are members of a sexual class and as such are excluded from liberal democratic rights. This understanding of women as a sexual class conflicts with the liberal individualism of bourgeois thought. Although many liberal feminists are not self-consciously aware of this conflict, it remains potentially subversive to liberalism and the capitalist patriarchal state, particularly as long as women are involved in the struggle for their equality. It is through this repeated struggle that woman's understanding of herself as part of a sexual class develops. Actually, persons in political power are more aware of this potentiality than many feminists are.

Although there are sectors within liberal feminism that are not radicalizing their demands, the state is the most concerned with the factions that are. It is important at this moment in our history to understand that President Carter actively tried to demobilize the radical faction of the liberal feminist movement, those who sought to change the everyday conditions of the majority of women by focusing on women's sexual-class identity across economic class and racial lines. (In this sense one could argue that he laid the foundation for Reagan's antifeminist election platform.) Carter's firing of Bella Abzug was toward this end. But Abzug's firing also reflected the high level of factional conflict within the state over woman's role in society. While part of this conflict is manifested in different solutions for salvaging the troubled traditional nuclear patriarchal family, another part occurs in different state strategies for demobilizing the radical tendencies of the liberal feminist movement. As we shall see, Carter's and Reagan's election platforms were indicative of this instrastate conflict.

Abzug's dismissal as co-chair of the National Advisory Committee on Women was explained as a personality clash between her and President Carter. It is said that she (as well as her committee) overstepped the bounds of legitimate criticism. The controversial report by the committee questioned Carter's anti-inflationary program as ignoring women's particular needs and their role in the economy; it criticized the large expenditures in military and defense as extravagant; and it requested a firmer commitment toward the ERA from the administration. It also condemned the administration for the ban on Medicaid abortions.

In several interviews after her firing, Abzug said that what really angered Carter was that women spoke out on economic issues, that women had strayed from women's issues as they had been narrowly defined by the administration. They had supposedly entered the male domain. Her committee made clear that the economy is a woman's issue when women earn fifty-nine cents for every dollar earned by a man. Inflation hits women harder, an inequity present state policies do not recognize. The committee criticized Carter's anti-inflation program for imposing

> additional and disproportionate burdens upon women because of possible increases in unemployment rates, slashing social and other human needs programs . . . absence of child care programs, so urgently needed by women, and the failure to address the widespread poverty and the financial plight of our cities, where a majority of women and all Americans live.[13]

The major fear the Carter administration had was that women were beginning to connect the relationship in their lives between economic exploitation and sexual subordination. This is what Carter had to stop—the radical elements within the liberal feminist movement that identify the sexual-class nature of women's oppression and its specific impact on women of different races and economic classes.

Abzug's dismissal was an effort by Carter to further legitimize the narrow legalistic interpretation of the ERA, rather than the broader view that connects women's rights to questions of the economy, abortion, and homosexuality. Whether Abzug herself was actually any more progressive than her temporary replacement, Marjorie Bell Chambers, was irrelevant; she had come to represent these broader political issues to the public. Whatever else Chambers was, she was not connected to the more radical elements of liberal feminism. The New York Times reported that while she had been active in fighting for improvements in the legal status of women, she generally stayed away from the controversial issues, such as abortion and lesbian rights. At the time of her temporary appointment, Chambers was instructed by Carter to stick to "women's issues" and that the economy was not considered a woman's issue. Abzug's permanent replacement, Lynda Byrd Robb, was explicitly chosen to represent the narrow concerns of liberal feminism, as opposed to Abzug's concern with poor women and Medicaid abortion, wage-earning women and questions of inflation.

Another example of an attempt to deradicalize feminism can be seen in the threat to draft women put forward by liberals in the Carter administration as well as by members of the New Right such as Jerry Falwell and Phyllis Schlafly. The issue of drafting women in 1980 was intended to confuse the issue of women's equality and thereby demobilize the current women's struggle for sexual equality. After all, how does one fight for equality when it is defined as the drafting of women into the armed forces?[14] The issue of drafting women has been raised specifically within the larger political context of antifeminism and is an attempt to stifle feminists' more radical demands. Once one understands this political context, I think it is much easier to recognize that the drafting of women has little if anything to do with being for the equality of women.

If women are drafted, they will be drafted into non-combat positions in the army, that is, cooks, clerks, and so forth. When asked whether he supported the drafting of women, a young man is quoted as saying, "Yes, my sister would make a good cook." The draft would merely reproduce the sexual hierarchy within society inside the military. In this instance, the drafting of women would only further burden women with more responsibility and duplicate their lack of freedom.[15]

Actually, one might speculate that the call to draft women has been used as a punishment to feminists (specifically the ERA) for demanding equality and reproductive freedom. But it is also true, as Sara Ruddick has argued, that "by allowing men exclusive control over the means of violence one endorses the division between protector and protected and sustains masculinist ideologies."[16] While the issue is not a simple one, the drafting of women will be acceptable only *after* the *real equality* of women (not merely equal legal rights) is established. If we recognize that the state never has women's sexual equality at heart, then we must always try to decipher what the real interest of the state is. In this instance, the threat of registering or drafting women is used to confuse and thus contain the struggle for women's equality.

Sexual Politics in the 1980 Election

A study of the platforms of the Democratic and Republican parties is important in sorting through the question of sexual politics for the 1980s. What quickly becomes evident is that the platforms represent different ideological stances on the issues of reproductive rights and hence abortion, questions of sexuality, and inadvertently the family, and women's equality, that is, the ERA. The Republican party platform specified its commitment to women's equality, but not the ERA, clearly opposed abortion, and embraced the values of the traditional patriarchal family:

> We reaffirm our party's historic commitment to equal rights and equality for women. We support equal rights and equal opportunities for women, without taking away traditional rights of women such as exemption from the military draft. . . . We oppose any move which would give the Federal Government more power over families. . . . As champions of the free enterprise system, of the individual, and of the idea that the best solutions to most problems rest at the community level, Republicans must find ways to meet this [child care], the working woman's need. . . . We reaffirm our belief in the traditional role and values of the family in our society. . . . We affirm our support of a constitutional amendment to restore protection of the right to life for unborn children. . . . We protest the Supreme Court's intrusion into the family structure through its denial of the parents' obligation and right to guide their minor children.

The Democratic party platform presented a counterview. It supported the ERA, reproductive freedom, and the legalization of abortion, and was critical of the Hyde Amendment:

> The Democratic Party commits itself to a Constitution, economy and society open to women on an equal basis with men. The primary route to that new horizon is ratification of the equal rights amendment. . . . The Democratic Party shall withhold financial support and technical campaign assistance from candidates who do not support the E.R.A. . . . The Democratic Party supports the 1973 Supreme

Court decision on abortion rights as the law of the land and opposes any constitutional amendment to restrict or overturn that decision. . . . The Democratic Party recognizes reproductive freedom as a fundamental human right. We therefore oppose government interference in the reproductive decisions of Americans, especially those governmental programs or legislative restrictions that deny poor Americans their right to privacy by funding or advocating one or a limited number of reproductive choices only.

In contrast to the stated differences on issues related to women, the platforms were strikingly similar on issues related to the economy, defense, and military spending. Both platforms share the New Right and neoconservative analysis that government has grown too big in the social service areas and has become too small in defense-related activities. One is left to ponder how and why the issues of sexual freedom and family life were brought to center stage and approached so differently. Actually, this was done primarily by the Republican party and Reagan. I would argue that if Carter had had his way, he would have chosen to keep questions of the working mother and family life out of the campaign because it brought attention to the reality that he had done very little for women. The ERA was not ratified, women lost ground in the struggle to obtain access to abortion during his tenure, and the economic position of women worsened. Carter's $16 billion slash in domestic spending hit many of the programs affecting women the hardest, because they are a majority of the low-wage earners, the poor, and the welfare population to begin with. Women's unemployment rate continues to be higher than men's, with third world women having the highest jobless rate. Although Carter claims to have appointed more than 1,990 women to top policy jobs, these were only 22 percent of his major appointments, and about 1,000 of these women were named to honorary, unpaid, temporary posts.[17] In actuality, about 11 percent of his appointments were women. And as Mim Kelber noted in an article in The Nation, Carter told his Bible class that "women have gone about as far as they ought to go now."[18]

How was one to take seriously a candidate who politically mouths women's equality and whose record stands as such? It is true that it appeared that the issue of women's equality was really at stake in this election. What was not clear, however, was whether there would be a difference between Carter's and

Reagan's attempts to actualize women's equality. Carter did differ from Reagan in that Carter believed that the state must, in today's age of the wage-earning mother, embrace the ideology of liberal feminism, but in its narrowest, most legalistic, form. However, he did little of substance about even this limited version. As a result, although it might appear that he should have used liberal feminist rhetoric against Reagan's use of New Right, "pro-family" rhetoric, he could not; his record tied his hands.

Reagan thought he had nothing to lose by centering his campaign on an antiabortion and so-called pro-family politics. He assessed the situation in purely instrumental terms, and that means he courted the segment of the population with a high voter turnout that could be counted on to support his antifeminist platform. He assured himself of an interested and dedicated section of the electorate, even if it was a small minority of the potential voting population. Because the voting electorate is shrinking, Reagan fought for the few who do vote. When one looks at who votes, one sees that "among married women close to two-thirds vote in most elections, whereas fewer than half of single women do."[19] The median age of the American electorate is fifty. In recent presidential elections, persons from forty-five to sixty-four years of age voted in the largest numbers. If married women between the ages of forty-five and sixty-four are the high-voting-turnout bloc, it becomes understandable how Reagan thought he was courting the vote with his "pro-family" politics. Many of the women in this age group are frightened by the ERA in that they fear it will deny them the security and protection they feel (and may need) from the traditional patriarchal family, which still defines their lives to a large extent. The ERA, in their estimation, has come too late for them. At the age of fifty, after raising their children, they do not want to think about their "rights" within divorce. The women the Republican party courted are the women who are economically dependent on their husbands and therefore do still obtain security within the nuclear family. One may hazard a guess that the Republican strategy worked. One should not forget, however, that it was men who disproportionately voted for Reagan, not women.

The women who did vote for Reagan reflect the backlash effect of a society in transition. Alan Crawford writes more generally about this element of the New Right when he states:

> It is in this sense a status revolt, growing out of deep anxieties on the part of those Americans who . . . are unyoung, unpoor and unblack, middle-aged, middle income and middle minded, who fear that the culture is being controlled, more and more, by "new morality" liberals.[20]

In particular, women who support the New Right and/or the right-wing faction of the Republican party fear equality (whatever this may mean to them) and prefer "preferential treatment." Their politics grow out of their particular position within the traditional patriarchal family even though this family form is itself undergoing serious transformation.

Therefore, Reagan's support of the New Right's "pro-family" platform embraced the ideology of the sanctity of motherhood and the traditional nuclear family. This, however, is an outmoded ideology for a society that requires that more than 50 percent of its married women enter the labor force as well as care for their families and their homes. The woman who functions exclusively as a mother in the home represents a dying breed. But if this is so, why did the Republican party take this position? Clearly they thought they could win with it, and they did. This, however, says little about what they will, or can, do with it after having won the election. This question becomes even more significant once one recognizes that a majority of American women, and even a large proportion of American men, are liberal feminists in that they believe in equality before the law, freedom of choice, and individual rights for women. Peter Steinfels, in *The Neo-Conservatives: The Men Who Are Changing America's Politics*, has written about the American public's commitment to liberal values: "They are Americans, and Americans are optimistic liberals. That is, 'equality, no matter how abused or disused,' has always been the prevailing American norm."[21] It is this attachment to liberalism, particularly when applied to women, that the New Right and conservative factions of the Republican party have reacted against. And yet it is these liberal values that may serve as a brake on the militarism and antifeminism of the New Right.

What must be remembered is that a majority of both men and women have been found to be pro-equality. The liberal values of individual rights and freedom of choice underlie the support of the ERA and abortion rights.[22] This is why there is such wide support for both by the public as a whole, which embraces the ideology of liberal individualism. When asked if a woman and her doctor should make the decision about abortion, approximately 74 percent of those polled said yes. Sixty percent of the public supported the Supreme Court's decision to legalize abortion in the first trimester of pregnancy.[23] The liberal values of individuality and equality lay the basis for the wide level of support for liberal feminism; it seems only logical to apply these same values to women. The problem is that it may appear logical to feminists, but in the end there are contradictions between liberalism and feminism that Carter tried but was unable to resolve. This is why the attack by Reagan has been against liberal feminism itself, that is, the ERA and abortion rights.

Much of Carter's attempt to deradicalize the women's movement was done by making liberal feminists think he supported their concerns by giving lip service to the ERA. It is hard to say which program will prove to be more damaging in the long run: Carter's, which allowed important notions of women's equality to be made vacuous by not implementing them, or Reagan's, which asserts an antifeminist position. I would argue that both are severely damaging to the struggle for women's equality. Both positions use and abuse issues related to establishing women's greater freedom and sexual equality.

In essence, I am arguing that the supposed differences between Reagan and Carter on the family, reproductive rights, and sexuality operated more on the level of ideology than in substance. In fact, the clarification of these differences is what the 1980s are about. For now it seems clear that the 1980 election presented us with *politics as ideology*. This is not to deny that there were real differences and political forces at work behind these ideologies. There was a real difference in the constituencies of the Republican and Democratic parties, which had an impact on the ideologies of this campaign. The National Organization for Women's refusal to endorse Carter in the 1980 election and its decision to campaign actively against the New Right forces within the Reagan camp is testimony to liberal feminists' belief that politics as ideology, with no real gains for women, is no longer permissible.

Militarism and Antifeminism

The theme of the 1980 election was the need to make America strong—by strengthening the family, the economy, and the military. The neoconservative and New Right analysis of the crisis of American democracy explains it as a crisis of the authority of the state and of the family, respectively. The New Right answer to the problem is to reconstitute the traditional patriarchal family and to reconstruct what neoconservatives envision as authoritarian democracy, or what Bertram Gross calls "friendly fascism."[24] Pro-family politics, which is basically antifeminist, anti-detente, anticommunist, and anti-affirmative action, provided the ideological language for arguing for a strong America. The present instability of society must be remedied by reconstituting the authority of the family and the state—at home and abroad. In this sense, pro-family ideology helps to construct the militaristic mentality that seeks to justify the necessity of "moral mothers" (and the patriarchal family) and "moral wars" (the new militarism). *The point, then, is not that sexual politics merely served as a gloss in the 1980 election for the (real) politics of the unstable economy, but rather that the authority of the patriarchal family—the institutionalizing of hierarchical sexual structures—was seen as central to reconstituting and restrengthening America.*

To fully follow this argument one must understand the "institution" of motherhood as political.[25] Motherhood reflects much more than the biological differentiation of female from male because the female can bear children; it reflects the self-conscious political differentiation of woman from man. Therefore the state deliberately constructs the institution of motherhood as much as it constructs the military state apparatus. Females can sexually reproduce and lactate. These are biological facts. That women are *defined* as mothers is a political fact and reflects a political need of patriarchy, which is based partially in the biological truth that women bear children.[26] The transformation of the female from a biological being (childbearer) to a political being (childbearer and mother) is part of the conflict that is expressed in the politics of patriarchy. Patriarchy seeks to maintain the myth that patriarchal motherhood is a biological reality, rather than a politically constructed necessity. The state's embodiment of the public/private

division, which is fundamentally a man/woman division, aids in
this process. The state legitimates the notion that women function
outside the public realm as noncitizens and nonrational beings;
they are mothers. Patriarchy tries to enforce this vision so that the
equation between childbearing and childrearing is seen as natural
and inevitable.

Any system of power must have a purpose, and in this case it is
the creation of children and the mothers to rear them. Power implies the ability to limit choices for others. The priorities of patriarchy, as a system of power, are to keep the choices limited for
women so that their role as mother remains primary. Because
early child care is female-dominated, boys and girls alike learn
that it is women who will rear the children. This reproduction of
gender roles, and of new generations of mothers, supplies society
with the most basic form of hierarchical social organization and
hence order. The woman as mother is revealed most easily
through her role in the reproduction of the species. Derived from
this are the most subtle forms of patriarchal organization, that is,
the sexual division of labor in the labor force, the division between public and private life, the ideological separation of political and family life. The separation of woman from man
constructs a dichotomous worldview that limits insight into the
structure of patriarchal organization itself. Woman defined as
mother structures the either/or mentality. Therefore, when I argue
that patriarchy seeks to maintain the idea and reality of woman as
mother, I mean this in the broad political sense of the term as well
as in the narrower biological sense. The biological definition of
motherhood grasps only a small part of its meaning in patriarchal
society. Motherhood also involves the notion of woman as a caring, emotional, dependent being. This reflects the political construction of motherhood, which means that there is nothing
natural about it; it is consciously organized and deliberately constructed to meet particular social requirements.

Relegated to her supposedly biological role as a mother, woman
is sidelined into the private sphere of the home and the family.
Because patriarchal ideology presents motherhood as natural,
woman's assignment to the private sphere and dismissal from the
public realm is argued as a defense of the natural order of things.
The logic derives from patriarchal needs themselves. The confus-

ing issue is that the politics of assigning women a sphere different from men can be mystified by using women's biology. The complicated reality is that women do bear children, but until this biological fact is distinguished from the political motivations of patriarchy, one cannot recognize the role of patriarchy in the assignment of woman to the private sphere, man to the public. Patriarchy erases the evidence of its presence on this individual level through the invocation of woman's biology to determine her social and political condition.

The antifeminist stance of Reagan, presented through the "pro-family" argument, seeks to reestablish the traditional patriarchal foundations of society by defining woman as a mother in the political sense. This antifeminist stance underlines the militaristic mentality of restrengthening America: restrengthen the authority of the father and one will reestablish the "moral mother" and the "moral society." The moral mother is defined by the New Right as the woman who is circumscribed by her duty to others. Her life is ordered by her responsibilities within the patriarchal division of labor: she is a mother and wife before she is anything else. The moral society merely reflects the hierarchical order between man and woman. In this sense, according to the New Right's conception, the moral mother cannot be a feminist.

The stance that is implicit in the antiabortion movement seeks to posit the rights of the unborn in opposition to the rights of women. The concern with "reproductive freedom" is presented as self-indulgent and narcissistic. Women are said to take their own needs too seriously and have supposedly forgotten about their commitments to "others." The antiabortion campaign treats the "other" as the unborn children, but the "other" is also one's husband, one's children, one's aged parents, and so forth. "Pro-lifers" pose narcissistic woman (the feminist) against the moral woman. The moral woman puts others before herself; by definition she is a mother, that is, one who lives for others, for her child or her country. That she should have the right to choose to do so becomes an irrelevant category within the moral system of the antiabortion movement.

The struggle for the morally ordered society, of which the antiabortion movement is a part, also requires the reconstitution of the traditional family. It is interesting to note that when Rousseau sought to reconstitute the authority of the family and the moral mother in eighteenth-century France, he did not recognize the contradictory nature of the traditional patriarchal family form he envisioned and the necessities of a capitalist society in economic transition. The New Right does not recognize these necessities either. Carter did, however, and this is why he did not invoke images of the traditional nuclear family constructed around the "institution of motherhood," but rather praised "working mothers" and even set aside a day to recognize these women, who constitute more than 50 percent of married women. What we see, then, is that there are different views in the state on how to save the "institution of motherhood." Reagan speaks of reinventing the traditional patriarchal model. Carter recognized that a revised version of the traditional patriarchal family was needed to fit the needs of a changing economy, one that recognizes the wage-earning position of women rather than the housewife role. Whereas Reagan's model reflects the New Right antifeminist stance, Carter's assumes what I will later discuss as the neoconservative position on feminism and family life. What is clear about both is that neither recognizes the sexual equality of women within the home or market. As a "mother," woman is politically differentiated from man and denied equality.

Antifeminism and the Politics of Sexuality

What does it mean in actuality to say that antifeminism is central to the politics of the eighties? It means that the New Right is using the abortion issue to try to gain control of the issues of good and evil, morality, and self-indulgence. The New Right argues that it is presenting a "moral" politics for an "immoral" society, and "moral" politics for it requires a restrengthened family, with clear differentiation between mother and father, their rights and responsibilities. One only need read Senator Paul Laxalt's original bill—presented before the Senate in June 1979—the so-called Family Protection Act ("To strengthen the American family and promote the virtues of family life through education, tax assistance, and related measures")—to understand that pro-family politics is antifeminist. Laxalt suggested, among other proposals in this first bill, that federal funding be removed from any institution of learning that engages in the questioning of "traditional sex roles." It should not be lost on the reader that Laxalt has key positions of responsibility in the Reagan administration and is a close personal associate of Reagan's, or that he has recently backtracked on some of his initial concerns, leaving the redrafting of the bill to Senator Jepsen.

Given the role sexual politics played in the 1980 election, it is important to recognize the New Right's continued double-edged use of it. The New Right's antifeminist, antiabortion politics remains not merely a cover for right-wing militarism and interventionism, but is also a central aspect of this militarism; *the politics of restrengthening America is implicitly a sexual politics. Antifeminism is simultaneously being used as a supportive rallying cry to create a morally strong society and as a central aspect of how one will create the moral society.* Exactly what the new "moral" family will look like is unclear—but it definitely will not be the traditional nuclear unit of a housewife, working husband, and two children. This vision already holds true for only 17 percent of the population.[27] What is clear is that the institution of motherhood and housewifery will remain central to the family if the New Right has anything to say about it. They wish to recreate honor for the institution of motherhood and thereby enhance the honor of the state.

In reality, the conflicts between patriarchy—the need for woman as "mother," which is not merely a biological concept, but rather a political one, constructing her life in the family for the care of children and men—and capitalism—including the need for the woman as wage-earner, given the structural changes in the labor force and inflation—still exist. They are precisely what Reagan will have to continue to deal with, and will act as constraints on Reagan's policies. Reagan and the faction of the state he supports will continue to have to contend with the center-liberals and neoconservatives whom Carter represented. There is little agreement among these factions on how to deal with abortion policy and legislation affecting the family, or on how to deradicalize feminism. Within his own party, Reagan will have to create a cohesive policy that spans the differences between Paul

Laxalt, the Moral Majority, and the Republican centrists. Already members of the New Right are asking whether Reagan is really a Reaganite. I would say he probably is not a Reaganite, or if he is, he will not remain one for long because he will be unable successfully to mediate the conflicts between the traditional patriarchal nuclear family he celebrates and the needs of the advanced capitalist patriarchal economy.

In conclusion) while the differences between the two parties were not merely ideological, the 1980 election presented us with politics as ideology. Whereas election politics and the state have become more conservative in this country, mainstream feminism—those who embrace the liberal feminism values of freedom of choice and the individual right to equality before the law—has become more progressive and radical. The consciousness of a majority of people in this country is liberal feminist, as polls on abortion indicate, and as a result the contradictions between liberal society and the position of women are being uncovered within mainstream politics itself.

The growing power of the New Right's antifeminist politics has developed in reaction to the changing nature of women's lives and the understanding by a majority of women that there are fundamental structural problems in a society that ghettoizes them in the home and/or in the labor force, and yet demands that they be responsible mothers. At issue here are the conflicts that appeared through the 1970s between patriarchy and capitalism. Women cannot be mothers and workers without understanding that their starting point in the "race of life" is unequal to begin with. As feminists they are moving beyond liberal politics. It is time to start from here to develop a mass-based feminist politics that grows from the understanding that we need to develop real political alternatives. If political struggle is a process, then it most definitely coalesced with NOW's refusal to endorse Carter and the promise to fight the New Right. Liberal feminism in this instance rejected the liberal political arena as insufficient for addressing the issues of women's equality and reproductive freedom. The radical potential of liberal feminism lies here—in beginning to formulate a feminist politics that grows out of mainstream liberalism, but no longer accepts its boundaries. I therefore argue that the assault against the New Right can be launched most effectively by mainstream feminism because it is the most active political movement today. Its true force remains to be fully organized and directed against the New Right and neoconservatism. But if feminists—of all different progressive political orientations—do not seek to work with and utilize this radical potential of mainstream feminism, the conservative forces within feminism itself, the New Right, and neoconservatives will win. So that we are better prepared to fight them, we need more specific analysis and understanding of the New Right and neoconservative attacks on liberalism and liberal feminism.

NOTES

1. Much of what I argue in this article is documented with data collected from a series of election polls. I use this information with caution, since to the extent that polls and compiled election data are always open to scrutiny, all the statistics should be considered as approximations. Nevertheless, I think the data call for a careful consideration. I want to thank my colleague Martin Brownstein for his assistance in gathering the voting statistics presented here.
2. See Michael Miles, The Odyssey of the American Right (New York: Oxford University Press, 1980), for an interesting discussion of the history of the American Right's assault on New Deal politics.
3. One can argue that these individuals could not find an alternative in John Anderson or Barry Commoner precisely because of the nature of the two-party system. In fact, most individuals who thought it mattered that Reagan be defeated voted for Carter, not Anderson or Commoner.
4. One can only speculate that this assessment carried over and set the context for senatorial races, even when there was a real choice on issues related to feminism. The defeat of these senators stands as a warning to the American public about the political direction of the voting electorate and poses a real dilemma for the nonvoting public.
5. See Leslie Bennetts, "Feminists Dismayed by the Election and Unsure of What Future Holds," New York Times, November 7, 1980, p. A16.
6. New York Times, November 5, 1980, p. 1.
7. See Bertram Gross, Friendly Fascism (New York: M. Evans, 1980), p. 118.
8. Adam Clymer, "Displeasure with Carter Turned Many to Reagan," New York Times, November 9, 1980, p. 28.
9. These data were compiled by an AP/NBC News Poll of about 11,000 voters.
10. Walter Dean Burnham, "The 1980 Earthquake: Realignment, Reaction, or What?" in Thomas Ferguson and Joel Rogers, eds., The Hidden Election: Politics and Economics in the 1980 Presidential Campaign (New York: Pantheon, 1981), p. 106.
11. The National NOW Times 11, no. 4 (April 1981): 2.
12. See Zillah Eisenstein, The Radical Future of Liberal Feminism (New York: Longman, 1981), for a fuller discussion of liberal feminism and its relation to the state.

13. Mim Kelber, "What Bella Knew," Ms. 12, no. 10 (April 1979): 98.
14. My criticism of the draft extends to the drafting of men as well. I think there is a set of specific and particular reasons why the drafting of women must be explored as a different phenomenon from the drafting of men—although they clearly are part of the same militaristic buildup.
15. There is significant opposition to the drafting of women by the New Right, many feminists, and antiwar activists, but for different reasons. Clearly the drafting of women appears antithetical to the image of the "moral mother," which elements within the state wish to support. But there are other factions within the state that seek to deradicalize liberal feminism by manipulating the issue of women's equality. They see the draft as a chance to invoke the ideology of equality for women, while in reality "giving" women nothing—not even the ERA. In the end the Supreme Court ruled that an all-male registration was constitutional and did not violate the Fifth Amendment because (1) Congress was not limited by a traditional view of woman in calling for an all-male draft, and (2) women were not eligible for combat, which is what the purpose of registration is in the first place. See Rostker v. Goldberg 69 L Ed 2d.
16. Sara Ruddick, "Pacifying the Forces: Drafting Women in the Interests of Peace," Signs 8, no. 3 (Spring 1983): 476.
17. Mim Kelber, "Carter and Women: The Record," The Nation 230, no. 20 (May 24, 1980): 627.
18. Ibid., p. 628.
19. Andrew Hacker, "E.R.A.-R.I.P.," Harper's, September 1980, p. 14.
20. Alan Crawford, Thunder on the Right: The "New Right" and the Politics of Resentment (New York: Pantheon, 1980), p. 148.
21. Peter Steinfels, The Neo-Conservatives: The Men Who Are Changing America's Politics (New York: Simon and Schuster, 1979), p. 221.
22. See Rosalind Petchesky, "Reproductive Freedom: Beyond 'A Woman's Right to Choose,'" Signs 5, no. 4 (Summer 1980): 661–85, for an important discussion of liberal theory and the reproductive rights movement. Also see her new book, Abortion and Women's Choice: The State, Sexuality and Reproductive Freedom (New York: Longman, 1984).
23. See Donald Granberg and Beth Wellman Granberg, "Abortion Attitudes, 1965–1980," Family Planning Perspectives 12 (September–October 1980): 250–61.
24. Bertram Gross, Friendly Fascism (New York: M. Evans, 1980).
25. See Adrienne Rich, Of Woman Born: Motherhood as Experience and Institution (New York: Norton, 1976), for a clarification of the distinction between biological childbearing and the political institution of motherhood. "The institution of motherhood is not identical with bearing and caring for children, any more than the institution of heterosexuality is identical with intimacy and sexual love. Both create the prescriptions and the conditions in which choices are made or blocked; they are not 'reality' but they have shaped the circumstances of our lives" (p. 42).
26. See The Radical Future of Liberal Feminism, chap. 2, for a detailed explanation of why I choose to use the term patriarchy to express the political structuring of woman's oppression.
27. Betty Friedan, "Feminism Takes a New Turn," New York Times, November 18, 1979, sec. 6, p. 92. Also see Heather L. Ross and Isabel V. Sawhill, Time of Transition: The Growth of Families Headed by Women (Washington, D.C.: The Urban Institute, 1975); and Ralph E. Smith, ed., The Subtle Revolution: Women at Work (Washington, D.C.: The Urban Institute, 1979).

2. The Sexual Politics of the New Right: The Crisis of Welfare State Liberalism

This chapter explores the New Right's analysis of the "crisis of liberalism" both as an economic philosophy and as a political ideology. The New Right critique, which amounts to an indictment of the welfare state, attributes this crisis to the changed relationship between the state and the family. The fundamental focus of present New Right politics is therefore on redefining this relationship. The New Right thinks that the welfare state is in some sense responsible for undermining the traditional patriarchal family by taking over different family functions, notably the health, welfare, and education of individuals. The New Right's critique of the welfare state in this way becomes closely linked to its understanding of the crisis of the family. I intend to ask whether this analysis is not a misreading of history. If the growth of the welfare state is as much a response to changes in family structure as it is a cause of those changes, then the New Right has wrongly identified the source of the crisis and as a result has provided us with anachronistic models of the family and the state for the 1980s.

From the perspective of the New Right, the problem of "the" family—defined as the married heterosexual couple with children, the husband working in the labor force and the wife remaining at home to rear the children as a housewife—stems from the husbands' loss of patriarchal authority as their wives have been pulled into the labor force. Richard Viguerie (the major fundraiser of the New Right), Jerry Falwell (a leading evangelist and head of the Moral Majority), and George Gilder (the economist whom David Stockman consults and the author of *Wealth and Poverty*) argue that in order to revitalize the capitalist economy, create a moral order, and strengthen America at home and abroad, policymakers must aim to reestablish the dominance of the traditional white patriarchal family. Because black women have always worked outside the home in disproportionate numbers to white women, whether in slave society or in the free labor market, the model of the traditional patriarchal family has never accurately described their family life. Yet with white married women's entry into the labor force this nuclear model no longer describes the majority of white families either.[1] This is why the "problem" of the family has become more pronounced and why the issue of the married wage-earning woman has now been brought to center stage by the New Right. In this fundamental sense the sexual politics of the New Right is implicitly antifeminist and racist: it desires to establish the model of the traditional white patriarchal family by dismantling the welfare state and by removing wage-earning married women from the labor force and returning them to the home.

The New Right's attack is directed so forcefully against married wage-earning women and "working mothers" because it is these women who have the potential to transform society.[2] The New Right correctly understands this. The reality of the wage-earning wife's double workday uncovers the patriarchal basis of liberalism and capitalist society.[3] As these women begin to understand the sexual bias in the marketplace (where a woman earns fifty-nine cents to the male worker's dollar) and continue to bear the responsibilities of housework and child care as well, they begin to voice feminist demands for affirmative action programs, equal pay, pregnancy disability payments, and abortion rights. They press for the equal rights promised by liberal ideology. The New Right focuses its attack on both liberalism and feminism precisely because mainstream feminist demands derive from the promises of liberalism as an ideology—individual autonomy and independence, freedom of choice, equality of opportunity, and equality before the law—and because they threaten to undermine patriarchy, and with it capitalism, by uncovering the "crisis of liberalism." Feminist demands uncover the truth that capitalist patriarchal society cannot deliver on its "liberal" promises of equality or even equal rights for women without destabilizing itself.

The New Right's antifeminism is projected as pro-family. It seeks to define an electoral position around questions of family life, a position the Left has always rejected as ineffective. Now that the New Right has effectively brought questions of family life into electoral politics—a verification of the feminist movement's early appreciation of the political nature of the family—it remains for feminists to try to use this new electoral focus on family politics for our own purposes. The issue is no longer whether a family politics that crosses lines of economic class and race can be built, but rather what kind of family politics will prevail.

Developing a policy for the family or for different forms of the family is as central to the politics of the 1980s as finding a remedy for inflation. Clearly this is the focus, as we shall see, of the Reagan–Stockman budgets. What is not clear is whether feminists, left-liberals, and leftists will be able to build a coalition around these issues, to agree in particular on the necessity of promoting a nonpatriarchal form of family life. One can only be skeptical about this possibility when one sees that Mark Green, former director of Ralph Nader's Congress Watch, still believes that "the issue of the 1980's is economic: how to generate and distribute wealth in a new era."[4] Until left-liberals and leftists recognize that New Right politics is fundamentally about the familial and sexual structuring of society, they will remain ineffective in the politics of the 1980s. And it will be feminists who have to "fight the Right."

The New Right vs. the "Liberal" Takeover of Government

The New Right represents a coalition of political, religious, and antifeminist groups that hope to dismantle the welfare state and reconstruct the traditional patriarchal family. The New Right's major fundraiser is Richard Viguerie, who started his mail-order funding drive in 1965.[5] Other New Right groups focus on election campaigns and governmental legislation: the Conservative Caucus led by Howard Phillips (a former Nixon appointee chosen to dismantle the Office of Economic Opportunity), the Committee for the Survival of a Free Congress led by Paul Weyrich, and the Conservative Political Action Committee led by Terry Dolan. Key senators identified with the New Right are Orrin Hatch of Utah, Paul Laxalt of Nevada, Jesse Helms of North Carolina, and James McClure of Idaho. Another major segment of the New Right, the "electronic church," is dominated by the Evangelical Right headed by the Moral Majority and Jerry Falwell. The third sector of the New Right comprises the antifeminist "pro-life," "pro-family" groups led by Phyllis Schlafly's Eagle Forum and Connie Marshner's Library Court. Although these three sectors of the New Right intersect and function as a coalition, they do not form one cohesive group.

According to Viguerie's book *The New Right: We're Ready to Lead,* the New Right's goal is to organize the conservative middle-class majority in America: citizens concerned about high taxes and inflation, small business people angry at governmental control, born-again Christians disturbed about sex in television and movies, parents opposed to forced busing, supporters of the right to life who are against the federal funding of abortion, middle-class Americans tired of Big Government, Big Business, Big Labor, and Big Education, pro-defense citizens, and those who believe America has *not* had its day and *does not* need to tighten its belt.[6]

Ultimately this list of concerns can be summarized as a criticism of what the New Right terms the "liberal takeover" of government that started with the election of Franklin D. Roosevelt in 1932.[7] According to Viguerie and the New Right, the liberals have made the United States a second-rate military power; given away the Panama Canal; created the massive welfare state; lost Iran, Afghanistan, Vietnam, Laos, and Cambodia; crippled the FBI and CIA; encouraged American women to feel like failures if they want to be wives and mothers; and fought for preferential quotas for blacks and women.[8] They identify Adlai Stevenson, Walter Reuther, George Meany, Martin Luther King, Nelson Rockefeller, Hubert Humphrey, and Robert Kennedy as the leaders responsible for the liberal takeover of government. They identify the National Organization for Women, Planned Parenthood, Gay Rights National Lobby, National Abortion Rights Action League, and Women Strike for Peace as the leading single-issue political groups of the "liberal establishment" that are responsible for the liberal takeover of the family. And they identify Andrew Young, William Sloane Coffin, Martin Luther King, and Father Robert Drinan as the religious leaders of the liberal establishment.[9] The New Right has therefore developed its politics to counter the liberal takeover of the state, the family, and the church.

The New Right, Liberalism, and the Welfare State

The New Right's indictment of liberalism reduces it to the policies, programs, and elected officials of the welfare state. In other words, the New Right's analysis of the "crisis of liberalism" equates it with a criticism of the welfare state that does not extend to a critique of liberalism itself as an ideology. We shall see, however, that the neoconservatives do extend their critique in this way, and in the end try to redefine and redirect the meaning of liberalism. The New Right instead uncritically adopts the notion of liberal individualism while rejecting welfare-state liberalism. The New Right continues to celebrate unselfconsciously much of the ideology of liberalism (in its particularly "patriarchal" form) in its rhetoric, which has often been described as populist. It is not at all clear that the term "populist" accurately describes the political motives of the New Right. Their concerns are limited by a politics that hopes to mobilize their supporters, and they care little if this extends to a majority of the populace. As Paul Weyrich has stated: "I don't want everyone to vote. Our leverage in the election quite candidly goes up as the voting populace goes down. We have no responsibility, moral or otherwise, to turn out our opposition, it's important to turn out those who are with us."[10]

Much of the New Right's ideology is liberal in that it adopts the values of individualism and equality of opportunity. Viguerie documents this point when he argues that he accepts the vision of the American Dream but not the welfare state's role in trying to bring it about for individuals. Phyllis Schlafly embodies the liberal individualist spirit perfectly in the attitudes underlining her anti-ERA position: "If you're willing to work hard, there's no barrier you can't jump. . . . I've achieved my goals in life and I did it without sex-neutral laws."[11] But there is little consistency in how the notion of equality of opportunity is used by the New Right. On the one hand it is assumed to structure and legitimate the American way of life, while on the other hand it is said to be mere pretense, because people are unequal to begin with.

> There is no way to equalize opportunity so long as the clever and energetic accumulate more wealth and power than the dull witted and lazy, so long as the handsome and wealthy are able to pick beautiful mates, so long as men are men and women are women.

Equal opportunity is one of those democratic ideas whose only effect is to widen the gap between men.[12]

The contradictory aspects of the New Right's position on equality of opportunity is clearest in their discussion about women's rights: "The worst effect of the craze for equal opportunity lies in the curious phenomenon of women's rights."[13] They argue that women already are guaranteed opportunity for employment equal to any man, and this has created strains for the family as husbands have begun competing with their wives. "The real effect of this collective delusion of women's rights is only to reduce the once sovereign family to a support system for various governmental agencies."[14]

Liberal ideology can also be seen in the New Right's "Right to Work Campaign" built on the argument that the individual should have the right to choose whether to join a union. This same liberal issue—an individual's right to choose—presents problems for the New Right's antiabortion campaign, which denies this individual right of choice to the woman. One can also see the deference to liberal ideology when President Reagan and Phyllis Schlafly carefully distinguish between their support for the equal rights of women—which recognizes the liberal individualist rights of a woman—and their lack of support for the Equal Rights Amendment, which they argue encourages state intervention into an individual's private life. One can, obviously, reject welfare-state liberalism and still be committed to liberal values in their patriarchal form, as the New Right is.

The New Right uses liberal ideology selectively and inconsistently, not recognizing how the ideology implies the welfare state, whereas neoconservatives, as the next chapter discusses, argue that the ideology itself needs redefinition. Hence, the New Right is caught in the same dilemma that created the welfare state in the first place: an ideology of equal opportunity and individual freedom coupled with a structural reality of economic, sexual, and racial inequality. By dismantling the welfare state the New Right will do nothing about the needs that produced this form of the state in the first place. Their commitment to liberal individualism and their rejection of the liberal welfare state simultaneously define their politics.

Instead of constructing a new vision of the welfare state, the New Right seeks to construct a society built around the traditional white self-sufficient patriarchal family. By so doing it hopes to establish the autonomy of the family from the state. In order to do this the family must be relieved of both its heavy tax burden and inflation, thereby freeing the married woman from work in the labor force. "Federal spending eats into the family's income, forcing mothers to go to work to pay for food, clothing, shelter and other family basics."[15] The New Right argument is this: welfare-state expenditures have raised taxes and added to inflation, pulling the married woman into the labor force and thereby destroying the fabric of the traditional patriarchal family and hence the moral order of society.

While the neoconservatives want to restructure the "new class"—the administrators of the welfare state—by redefining the responsibilities of the state, members of the New Right have targeted wage-earning women to be the agents of the family's social services once they are returned to the home. Thus the attack on the welfare state becomes antifeminist and not merely anti-new class. The attack is also racist in that many members of this new class who are currently being "declassed" and purged from government are black. Dismantling the welfare state is not only intended to redirect surplus into the private sector in a period of declining U.S. industrial power; it also is supposed to make clear that equality of opportunity for black and white women and black men is a privilege reserved for times of plenty.

The antifeminism and racism of the New Right operate on two levels here. First, the presentation of the traditional patriarchal family as the desired model denies the reality(ies) of the black family and the reality of the married wage-earning woman in both the black and white family. Second, the indictment of the welfare state and its Great Society programs is being used to turn back whatever gains have been made by black and white women and black men.

As we shall now see, according to Falwell and Gilder, married women have entered the labor force because of the high taxes and inflation caused by the continued growth of the welfare state. And married women's entrance into the labor force has eroded the traditional (white) patriarchal family structure necessary to the moral fabric of society and economic vitality. There is, however, another analysis to be considered: the argument that the welfare state is as much a consequence as a cause of changes in the economy and the family (for example, women's entrance into the labor force, new sexual mores, and higher divorce rates). If this is true, the traditional (white) patriarchal family cannot be re-stabilized by dismantling the welfare state, because the welfare state developed out of the dissolution of the traditional patriarchal family. The New Right's vision of the state and of the family is outmoded, as some of them have begun to recognize. Jeffrey Hart, writing in the *New Right Papers*, suggests that the New Right needs to develop a futuristic, modern approach to replace its tradition-bound outlook, particularly on issues surrounding questions of sex.[16]

The New Right and the Traditional Patriarchal Family

By reasserting the power of the family against the state, the New Right more accurately intends to reestablish the power of the father. According to Jerry Falwell in *Listen America*, government has developed at the expense of the father's authority: "The progression of big government is amazing. A father's authority was lost first to the village, then to the city, next to the State, and finally to the empire."[17] Falwell is also angry and critical of the inflationary economy because it has undermined the father's authority. He states that children should have the right "to have the love of a mother and father who understand their different roles and fulfill their different responsibilities. . . . to live in an economic system that makes it possible for husbands to support their wives as full time mothers in the home and that enables families to survive on one income instead of two."[18] He wants to create a healthy economy and limit inflation in order to establish the single wage-earner family. "The family is the fundamental building block and the basic unit of our society, and its continued health is a prerequisite for a healthy and prosperous nation. No nation has ever been stronger than the families within her."[19] Thus Falwell's fight against inflation is also a fight to reestablish the father's authority and to put women back in the home.

One sees this argument further developed in George Gilder's *Wealth and Poverty,* the book that Reagan has distributed to members of his cabinet. According to Gilder, the economy has become sluggish because the welfare state has created an imbalance between security (investment) and risk by creating an insurance plan for joblessness, disability, and indigent old age. This reduces work incentives, cuts American productivity, and in the end perpetuates poverty.[20] If the welfare state perpetuates poverty, Gilder sees the deterioration of family life as an apparent cause. Welfare benefits destroy the role of the father: "He can no longer feel manly in his own home." In welfare culture money becomes not something earned by men, "but a right conferred on women by the state." The male's role is undermined, and with it the moving force for upward mobility "has been cuckolded by the compassionate state."[21] Welfare erodes both the work ethic and family life and thus keeps poor people poor; unemployment compensation only promotes unemployment; Aid to Families with Dependent Children (AFDC) only makes families dependent and fatherless.[22] According to Gilder, "The only dependable route from poverty is always work, family, and faith," not the welfare state.[23]

A principle of upward mobility for Gilder is the maintenance of monogamous marriage and the family. Disruption of family life creates disruption in the economy because men need to direct their sexual energies toward the economy and they only do so when they are connected to family duty. Marriage creates the sense of responsibility men need: "A married man . . . is spurred by the claims of family to channel his otherwise disruptive male aggressions into his performance as a provider for a wife and children." This is not true for women, however. "Few women with children make earning money the top priority in their lives," whereas men's commitment to children and to this sense of future spurs them to new heights. "These sexual differences alone . . . dictate that the first priority of any serious program against poverty is to strengthen the male role in poor families" and to maintain it in middle- and upper-class families.[24]

One can discern from Gilder's discussion of the poor family that the model of the successful family is one in which the male earns wages. Woman's involvement in the labor force has challenged the man's position of authority in the family, reduced his productivity at work, and thereby "caused a simultaneous expansion of the work force and a decline in productivity growth."[25] As a result, the husband's drive to succeed in his career has been deterred because "two half-hearted participants in the labor force can do better than one who is competing aggressively for the relatively few jobs in the upper echelons."[26] In the end Gilder believes that it is *familial anarchy*, not capitalism, that causes poverty by creating a nonproductive economy.[27] Women's participation in the labor force promotes family dissolution either by facilitating divorce or by challenging the patriarchal authority necessary to a "productive" economy. This leads to Gilder's indictment of the welfare state. One can stabilize the family by reasserting the authority of the father in the family and by removing women from the wage labor force, and this can be done if taxes and inflation are reduced.

The New Right and the Married Wage-Earning Woman

From the preceding discussion one can see that the United States is as patriarchal as it is capitalist. This means that the politics of society is as self-consciously directed to maintaining the hierarchical male-dominated sexual system as to upholding the economic class structure. The forms of order and control in both systems remain mutually supportive until changes in one system begin to erode the hierarchical basis of the other. For example, such erosion in the patriarchal system began to occur when structural changes in the marketplace, changes in the wage structure, and inflation required white married women to enter the labor force.

When I say that there have been structural changes in the economic marketplace, I mean that the service and retail-trade sectors of the economy have grown at the expense of the industrial sector. According to Emma Rothschild, 43 percent of all Americans employed in the private nonagricultural part of the economy in 1979

worked in services and retail trade.[28] From 1973 to 1979 the major
growth sectors of the economy, which supplied more than 40
percent of the new private jobs, were fast-food places, business
services (personnel supply services and data processing), and
health services (including private hospitals and nursing homes).
These new jobs have been the primary source of employment for
married women. Some of the women in this service sector supplement their husbands' earnings, but many are single parents. Either
way, their labor force participation is essential to maintaining
their families and this sector of the economy.

Women accounted for 41 percent of all wage-earners in 1979: 31
percent of all manufacturing workers, 56 percent of all employees
in eating and drinking places, 43 percent in all business services,
81 percent in all health services.[29] "Waiting on tables, defrosting
frozen hamburgers, rendering services to buildings, looking after
the old and the ill, is 'women's work.' "[30] And this is low-hour and
low-pay work. Wages in the private service sector averaged $9,853
in 1979 (measured in 1972 dollars); in the industrial sector they
averaged $21,433.[31] In nursing and personal service work, in
which 89 percent of the workers are women, the average wage in
1979 was $3.87 per hour compared with the average hourly wage
of $16.16 in the entire private economy.[32] Most private service
sector jobs are also deadends that offer no possible advancement
to a supervisory level; for example, 92 percent of the jobs in eating
and drinking places are nonsupervisory. "The United States, in
sum, is moving toward a structure of employment ever more
dominated by jobs that are badly paid, unchanging, and unpro-
ductive."[33]

But what is really interesting about the private sector is that its
growth reflects the market's response to changes in the family, as
well as changes in the relation between the state and the family.
Increases in state welfare services, nursing homes, and fast-food
restaurants all reflect new trends in family life, particularly the
changes in woman's place within the family and within the market. Work once done in the home has been increasingly shifted to
the market, and particular responsibilities of the family have been
shifted to the state. We shall see, however, that Reagan's plan is to
redirect these shifts. How can he do this, given the present
realities of the family, the economy, and the intersection of the

welfare state and the economy? And *why* do he and the New Right want to redirect the relationship between the state and the family? I think it is because they believe this will ultimately remove married women from the labor force.

The capitalist need for women workers has developed along with the not always successful attempt to protect the system of patriarchal hierarchy through the sexual segregation of the labor force. Women have been relegated to the low-productivity sector of the market, and their pay is unequal to men's even when the work is of the same or of comparable worth. Some women may accept the patriarchal organization of their family life, considering it "natural" that women cook the meals or do the laundry (although many do not), but I have yet to hear one of the secretaries in my office say that she does not have the right to earn the same as a man. Women as workers come to expect equal treatment in the market whether they expect it in their familial relations or not. Relations at home are supposedly regulated by love and devotion; the wage regulates women's relations at the workplace. Her boss is *not* her husband. In other words, even though capitalism has reproduced a patriarchal structure within the market, the liberal ideology of the bourgeois marketplace—equality of opportunity, equality before the law, individual aggressiveness and independence—remains. As the working woman internalizes and applies these values to herself as she operates within the market's patriarchal structure, she develops a consciousness critical of her deadended work life. In the market, one's sex is supposed to be irrelevant. People are supposedly individuals, not members of a sexual class. Hard work is supposed to be rewarded. To the extent that the married wage-earning woman accepts these values when she enters the market, she embodies a contradiction. As a worker she is supposedly an individual, and as a married woman she is a member of a sexual class. Her sexual-class identity is highlighted in the market specifically because it is not supposed to matter there.

This highlighting of woman's differentiation from men in the market begins to create a consciousness we can term feminist. We are back to the point that because the majority of married women work in the labor force today and expect equality—even if it is only equality in the workplace—the promises of liberalism are being challenged. The New Right's objection is not merely that equalizing pay between men and women would cost billions of dollars, although the cost to the capitalist or profit maintenance is always at issue. More important is the fact that establishing equality in the workplace would erode a major form of patriarchal control presently maintained as much in the market as in the family and the home.

Here then is the contradiction: advanced capitalism, because of structural changes and inflation, has required married women to enter the labor force. Although the structure of the capitalist market is patriarchal, its ideology is definitely liberal. Married wage-earning women have the potential to perceive the conflict between liberalism as an ideology about equality and the sexual inequality of patriarchy as a structural requisite of the capitalist market. In their discontent, however limited, they can begin to recognize and reject this patriarchal structuring of opportunities in the market. When you put this awareness together with a married woman's double workday—the work of her home and children as well as her outside job—the *possibilities* for feminist consciousness increase. The New Right attack on married wage-earning women lies in this reality; in demanding equality before the law and in wages, wage-earning women have begun to challenge the patriarchal organization of the market. Therein lies a major crisis for liberalism: the contradictory reality of patriarchal inequality in an ideology of (liberal) equality is being uncovered by the married wage-earning woman.

The New Right's attack on married wage-earning women also reflects women's greater unification as a sexual class. First, white married women have joined black married women in the labor force. Although racial divisions still exist, black and white women share the world of the market more than ever before, and their attitudes reflect this. In 1972 a Harris poll for Virginia Slims cigarettes found that black women outscored white women 62 to 45 percent in support of efforts to change the status of women and 67 to 35 percent in sympathy with women's liberation groups.[34]

Second, married middle-class and working-class women find themselves sharing the service sector of the economy. A majority of wage-earning women find themselves in the low-paying service and clerical fields, with only a small minority of women occupying professional jobs. The notion that feminism or feminist consciousness is limited to the white middle-class woman has never been more untrue than it is today. As Philip S. Foner has documented so well in *Women and the American Labor Movement*, working-class wage-earning women often define themselves as feminists.[35] The redefinition of women's lives, given the increasing number of women in the labor force, has actually made it necessary for feminism to address the needs of wage-earning women. And the reality of married wage-earning women cuts through traditional economic class lines.

The New Right, Sexuality, and Sexual Difference

In order to understand more fully the New Right attack on the welfare state and the wage-earning married woman we need to understand the New Right belief that the differences between the sexes are the single most important motivating force in human life.[36] According to George Gilder: "There are no human beings; there are just men and women, and when they deny their divergent sexuality, they reject the deepest sources of identity and love."[37] The sexual constitution of society is as important as the legal constitution.[38] "For sex is the life force—and cohesive impulse of a people, and their very character will be deeply affected by how sexuality is managed, sublimated, expressed, denied, and propagated."[39] It is men's sexuality, according to Gilder, that needs to be controlled and contained and much of the politics of society must be aimed at doing this by reaffirming the role of husband. The role of the male, as husband and breadwinner, is a "cultural contrivance," which can be destroyed unless it is protected. Gilder believes that the male role of husband, defined as father and breadwinner, is absolutely necessary for a moral, ordered society. It creates the sense of obligation and importance that men need for guidance.

Gilder believes, somewhat reminiscent of the thinking of Rousseau, that women are superior to men because they can bear children and they control the realm of the erotic. "Women control not the economy of the marketplace but the economy of eros: the life force in our society and our lives. What happens in the inner realm of women finally shapes what happens in our social surfaces, determining the level of happiness, energy, creativity, and solidarity in the nation."[40] The problem, according to Gilder, is that the differences between the sexes are totally important and necessary, and yet these differences—in terms of childbearing and eros—make women superior to men.

Because women hold such power as sexual and reproductive beings, controls must be set up to contain women and to establish the "equally" important role of man as breadwinner. Gilder therefore argues for inequality between men and women in the economic realm in order to establish the importance and privilege of man as breadwinner, to counter the "natural privilege" of women: "The reasons for unequal pay thus are numerous: (1) the need for male social initiation; (2) the need to give men a way to counterbalance female sexual superiority; (3) the need to give money a positive effect on family relation and maintenance."[41] Since economic superiority of men is necessitated by the sexual superiority of women, the only way society could allow the economic equality of men and women is if women renounced their sexual superiority.[42] This is impossible, according to Gilder, because it would lead to sexual suicide: the abolition of biological differences between men and women and an end to "procreative energy."[43]

Women's economic equality of opportunity undermines the sexual constitution of society and leads to a breakdown of morality. The economic superiority of men is needed to enforce the male-provider role and limit domination of men by women. As such, sexual discrimination in the economy is necessary to enforce the male role:

> Men *do* get paid more than women; women *are* persistently discouraged from competing with men; when sufficiently motivated women individually *can* perform almost every important job in the society as well as men; job assignments by sex *are* arbitrary and illogical; most women *do* work because they have to; the lack of public child-care facilities does prevent women from achieving real financial equality of opportunity.[44]

Discrimination against women, which establishes the (economic) superiority of men, is not problematic for Gilder because he believes "these practices are not oppressive."[45]

It is never quite clear whether Gilder is trying to establish equality between men and women or the superiority of men. He is critical of the term "equality" because he says it usually means that men and women are the same, which he rejects as resulting in sexual suicide. For Gilder, procreative sexuality requires masculine superiority—at least in the economy, and he attacks the feminist movement for challenging this patriarchal conception of woman's inequality in the economy.

Gilder is critical of feminism because he thinks it is hostile to sexual difference and family life, "that as a movement it is devoted to establishing the career woman as the American ideal, supported by federal subsidies and celebrations."[46] He says this is true of the moderates as well as the revolutionaries, since while the moderates say that they wish only to improve relations between the sexes through liberal reforms, their reforms, if adopted, would be revolutionary.[47] Gilder understands somewhat accurately that in the end, if woman's real equality were established, it would erode male privilege and the notion of masculinity as it presently exists. As he states: "The reason the revolutionaries are right and the moderates revolutionary is that the movement is striking at the Achilles' heel of civilized society: the role of the male."[48]

Gilder identifies the feminist movement with a form of loose sex that he believes is also suicidal. Sex that is separate from procreation endangers society at its core because pregnancy and the obligations it creates set up a series of controls on sex. Without these controls, the desire for sex (as pleasure) becomes endless. He sees feminists, pornographers, male chauvinist Playboys, and so forth, as equal collaborators in a sexual suicide society.[49] The concern with sexual pleasure now threatens the very fabric of the monogamous family: "It is a time of wife swapping, group swinging, and gay liberation; a time of dildos in drugstore windows and perfume sprays in men's rooms; a time of oral sex and vaginal sundaes, with a Howard Johnson's array of flavors advertised in McCall's."[50] Instead of sexual freedom Gilder opts for the monogamous family, believing that marriage constrains sexual passion. Sexual freedom is seen as destructive of the moral fabric of society, whereas "monogamy is egalitarian in the realm of love. It is a mode of rationing."[51]

In sum, Gilder argues in favor of sexual difference and against economic equality and sexual freedom. His rejection of egalitarianism between men and women, in both the sexual and economic realms, extends into a rejection of equality of opportunity. Gilder adopts a conservative and antiliberal stance on the positioning of women in the (economic) "race of life." They should be excluded from the competition with men because of the challenge and instability this poses for the role of men as breadwinners. Even though Gilder excludes women from "the race" on the basis of their supposed (natural) superiority, the exclusion is based on the ascribed status of women as (pre)determined by being female.

This particular New Right antifeminist position, which argues for separate sexual spheres, is very similar to the antifeminist position of Phyllis Schlafly, which embraces the notion of equality of opportunity while applauding the doctrine of sexual spheres, as well as to the neoconservative position on feminism, which supports equality of opportunity but not egalitarianism. Gilder, Schlafly, and the neoconservatives also share a similar position on the issue of sexual freedom and freedom of sexual preference, as we shall see. Instead of applauding freedom in the realm of sex, as they do for the economic marketplace, they reject it as breeding sexual license and hedonism and a breakdown of (heterosexual, monogamous) family life. It is important to note that the rejection of sexual egalitarianism is very much tied up with a denial of sexual freedom and freedom of sexual preference. Instead of sexual freedom, they call for either constraint, as in the case of Gilder, or protection, as in the case of neoconservative Midge Decter. Constraint and protection presume the notion of sexual difference between man and woman but not their sexual equality.

On the whole, the New Right adopts much of Gilder's position: his fear of sexual license and freedom, his commitment to sexual difference rather than sexual equality, his concern with protecting the traditional patriarchal family while never utilizing an explicit argument for women's inequality. Although he and Schlafly construct their arguments somewhat differently, as we shall see in Chapter 7, they both argue for the protection of women rather than their equality. Richard Viguerie adopts this same view when he argues in the New Right journal *Conservative Digest* that the New Right needs to focus on women's "real" issues like soft- and hard-core pornography and rape in order to mobilize the woman's vote.[52] The focus once again is on woman's need for protection—especially protection from sexual abuse and sexual excess. This is the same perspective held by New Rightist Joseph Sobran, who states: "Just as welfare destroys the work ethic, so abortion destroys the family ethic."[53] Family life supposedly protects and requires sex that is tied to childbearing, whereas abortion allows for the possibility of sex for pleasure, which in the end destroys the moral fabric of the family and society. "We seek to preserve not the selfish and irresponsible individual, but an individual who respects law—divine and human—and who nurtures the community that gave him life and protection."[54]

In the 1980 election, the New Right successfully mobilized support around these sexual issues, especially abortion, thus helping elect Reagan. But they have been less successful in actually passing legislation related to this antiabortion, antisex stance, or in gaining legitimacy for this position within the Reagan administration. The Laxalt Family Protection Act, which sought to promote traditional family mores, has run into considerable criticism and is presently undergoing complete revision. Different proposals suggesting a constitutional amendment banning abortion, like the Hatch Act, have also run into significant trouble. Sandra O'Connor was appointed to the Supreme Court over the objections of the New Right, which considered her to be pro-abortion at that time. When Richard Schweiker resigned as head of the Department of Housing, Education, and Welfare and Drew Lewis resigned from the Department of Transportation they were replaced by Margaret Heckler and Elizabeth Dole, respectively, neither of whom is considered a "Reaganite" according to the *Conservative Digest*. This same journal criticized these appointments as giving in to "liberal" pressure. "For Reagan, the great critic of affirmative action, to be propitiating the clamorous press by playing the women—and blacks—game at this level suggests a lack of seriousness and a loss of purpose."[55] New Rightists have also expressed grave concern and upset that Joseph Spediel, a Carter appointee, remains the acting director of population-control programs in the Agency for International Development (AID) because they consider him pro-abortion.[56]

The dissatisfaction of the New Right with Reagan can be fully understood only when we recognize the role and place of neoconservatism within the state today. Much of the present conflict

within the state exists between the New Right and neoconservatives as the latter appear to be consolidating their power in the
Reagan administration. Although New Rightists and neoconservatives share an indictment of the welfare state, neoconservatives do
so in the hopes of revising it, while the New Right hopes to destroy it. The neoconservatives, as revisionist liberals, have been
more successful than the radical New Right because they do not
reject liberalism; rather, they wish to redefine it away from its
radical possibilities. Without rejecting the notion of equality of
opportunity between the sexes, the neoconservatives also attempt
to revise the meaning of equality to recognize "sexual difference."
The neoconservative attack on liberalism has gained more legitimacy within the state than that of the New Right because its moorings are to be more systematically found in liberalism itself.
Neoconservatives accept and utilize the division between public
and private life more than the New Right does. They therefore
have much less to say about family life and/or abortion (private)
and much more to say about affirmative action programs that apply to the market (public). Although the New Right's focus on
sexual issues might have mobilized enough of a minority to win
the 1980 election, these concerns limit its potential to consolidate
its power. The New Right intervention into the private life of
family and sexuality is a radical break with the liberal notion of
privacy. It also appears to demystify the commitments to its patriarchal arrangements within the family by trying to reestablish the
patriarchal controls that have formerly been implicit in liberalism. One cannot successfully argue that we need to get government off the backs of the people and simultaneously legislate
sexuality. Against this backdrop, the neoconservatives are putting
in place a state that rejects equality between the sexes and opts for
sexual difference, but within the liberal rhetoric of equality of
opportunity. As such, they do not assert an antifeminist stance but
rather a neoconservative one, where the issues of sex and politics
and the personal as political are mystified once again. The New
Right espouses and defends the patriarchal aspects of family life
and therefore rejects liberalism in the realm of family and sexuality; neoconservatives attempt to redefine and modernize the patriarchal aspects of liberal society in the hopes of deradicalizing
liberalism itself. Chapter 3 will examine exactly what this means.

NOTES

1. The criticism of female wage-earners' effect on family life emerged in Patrick Moynihan's 1965 report, "The Negro Family, the Case for National Action," in Lee Rainwater and William Yancey, eds., *The Moynihan Report and the Politics of Controversy* (Cambridge: MIT Press, 1967), pp. 39–424. Moynihan, using the model of the traditional (white) patriarchal family, argued that the deterioration of the Negro family was in large part due to the emasculation of the black male by his female counterpart who was working in the labor force and/or heading a household. Believing that "the very essence of the male animal, from the bantam rooster to the four-star general, is to strut" (p. 62), he argued that the challenges to the black male's authority by black women made a stable family relationship impossible.

2. The New Right's attack on the married woman wage-earner is at one and the same time a criticism of what it terms the "working mother."

3. See *The Radical Future of Liberal Feminism* (New York: Longman, 1981) for a fuller account of this point.

4. Mark Green, "The Progressive Alternative to Cowboy Capitalism," *The Village Voice*, March 18–24, 1981, p. 10. I also remain skeptical about this possibility, given the left analysis of family life provided by Christopher Lasch in *Haven in a Heartless World* (New York: Basic Books, 1977) and his lack of recognition of feminism *as a progressive political force* for the 1980s in his "Democracy and the Crisis of Confidence," *Democracy* 1, no. 1 (January 1981): 25–40. This denial of the importance of the feminist movement in guiding or at least participating in a progressive coalition is evident in several left or left-liberal journals. A recent example of this is *Democracy*, founded in order to address the present antidemocratic tendencies in the United States, which so far has not discussed feminism as having a role to play in fighting antidemocratic forces. Also see *Radical America*, "Facing Reaction" 15, nos. 1 and 2 (Spring 1981), especially Barbara Ehrenreich's, "The Women's Movements: Feminist and Antifeminist," which denies the viability of the feminist movement in fighting the right-wing reaction. See the interesting discussion by Stacey Oliker, "Abortion and the Left: The Limits of Pro Family Politics," *Socialist Review* 11, no. 2 (March–April 1981): 71–96, about the left's wavering support for reproductive rights. Also see Michael Walzer, *Radical Principles* (New York: Basic Books, 1980) for an example of a leftist analysis of the challenges to liberalism to the exclusion of feminism.

5. Viguerie started his company with lists made up of contributors (of $50 or more) to the Goldwater campaign. According to Viguerie, the New Right became politically mobilized in 1974 when Ford chose Rockefeller for vice-president because they identified Rockefeller with the liberal establishment of the eastern Trilateral Commission. See Richard Viguerie, *The New Right: We're Ready to Lead* (Falls Church, Va.: The Viguerie Company, 1980).

6. Ibid., pp. 15–16. For interesting discussions of New Right politics see Alan Crawford, *Thunder on the Right* (New York: Pantheon Press, 1980); William Hunter, *The New Right: A Growing Force in State Politics* (Washington, D.C.: Conference on Alternative State and Local Politics/Center to Protect Workers' Rights, 1980); and Thomas McIntyre and John Obert, *The Fear Brokers* (New York: Pilgrim Press, 1979).

7. Viguerie identifies the major victories of the liberal establishment as (1) Johnson's Elementary and Secondary Education Act of 1965, which shifted deci-

sion-making power from parents and local school boards to teachers unions and state and federal bureaucracies; (2) the congressional endorsement of the ERA in 1972; (3) the 1973 Supreme Court decision to make abortion legal; (4) the creation of the Department of Education in 1979, which extended federal control over education (*The New Right*, pp. 20–21).

8. Ibid., pp. 5, 9.
9. Ibid., p. 105. Viguerie argues that the New Right's use of religion in politics is nothing new because the National Council of Churches has always taken political stands. They advocated admission of Red China to the United Nations as early as 1958, spoke out against prayer in public schools and against the Vietnam war, and endorsed the need for a guaranteed national income.
10. As quoted by Thomas Ferguson and Joel Rogers, "The Reagan Victory: Corporate Coalitions in the 1980 Campaign," in Ferguson and Rogers, eds., *The Hidden Election: Politics and Economics in the 1980 Presidential Campaign* (New York: Pantheon, 1981), p. 4.
11. Quoted in Carol Felsenthal, *The Sweetheart of the Silent Majority: The Biography of Phyllis Schlafly* (New York: Doubleday, 1981), pp. 55, 58.
12. Thomas Fleming, "Old Rights and the New Right," in Robert Whitaker, ed., *The New Right Papers* (New York: St. Martin's Press, 1982), p. 196.
13. Ibid., p. 195.
14. Ibid., p. 197.
15. Viguerie, *The New Right: We're Ready to Lead*, p. 207.
16. Jeffrey Hart, "The Intelligent Woman's Guide to a Modern American Conservatism," in Whitaker, ed., *The New Right Papers*, p. 38.
17. Jerry Falwell, *Listen America!* (New York: Doubleday, 1980), p. 26.
18. Ibid., p. 148.
19. Ibid., p. 121.
20. George Gilder, *Wealth and Poverty* (New York: Basic Books, 1981), p. 67.
21. Ibid., pp. 114, 115.
22. Ibid., pp. 127, 111.
23. Ibid., p. 68.
24. Ibid., p. 69.
25. Ibid., p. 14.
26. Ibid.
27. Ibid., p. 71.
28. Emma Rothschild, "Reagan and the Real America," *New York Review of Books*, February 5, 1981, pp. 12–18, esp. p. 12. Also see Harry Braverman, *Labor and Monopoly Capital* (New York: Monthly Review Press, 1974).
29. Rothschild, "Reagan and the Real America," p. 12.
30. Ibid., pp. 12–13.
31. Ibid., p. 14.
32. Ibid., pp. 12–13.
33. Ibid.
34. See Philip S. Foner, *Women and the American Labor Movement*, vol. 1, *From World War 1 to the Present* (New York: Free Press, 1980), p. 488.
35. Ibid., p. 478.
36. George Gilder, *Sexual Suicide* (New York: Quadrangle/The New York Times Book Co., 1973), p. 7.
37. Ibid., p. 43.
38. Ibid., p. 131.
39. Ibid., p. 1.
40. Ibid., p. 25.

41. Ibid., p. 98.
42. Ibid., p. 14.
43. Ibid., p. 3.
44. Ibid., p. 103.
45. Ibid.
46. Ibid., p. 67.
47. Ibid., p. 192.
48. Ibid., pp. 193–94.
49. Ibid., p. 32.
50. Ibid., p. 2.
51. George Gilder, "In Defense of Monogamy," *Commentary* 58, no. 5 (November 1974): 34.
52. Richard Viguerie, "The Real 'Women's Issues,'" *Conservative Digest* 8, no. 10 (October 1982): 64.
53. Joseph Sobran, "Why Conservatives Should Care about Abortion," *Conservative Digest* 7, no. 11 (November 1981): 14.
54. Ibid., p. 15.
55. Patrick Buchanan, "Reaganism in Retreat," *Conservative Digest* 9, no. 2 (February 1983): 6.
56. Donald Lambro, "Carter Holdover Promotes Foreign Abortions," *Conservative Digest* 9, no. 3 (March 1983): 6.

3. Neoconservatives and the Crisis of Liberal Equality

The term "neoconservative" does not encompass a completely unified set of assumptions. There are several differences that exist among today's leading neoconservatives: Daniel Bell, Irving Kristol, Norman Podhoretz, Nathan Glazer, Edward Banfield, Daniel Moynihan, Midge Decter, and Jeane Kirkpatrick.[1] But there is a unifying theme that defines neoconservative ideology, and that is the criticism of liberalism for overextending itself. As revisionist liberals, neoconservatives seek to save liberalism from itself. This is distinguished from the New Right rejection of liberalism, which attempts to replace welfare-state liberalism with a pseudo-populism rooted in Old Right patriarchal politics. In order to understand present-day New Right patriarchal politics, one must place those politics within the neoconservative stance on feminism in the state today, which is a carryover from the Carter administration. The elitism of neoconservatives and the pseudo-populism of the New Right are very different ideologically, appealing to different constituencies. Whereas the New Right can be viewed as right-wing radicals, neoconservatives are reformist liberals. However, both groups believe liberalism is in crisis and share a basic indictment of the welfare state.

Liberalism and the "Race of Life"

Neoconservatives reject the Great Society version of the welfare state because they think it has created what they term the "excesses of democracy," which supposedly means too much equality.[2] They criticize the present welfare state for trying to create equality of conditions rather than equality of opportunity, for destroying the differences between liberty and egalitarianism. Liberty is the freedom one should have to run the "race of life."[3] But there can be no guarantee that each competitor in the race should or will win. A truly liberal society allows everyone to compete, but a race in and of itself requires winners and losers. According to the neoconservatives, the problem is that everyone today claims the right to win. This has led people (particularly white and black women and black men) not only to expect equality of opportunity but to expect equality of outcomes or conditions. The neoconservative believes these expectations destroy true liberty—which is about freedom, not equality. Daniel Bell articulates this position when he states, "One has to distinguish between treating people equally and making them equal."[4] Thomas Sowell also makes this distinction when he argues that "uneven is not necessarily inequitable."[5] President Reagan's Commission for the Study of Ethical Problems in Medicine and Biochemical and Behavioral Research assumed this position when they found: "Equitable access is the 'ethical obligation' and 'ultimate responsibility' of federal government. . . . The cost of achieving equitable access ought to be shared fairly, but equity does not require equal access." This is why Irving Kristol argues that liberalism needs redefinition: he does not want to repudiate liberalism but rather wants to revive the distinction between equality and liberty.[6]

The Great Society programs such as Medicaid, Medicare, the Civil Rights Act of 1964, affirmative action programs, the expansion of training programs, and the establishment of the Office of Economic Opportunity, Job Corps, and Model City Programs are viewed as having unleashed a set of expectations that are endless. In the period from 1964 to 1975 a series of laws was established to prohibit discrimination in federally assisted programs and activities. In particular, Title VI of the Civil Rights Act barred discrimination on the basis of race, color, or national origin. In 1975 the nondiscrimination principle was extended to women in employment and educational programs. The Equal Rights Amendment (ERA), however, which would make sex a "suspect category" like race, has yet to be ratified. The Great Society programs are criticized for overextending the role of government in (supposedly) guaranteeing an individual a place in the "race of life." Edward Banfield comments on this problem of expectation:

> As Americans become more affluent, schooled and leisured they discover (and also invent) more and more "social problems" which

(they fondly suppose) can be "solved" if the government "really cares" (that is, if it passes enough laws, hires enough officials, and spends enough money).[7]

James Wilson echoes this same concern: "There is no nation on earth that has so expanded the catalogue of individual rights and no democratic nation on earth that has made subject to regulation so many aspects of otherwise private transactions. . . . The more we extend the scope of rights, the harder it is to regulate and to improve, and vice versa."[8] David Stockman, as director of the Office of Management and Budget, articulates this same position for the Reagan administration: "The idea that has been established over the last ten years, that almost every service that someone might need in life ought to be provided and financed by the government as a matter of rights is wrong. We challenge that. We reject that notion."[9]

Besides the fact that neoconservatives think that Americans have come to expect too much from government, they also believe that people expect the wrong thing. At best, individuals should expect that they be free to compete, and this is different from assuming that equality should be part of the competition. The problem, according to Daniel Bell, is that equality has been redefined by the Great Society programs. In the nineteenth century, equality meant equality of opportunity; it was used to destroy the hierarchy of ascription. Now it is being criticized as hierarchical itself. There is a demand for "the reduction of all inequality, or the creation of *equality of result*—in income, status, and power—for all men in society. This issue is the central value problem of the post industrial society."[10]

Bell embraces the nineteenth-century conception of equality (as equality of opportunity) and argues "that what it meant in effect, was that no one should take on the air of an aristocrat and lord it over other men."[11] The notion of equality comes down "to the sentiment that each man was as good as another and no man was better than anyone else."[12] In this sense the nineteenth-century notion of equality emphasized personal achievement, a lack of deference to formal barriers and prescribed positions. Bell supports a notion of meritocracy that recognizes the differences between individuals rather than the equality between them. "It is to that extent that a well-tempered meritocracy can be a society not of equals, but of the just."[13] Equality of opportunity posits the classic liberal view of the individual, and it is assumed that individuals will differ "in their energy, drive, and motivation, in their conception of what is desirable—and that the institutions of society should establish procedures for regulating fairly the competition and exchanges necessary to fulfill these diverse desires and competencies."[14]

Irving Kristol adopts a similar stance, asserting that inequality is necessary for a particular ideal of human excellence and achievement.[15] He rejects the notion that the only true equality of opportunity requires guaranteeing equality of conditions from the outset. Kristol argues that "the insatiability of the egalitarian passion" makes it an untenable political principle.[16] It is interesting, however, to note that Kristol has not always held this antiegalitarian view. In a *Commentary* symposium in 1960 he stated his support of programs that would attempt to redress unequal opportunity:

> What seems necessary now, if we are to be governed as a democracy in some spirit of equality, is unequal opportunity. In other words, the disadvantaged groups do not need to be given less chance than anyone else, they need to be given far more opportunity than anyone else. This requires government action. They will be accorded privileges under the name of equality for all.[17]

Kristol no longer holds this view and instead shares Bell's indictment of affirmative action as denying individual expression and difference in favor of an individual's ascribed status as a member of a group. Whereas liberalism is supposed to reject ascribed status in favor of individual achievement, affirmative action is rejected by neoconservatives because it identifies the individual in terms of ascribed group status. "But now it is being demanded that one must have a place primarily because one possesses a particular group attribute."[18]

Reconsidering Affirmative Action

Neoconservatives are critical of affirmative action programs because in their judgment they predetermine the outcome of a competition. They view affirmative action as promising and creating equality of results, rather than establishing equality of opportunity. In the Heritage Foundation's mandate-for-leadership report, *Agenda '83*, which outlines neoconservative concerns, affirmative action is specifically targeted as a problem to be redressed. The agenda states that "schools must not be required to bear the burden of proving that they do not discriminate. Also, the legislation should state that only a concrete specific act against a specific victim constitutes discrimination—not the absence of affirmative action or numerical quotas."[19] It is also argued that intentional discrimination should be distinguished from unintentional discrimination as the problem that needs redressing.

> The more troublesome issue is unintentional-uneven results. In these cases, the focus is not on the denial of opportunity but on the results . . . in these cases, no individual is identified as a victim; an entire subset of the population is deemed to be an injured party . . . clearly, members of society have an equal opportunity to strive for and achieve different goals. Proponents of equality-of-results definitions of discrimination forget that an uneven result is not necessarily an inequitable result.[20]

This notion of "intentional discrimination" that affects "identifiable victims" once again serves to mask the unintended (as well as intended) reality of individual discrimination defined by one's racial or sexual class identity. This is readily evident in the following statement, also in *Agenda '83*: "No woman can be found who was denied a slot on a professional football team just because she was a woman."[21] In much the same way, veterans' preference laws in government hiring have been found to be nondiscriminatory toward women; they are rather said to discriminate against nonveterans. As such, women's identity as a member of a sexual class is denied and through this denial discrimination toward an individual, as a member of a sexual class, is made impossible. How can one prove sexual discrimination as an individual woman when the sexual-class identity of "woman" is not recognized?

This neoconservative view has been adopted by the Reagan administration. The dismantling of affirmative action programs is now justified on the grounds that *individual identifiable victims*, rather than a generalized notion of an individual as a member of a particular class, must be at the base of affirmative action suits. Under the new proposed Labor Department rules one needs "identifiable victims" of job discrimination (for relief such as back pay) rather than "affected classes," where the presumption is that everyone in the class suffered discrimination. Instead of the employer's having to prove that discrimination does not exist, the individual will now have to prove that it does exist.[22]

Discrimination is redefined in relation to the individual rather than in terms of the individual's identity within a particular class. This switch is significant in that it attempts to erase the feminist indictment of (liberal) equality of opportunity for its commitment to the ascribed status of white and black women and black men according to their race and/or sexual class. Once one acknowledges the sexual-class identity assigned to women by the patriarchal bias of liberalism, the demand for sexual equality becomes potentially subversive. The recognition of woman as a member of a sexual class challenges the patriarchal foundations of the individual right to run in the "race of life." As such, liberal individualism, or equality of opportunity, is exposed as a form of male privilege. The identification of the individual as a member of a particular racial category also exposes racial privilege as an aspect of "individual rights." Affirmative action, to the extent that it acknowledges previous discrimination on the basis of one's sexual-class identity, challenges the patriarchal foundations of equality of opportunity. The neoconservatives recognize this challenge and seek to dismantle affirmative action programs for this reason. Equality of opportunity for the neoconservative requires the patriarchal sexual-class and racist aspects of the race of life.

According to the neoconservative analysis, the welfare state is in crisis because it cannot and will never be able to satisfy the demand for equality, which only breeds more demands for greater equality. Hence, the neoconservative believes that only when expectations are lowered will government be able to satisfy the people again; if people expect less of government, government will be able to perform better.[23] This of course has a certain logic because the welfare state cannot create an egalitarian society and protect capitalist patriarchy at the same time. However, I would argue that the welfare state has never attempted to create equality of conditions, but rather opportunity, and that the crisis of liberalism reflects its incapacity to absorb equality of opportunity along sexual-class and racial lines.

The Neoconservative Welfare State

The major attack on the welfare state is leveled against what Irving Kristol calls the "new class": "scientists, lawyers, city planners, social workers, educators, criminologists, sociologists [and] public health doctors" who work in the expanding public sector of the welfare state as "regulatory officials."[24] Kristol sees this class as the people "whom liberal capitalism has sent to college in order to help manage its affluent, highly technological, mildly paternalistic, 'postindustrial society.'"[25] According to Kristol, the welfare state does not just support the nonworking population, it actually supports the "middle-class professionals who attend to the needs of the nonworking population (teachers, social workers, lawyers, doctors, dieticians, civil servants of all descriptions)."[26] A review of the Reagan budget cuts will show that they are aimed as much against this "new class" as they are aimed at the working poor.

Kristol does not want to do away with the welfare state, but rather seeks to create a conservative welfare state based on the American values of self-reliance and individual liberty: "Wherever possible, people should be allowed to keep their own money—rather than having it transferred (via taxes) to the state—on condition that they put it to certain defined uses."[27] He wants to reconcile the purposes of the welfare state with the maximum amount of individual independence and the least amount of bureaucratic coercion. A fuller version of the neoconservative welfare state is outlined by Jack Meyer in the American Enterprise Institute's publication *Meeting Human Needs: Toward a New Public Philosophy:*

> (1) remove the non-needy from income maintenance programs; (2) improve the work incentives of social programs; (3) tighten up claims review, returning programs to their original intent; (4) redesign programs with uncontrollable cost increases; and (5) rely to a greater extent on the resources of the private sector to meet our social needs.[28]

This streamlined welfare state will reduce bureaucracy and allow for a reduction in taxes, which Bruce Bartlett in *Agenda '83* argues will provide a real income in after-tax incentives for work production and saving.[29]

The neoconservative revision of the welfare state calls for a reprivatization of many of the functions of the present state apparatus. Meyer believes that wherever the private sector can offer an alternative to government services, government programs should be eliminated. When this is not possible, user fees should be levied on those who benefit from the services.[30] However, many neoconservatives, like Robert Woodson, caution against "shifting responsibility and authority from large publicly supported bureaucratic social agencies of the welfare state to large corporations and large foundations with the tacit expectation that they will fill the gap left by cuts in social programs in the name of private sector initiative."[31] He argues that private and public "mega-structures of society" do not necessarily hold the answer; instead we need to turn to mediating structures within the social system. He adopts what has come to be termed the Berger-Neuhaus thesis: "that when faced with crises, low-income residents turn to friends, relatives, churches, families and other mediating structures."[32] The neoconservative view turns toward the private market and the private realm of mediating structures, away from the state. The neoconservative version of the welfare state attempts to reprivatize social life and reestablish the distinction between the state and the market and the family and the state. Neoconservatives attempt to revise the liberal (patriarchal) state toward its former self, while recognizing that traditional patriarchal family forms are outmoded. They therefore focus attention on the public sphere of the market, rather than the private sphere of the family, to reconstitute the necessary patriarchal controls for capitalist society. Whereas most New Right legislation has focused on family life and sexuality, neoconservatives have been more concerned with affirmative action programs, which directly affect the market and indirectly impact on family life. Because this approach appears focused on public matters, neoconservatives are better able to disguise their commitments to patriarchal social relations than the New Right.

Both Bell and Kristol recognize that with liberalism in crisis, capitalism needs a new moral vision. Kristol argues that "the enemy of liberal capitalism today is not so much socialism as nihilism. Only liberal capitalism doesn't see nihilism as an enemy, but rather as just another splendid business opportunity."[33] Bell contends that the crisis of liberalism lies in the cultural contradiction of capitalism, which reflects "the disjunction between the kind of organization and the norms demanded in the economic realm, and the norms of self-realization that are now central in the culture."[34] Hedonism, pleasure as a way of life, has replaced the Protestant ethic and the Puritan temper of "sobriety, frugality, sexual restraint, and a forbidding attitude toward life."[35] Bell criticizes the consumer mentality in capitalism that corrupts society with rampant individualism and leaves little sense of community or public purpose. Former President Jimmy Carter spoke of this problem of self-interest in his famous "malaise" speech, July 1979, when he warned against the breakdown of America's sense of community and resurgence of self-indulgence and consumption. Neoconservatives, rightly concerned with the selfish aspects of liberalism, ask: "As liberalism's national community erodes, how are we to avoid slipping into mean spirited individualism?"[36]

In the neoconservative revision of twentieth-century liberalism, inequality is preferred to equality; equality of opportunity is preferred to equality of conditions or starting places. As Charles Frankel has stated: "It could be argued, indeed, that social inequality is itself the principal incentive that makes people work in an affluent society."[37] This redefinition demonstrates the reactionary impulse inherent in liberalism. Arguing that this impulse has always been a part of liberalism itself, Kristol thinks the term "neoliberal" is more appropriate than neoconservative for describing this position.[38] But the term "neoconservative" is more apt, in my mind, because neoconservatism attempts to redirect liberalism away from its democratic potential and emphasizes the conservative elitism inherent in liberalism. Neoconservatives attempt to reestablish the justification for hierarchical relations within liberal society. They seek an order and authority that will once again stabilize society by redefining people's expectations. In this sense, neoconservativism merely rearticulates the conservative commitment to hierarchy while emphasizing the necessity of inequality for a system based on equality of opportunity.

Liberalism and neoconservatism are not theories about equality or sexual equality. Liberalism is a theory about economic and political freedom, while conservatism is a theory about political hierarchy, authority, and inequality. Neoconservatism tries to blend the two: it is a theory about equality of opportunity with a defense of the inequities necessary to competition. Neoconservatism retains the liberal commitment to individualism and individual freedom of choice but does so with the added commitment to inequality and authority implicit in liberalism and explicit in conservatism. As such, it moves away from liberal democracy toward an authoritarian democracy that emphasizes the importance of authority and order in a specifically revised patriarchal form. It is not clear what is left of the progressive or radical aspects of liberalism once we redefine it in conflict with a democracy committed not only to freedom but to equality as well. Patrick Moynihan's statements about an ordered society reflect the priorities and problems with the neoconservative view. In arguing against the equal participation of all he states: "An 'information-rich society' is not necessarily a society better able to handle itself. For people, as for rats, too much contradictory information is disorienting."[39] A theory that rejects equality becomes antidemocratic even if not antiliberal.

Neoconservatives must recognize that the elitist liberalism they espouse will not work any better than the supposed egalitarian liberalism they so fear. Liberal democratic ideology, with its egalitarian promises, functioned well as an ideology for competitive capitalism, but it functions less well for advanced monopoly capitalism. Once society is forced to emphasize the elitist bias of liberalism—liberty rather than equality, equality of opportunity and not egalitarianism—the very ideological force of liberalism is undermined. In actuality liberalism has always had its elitist aspects. But once policymakers seek to protect and further articulate liberalism's elitist (economic, sexual, racial) nature rather than its democratic qualities, they no longer have an ideology that is both liberal *and* democratic. Kristol might learn from himself when he criticizes a politics of nostalgia: "There is no more chance today of

returning to a society of 'free enterprise' and enfeebled government than there was, in the sixteenth century, of returning to a
Rome-centered Christendom. The world and the people in it have
changed. One may regret this fact; nostalgia is always permissible.
But the politics of nostalgia is always self-destructive."[40] In the
end, the neoconservative criticism of the welfare state is a criticism of the democratic aspects of liberalism and the potential of
its ideology to promise egalitarianism. The neoconservatives seek
to protect liberalism (and with it capitalist patriarchy) by replacing the democratic potential of its ideology with authoritarianism.
In doing so, they attack the democratic aspects of liberalism.

Neoconservatism and the Excesses of Feminism

Neoconservatism has defined the crisis of liberalism as rooted
in the confusion between equality of opportunity and equality of
conditions. Liberal society requires the first, not the second. The
feminist movement, with its demands for affirmative action, abortion rights, and the Equal Rights Amendment, is viewed by
neoconservatives as an "excess" of liberalism. Women have come
to demand too much (sexual) equality and have denied the reality
of difference (or inequality) in the "race of life." Neoconservatives
opt for the notion of "sexual difference" rather than "sexual equality"; and they support equality of opportunity rather than egalitarianism between the sexes.

Michael Levin, in Commentary, a leading neoconservative journal, criticizes the feminist movement for assuming that there are
no important biologically based differences between men and
women—as though if they were raised identically they would
develop identically.[41] He argues that "we come into the world not
as bits of prime matter, but as males or females."[42] Putting aside
Levin's assumptions about what feminists think about the issue of
biological difference, one needs to recognize that neoconservatives believe that the differentiation of the sexes, of woman from
man, is necessary to social life. Levin therefore rejects what he
calls sexual egalitarianism, which requires androgynously equita-

ble outcomes.[43] Ruth Wisse, also in *Commentary*, discusses the issue of whether women should be allowed to become rabbis in terms of this issue of difference: "We may then find it increasingly difficult, when the distinctions between women and men have no known consequence or meaning, to maintain Judaism's unyielding differentiations between wool and linen, between milk and meat, between Sabbath and week, between Israel and the Nations."[44]

In another leading neoconservative journal, *The Public Interest*, the point that men and women are different is made continuously while discussing the problem of affirmative action. "We should strive for equal treatment [opportunity] of individuals rather than equal results [conditions] for men and for women."[45] The problem of women's advancement is understood as not a lack of opportunity but rather a reflection of the differences between men and women. Hence, we need a reward system that recognizes "initiative, leadership, knowledge of the job and competitive spirit rather than a reward system that tries to equalize the sexes.[46] "The law should open opportunities and expand the range of choices for individuals—not interfere with rational business practice, individual decisions, or the fundamental institutions of society."[47]

Neoconservatives attack feminism for its commitment to equality that derives from the ideology of liberal individualism: that each individual is autonomous and equal. In the eighteenth and nineteenth centuries, although the concept of individual and citizen was in actuality limited to white male individuals, liberal ideology held out the promise of equality for men and women. Once Mary Wollstonecraft, Elizabeth Cady Stanton, Susan B. Anthony, and others chose to argue the concept of individual rights for women, a subtle, subversive challenge to the patriarchal underpinnings of liberalism was initiated.[48]

A similar dynamic developed out of the progressive movements of the 1960s. The feminist movement of the 1970s, although not limited to a critique of the male bias of liberalism (it was as much an indictment of the male privilege of the New Left and civil rights movement), was very much rooted in acting on the progressive aspects of liberal ideology's commitment to equality.[49] And at the same time that the feminist movement of the 1970s grew out of a rejection of the patriarchal bias of liberalism it has also exacerbated the crisis of liberalism in that the demands for women's equality, in such limited aspects as ERA, have further articulated and legitimized the notion of (sexual) equality as an acceptable expectation. Demands such as those embodied in the ERA uncover the contradictory aspects of liberalism. On the one hand, the ideology of equality before the law and the individual right to achievement appears to be sex-neutral. On the other hand, the fact that the ERA was not ratified unmasks the ascribed status of women as less than equal as a reality. The Equal Rights Amendment does not demand equality of conditions, but merely legislates equality of opportunity. Equality before the law is defined by the patriarchal privileges encompassed within the law. This means that a woman starts out in a different (unequal) starting place in the race of life. However, if equality of opportunity as an ideological force continues to be as subversive as it was in the 1960s in that it leads to further demands for real equality, one can begin to see why the neoconservatives reject affirmative action, the ERA, and so on, as an "excess" of liberalism.

If liberal capitalist society cannot abide real equality between the sexes, and if equality of opportunity is subversive to itself in that once it is accepted as a "right" it leads to further expectations about a more substantial equality, and if feminism (particularly its liberal form, which is embodied in all forms of feminism—that is, the conception of woman as a full individual with requisite "rights") has been the major political movement of the 1970s to highlight the inadequacy of liberal ideology for creating real equality, then the importance of neoconservatives' reembracing the notion of so-called sexual difference in the attempt to reassert the necessity of (a form) of inequality in the race of life becomes clear. The concept of sexual difference is being used to curtail and define an acceptable notion of sexual equality that can then be used to further construct an acceptable notion of equality—meaning equality of opportunity and not equality of conditions. And the particular import of using the concept of sexual difference is that it can be used to underline and justify the notion of difference as natural and necessary. Once the race of life between men and women as a specific is justified as natural, the epistemological and political base of equality of opportunity in general is made. The natural differences (inequalities) in the (sexual) race of life justify the inequalities of the economic and social race of life.

Neoconservatives, Family Life, and Sexuality

The neoconservative position that there is an excess of democracy, meaning an excess of equality, leads them to argue for hierarchy as a necessity for social and political order. Hierarchy is not supposed to be predetermined (by ascribed rank) but rather is supposed to reflect the outcome of an open competition. In this sense, women are not to be kept out of the race within the neoconservative argument, but neither are they to be assisted in entering it. Margaret Bonilla of the neoconservative Heritage Foundation argues in this vein that "government interference in the marketplace is the greatest barrier to the success and advancement of women."[50] Rachel Flick, in *The Public Interest*, also adopts this position. She thinks men's and women's work in the market is not comparable but different, and that the male ethos and "masculine behavior" from employees is necessary to American business enterprise. At the same time, she does not exclude women from the opportunity to obtain a "masculine" job; she just does not want to make men's and women's work similar. "To the degree that women *want* the kinds of jobs and careers hitherto dominated by men, and to the degree that they are willing to alter their supposed 'womanly' outlook from 9–5—they can and will get 'men's jobs' within the framework of an open job market."[51]

Interference in the competition of the marketplace, such as affirmative action programs, merely tampers with the natural order. Neoconservatism subtly reasserts the patriarchal hierarchical ordering of woman from man in the name of "sexual difference," particularly in the marketplace. Unlike the New Right, neoconservatives do not explicitly call for a restrengthening of the power of the father in the family as an ascribed privilege. They rather argue for the necessity of family life, heterosexual marriage, and sexual difference while not limiting family life to the traditional patriarchal family with a housewife. They extend their view of family life to include the dual wage-earning family with the "working mother." However, the working mother should not expect assistance from programs designed to create greater equality (of conditions) between men and women, such as day care programs, job training programs, or affirmative action.

In The Public Interest, Allan Carlson asks what a family is. He argues that if one defers to a "pluralism of family forms"—which the liberals do—then one is left with no definition of family at all. "If there can be no definition that excludes any form of human cohabitation, then what is a family policy trying to save, or restore, or strengthen, or help?"[52] Although the neoconservative view of the preferred family is more often assumed than defined, the family itself remains at the core of an ordered, stable society. The family is viewed as one of the only places people get the love they need. "The family is also the institution where most of us, both as children and as parents, acquire a sense of continuity with the past and a sense of commitment to the 'future.'"[53] This notion of the family assumes the biological family as a necessity. "The burden of proof should fall upon those believing our humanness could survive even if the biological family does not."[54]

The neoconservative critique of family life rejects what it terms the liberal agenda, which requires government involvement in family life. "The disconcerting reality appears to be that state social intervention on behalf of families actually weakens or destroys families."[55] And by this is meant that many of the economic maintenance programs for the family, which have by now been dismantled but which were established through the 1960s, lead to further disintegration of the family. Full employment, national health insurance programs, day care subsidies, and the like may bring about certain improvements in family life, "but these measures will not strengthen families."[56] It is assumed that the economic dependence of the woman on her husband holds families together more than does a woman's dependence on the state. And the inequities of the market are used to reinforce this dependence for wage-earning women.

Brigette Berger, also in The Public Interest, criticizes the state and its paid professionals for the invasion of family life. "The family has generally been 'battered' in our society, with public policy . . . tending to take children away from the family, and to decrease the family's authority and independence."[57] She argues that the family should be recognized as the central therapeutic unit with policies only offering support for the family as a unit unto itself.[58] As such, for the neoconservative, the family should be protected *from* the state, although I have argued that the family is already structured and protected *by* the state. This poses a real dilemma for the neoconservative view of family life. These conflictual needs of family life, which the neoconservatives attempt to protect, set up the problem of what the relationship should be between the state and family life.

According to Robert Nisbet, most theorists committed to equality (of conditions) argue against the family. If egalitarianism is taken to its logical conclusion it requires the destruction of the economic inequalities fostered through family structure. Interestingly enough, neoconservatives focus only on the way family life reproduces economic inequality; they are completely silent on the issue of how family life reproduces sexual inequality. Seymour Martin Lipset, discussing the Workingmen's Association of the 1930s, asks whether they understood the relationship between (economic) egalitarianism and the necessary destruction of family more clearly than do liberals today:

> For if one really wishes a society in which there is not merely formal equality of opportunity, but where class background has absolutely no relation to success, one must be willing to pay the necessary price. And that price would appear to include the practical abolition of the family. . . . As the Communist experience has shown, the abolition of capitalism, at least in itself, is by no means sufficient.[59]

Neoconservatives use the commitment to family life to reject the notion of egalitarianism and embrace the view of (natural) difference. If one accepts an equality premised on difference (inequality), the family poses no problem because egalitarianism is rejected in the first place.

Inequality is spoken of as difference, and difference is necessitated by the race of life *and* family life. The family is contradictory only to egalitarianism; it is not contradictory to equality of opportunity, which posits inequality as difference.

Why then is the family in crisis according to the neoconservative viewpoint? Because liberalism itself is in crisis. Once society begins to embrace and advocate egalitarianism—supposedly through interventions by the state—it begins to destabilize the family. The crisis of authority in the state is reproduced in a crisis of authority within the family. And I would argue that the problem on both state and family levels reflects a crisis of the patriarchal underpinnings of liberalism; equality of opportunity has been uncovered as still assuming an ascribed status for women. In this sense the neoconservatives are right: the authority of the state, the father, and husband is challenged when the guise of equality of opportunity is stripped of its ideological import as the ascribed sexual status of the race of life is demystified.

But for the neoconservatives, the crisis of liberalism is not merely a political crisis, it is also a cultural problem. The individual, which is the root concern of liberalism, has begun to be hedonistically centered on himself, or more likely herself. According to Daniel Bell, individuals have begun to wallow in their freedom, having lost the necessary ties and obligations that hold a society together. Hedonism, narcissism, and feminism become one and the same—the troublesome extension of liberal individualism. Feminism becomes defined as an excess—if not *the* excess—of liberal democracy.

Midge Decter more than a decade ago focused on the problem of feminism as reflecting an excess of freedom for women. The women's movement was really about "the difficulties women are experiencing with the rights and freedoms they already enjoy."[60] Feminism is presented in this case as a response to the fact that women are anxious over their increasing freedom: "For the middle class woman her opportunity to participate in the world beyond household—to educate herself, limit her family, go to work, and to an unprecedented extent make her life—have left her in a sometimes nearly overwhelming state of uncertainty."[61]

Sexuality itself poses a major problem for the feminist according to Decter in that the "new chastity" gives a woman boundless freedom. No longer expected to be chaste "and yet without the active force of lust to guide her, she finds herself without natural boundaries."[62] Decter assumes that women are passive in terms of sexual desire—giving rather than receiving pleasure—and the giving has supposedly become boundless. This is why women, in her view, seek marriage—it puts a lid on their freedom: " . . . marriage is an institution maintained and protected by women, for the sake of and at the behest of women, and in accordance with their deepest wishes."[63] Women marry because they want to and need to marry. And the feminist movement is really a reaction to the freedom that its own critique of marriage has supposedly created. Women do not need more freedom, more hedonism, more narcissism, or feminism. Rather, they need marriage and the family. It is interesting that we have shifted from a critique of equality to a critique of freedom—specifically sexual freedom. In the end if sexual freedom is a problem, then sexual equality is an impossibility, because if sexual freedom is a problem women need protection rather than equality. This is the nub of the neoconservative argument against sexual equality.

The issues of sexual freedom, homosexuality, and feminism are all bound together for the neoconservative as enemies of family life. Feminism and the so-called sexual revolution are viewed as direct assaults against family life, because sex and love become separate; masturbation and homosexuality become condoned: "No religious views, no community moral standards are to deflect him from his overriding purposes of self-discovery, self-assertion, and self-gratification."[64] The religious or moral view of sex is replaced by rampant narcissism and individualism. Homosexuality becomes an excess much like feminism. Robert Nisbet, commenting on Midge Decter's article "Boys on the Beach, " states:

> Militant homosexuality has become one of the most destructive of ideological influences on the family in our society. . . . Gay Liberationists ally themselves naturally with the same voices from radical Women's Liberationism; the single objective is the devastation—through contempt, ridicule, and derision—of the family.[65]

Militant feminism and militant homosexuality endanger the family and with it the moral order that could contain the excesses of liberalism, namely, sexual egalitarianism and freedom of sexual preference. The argument that nature requires family life is once again used but this time to indict homosexuality and its supposed narcissism. If heterosexuality can be claimed as "natural" and therefore "necessary" and "good," then marriage and the biological family remain intact. "To be sure, it would be a mistake to argue from the biological act to 'what ought to be,' that is, from 'is' to 'ought'; but certainly, the facts of biology lend much credence to the view that heterosexuality—and not homosexuality—is natural—and normal (both descriptively and prescriptively)."[66]

Homosexuality is viewed as unnatural: "Human bodies seem more obviously designed for heterosexual intercourse than for homosexual, both as to technique and as to purpose."[67] Heterosexual reproduction is viewed as natural and therefore homosexuality is characterized as an unnatural renunciation of childbearing. As such, homosexuality is seen as a direct assault on the biological family. "It is not surprising that an age which has, in other contexts, developed a considerable animus against the family and the production of children, should look more complacently upon homosexuality, the sterile practice of which is now in less clear contrast with marriage than it once was."[68]

Neoconservatives regard gender identity, the distinguishing of woman from man within the heterosexual and patriarchal context, as fundamental; thus the biological family takes on a natural and necessary status.[69] Liberalism and (liberal) feminism will have to be curtailed to the extent that they have become subversive to the heterosexual and patriarchal family. Equality of opportunity—which posits heterosexual, married men and women in the race of life—is all that the individual should expect. To demand that as individuals we have the right not to marry, or not to bear children, or to be lesbian or homosexual is an excess of equality and sexual freedom. For the neoconservative sexual equality and sexual freedom pose the dilemma of liberalism because once sexual equality is promised and is interpreted to mean a real equality of conditions, heterosexuality, marriage, and family life along with the legitimacy of the state are challenged.

The Neoconservative State and "Women's Issues"

Neoconservatives criticize the welfare state as identifying women as victims in need of help. They argue that the Reagan administration needs to abandon "women's issues" as they are currently defined because they are liberal issues.[70] Margaret Bonilla in *Agenda '83* rejects the advocacy position of government in establishing programs for women:

Typically, the proposed solutions include: free child care, government funding for abortions, and government funding for political advocacy groups who would then promote "correct" positions, which are pushed in government and society. These so-called reforms are in fact thinly disguised attacks on the concepts of personal responsibility, the traditional family and the free enterprise system itself.[71]

She instead opts for a neoconservative approach to women's issues: one that reduces state regulation, largely eliminates licensing requirements, and lessens the tax burdens associated with a second income. Then the Reagan administration will be able to "leave a legacy of genuine respect for those women who choose to be housewives and mothers, greater opportunities for women working outside the home in a market-oriented society, and creative options for part-time and home-based occupations."[72]

Bonilla argues that such a policy, one she terms a conservative policy (as opposed to a liberal one) for women, has to be developed by the Reagan administration. Such policies need to recognize "free markets, personal freedom, personal responsibility, limited government and a strong defense."[73] She criticizes Reagan for not appointing conservative women to positions in his administration and for utilizing the liberal agenda on women that assumes their victim status rather than developing programs that expand opportunities for them. The Reagan administration needs to move from aiding victims to offering opportunities.

> The key word is opportunity and the creation of an opportunity society in which part-time or home-based occupations offer greater choices to women than ever before. With technological advancement in computers, word processing, and accounting many other tasks can be performed by women who may choose to mix family and career without leaving their houses.[74]

This means increasing freedom for the individual without creating interference from the state. Federal paternalism, according to Bonilla, whether it is affirmative action or another form of state intervention, is abhorrent and insulting.[75]

The neoconservative position applauds equality of opportunity and individual freedom of choice for women. Women should be free to be housewives or wage earners. Women should not, however, expect equality if it assumes the "likeness" of women and men. The protection of sexual difference and individual freedom from government interference remain core elements of the neoconservative position on women's issues. Neoconservatism calls for a reprivatization of the state and a protection of family life. The major focus of the neoconservatives' critique of sexual equality is not "the" family per se because they abide by the liberal notion of the right to privacy. They therefore do not seek to legislate sexuality in the realm of the family through constitutional amendments against abortion, as does the New Right. Nor do they argue for increased rights of the traditional patriarchal father. But they do openly advocate heterosexuality and marriage even if they do not approve of using constitutional amendments to enforce such behavior. Interestingly enough, neoconservatives have written very little about their position on the Equal Rights Amendment. It is possible that they could support it as establishing equality of opportunity for women or reject it as an excessive demand leading to greater demands for equality of conditions. Instead they have focused on affirmative action, seeking to curtail the gains made by women toward equality within the market. They focus on the market to rearticulate and justify the notion of sexual difference, and reject the notion of sexual egalitarianism in their rejection of affirmative action programs. They argue for (sexual) equality of opportunity, rather than egalitarianism that is enforced by the paternalistic welfare state. Their language is one of personal freedom and independence for women; not equality, but equality of opportunity, which recognizes sexual difference. Neoconservatives do not argue that women are not equal to men; they say rather that women are different from men. Therefore equality of opportunity for women is fine; equality of conditions (which assumes sameness) is not.

Whereas the New Right demystifies the place of sex and family life within the political order by challenging the private/public split on these issues, the neoconservatives mystify the place of sexuality and the family by adhering to the liberal distinction between public and private realms. As such, the New Right is truly subversive to the liberal (patriarchal) state, whereas the neoconservatives wish to reform it—hence my point that the neoconservatives, as revisionist liberals, are more dangerous in a society defined by liberal ideology. The New Right sets up its own constraints to the extent that it is anti-liberal in the very realm of sex and family life. The neoconservatives attempt to preserve aspects of patriarchal privilege by arguing for sexual difference rather than sexual equality. They recognize the wage-earner role of women and their place in the market, while they argue to dismantle affirmative action programs because affirmative action supposedly denies individuals their personal freedom in the race of life. Woman is recognized as an individual, with no problematic sexual-class identity. There is therefore no need for feminism, or an interventionist state.

NOTES

1. For a discussion of neoconseravatism see Peter Steinfels, *The Neoconservatives: The Men Who Are Changing America's Politics* (New York: Simon and Schuster, 1979). Also see Daniel Bell, *The Cultural Contradictions of Capitalism* (New York: Basic Books, 1976); Nathan Glazer and Irving Kristol, eds., *The American Commonwealth* (New York: Basic Books, 1976); and Irving Kristol, *Two Cheers for Capitalism* (New York: New American Library, 1978).
2. See Steinfels, *The Neoconservatives*, for a full discussion of this point.
3. See Isaac Kramnick, "Religion and Radicalism: English Political Theory in the Age of Revolution," *Political Theory* 5, no. 4 (November 1977): 505–34, for an excellent discussion of equality of opportunity in bourgeois thought. For related critical discussions see C. B. MacPherson, *The Political Theory of Possessive Individualism: Hobbes to Lock* (New York: Oxford University Press, 1962) and *Democratic Theory: Essays in Retrieval* (New York: Oxford University Press, 1973); Carole Pateman, *The Problem of Political Obligation* (New York: John Wiley and Sons, 1979); Michael Gargas McGrath, ed., *Liberalism and the Modern Polity* (New York: Marcel Dekker, 1978); and Michael Margolis, *Viable Democracy* (Harmondsworth: Penguin, 1979).
4. Daniel Bell, *The Cultural Contradictions of Capitalism* (New York: Basic Books, 1976), p. 260.
5. See Thomas Sowell, *Affirmative Action Reconsidered* (Washington, D.C.: American Enterprise Institute for Public Policy Research, 1975) and "Are Quotas Good for Blacks?" *Commentary* 65, no. 6 (June 1978): 39–43, for a more complete discussion of this point.
6. Irving Kristol, "What Is a Liberal—Who Is a Conservative? A Symposium," *Commentary* 62, no. 3 (September 1976): 74. Also see Kristol, "About Equality," *Commentary* 54, no. 5 (November 1972): 41–59, and "An Exchange on Equality," *Commentary* 55, no. 2 (February 1973): 12–25.
7. Edward Banfield, "Nixon, the Great Society, and the Future of Social Policy—A Symposium," *Commentary* 55, no. 5 (May 1973): 33.
8. James Q. Wilson, "Policy Intellectuals," *Public Interest* 64 (Summer 1981): 35. Also see Samuel Huntington, *American Politics: The Promise of Disharmony* (Cambridge: Harvard University Press, 1981).
9. Quoted in David Rosenbaum, "Study Shows Planned Welfare Cuts Would Most Hurt Poor Who Work," *New York Times*, March 20, 1981, p. 1.
10. Daniel Bell, "Meritocracy and Equality," *Public Interest* 29 (Fall 1972): 40.

Also see Seymour Martin Lipset, "Social Mobility and Equal Opportunity," *Public Interest* 29 (Fall 1972): 90–108; Milton Himmelfarb, "Liberals and Libertarians," *Commentary* 59, no. 6 (June 1975): 65–70; and Robert Nisbet, "The Pursuit of Equality," *Public Interest* 35 (Spring 1974): 103–20.

11. Bell, "Meritocracy and Equality," p. 40.
12. Ibid.
13. Ibid., p. 68.
14. Ibid., p. 40.
15. Kristol, "About Equality," p. 41.
16. Irving Kristol and critics, "An Exchange on Equality," *Commentary* 55, no. 2 (February 1973): 24.
17. Ibid., p. 12.
18. Bell, "Meritocracy and Equality," p. 38.
19. Lucy Phelps Patterson, "Education," in Richard Holwill, ed., *A Mandate for Leadership Report, Agenda '83* (Washington, D.C. : The Heritage Foundation, 1983), p. 117.
20. Marshall Breger et al., in Holwill, ed., *Agenda '83*, p. 208.
21. Ibid., p. 209.
22. Further proposed changes in affirmative action regulations include: (1) only companies with a federal contract of $100,000 or more and with 100 or more employees would have to prepare affirmative action plans to increase the number of women and minorities; (2) the government would no longer have to review a company's compliance with the equal employment opportunity laws before awarding a contract; (3) a presumption would be established that an employer has reasonably utilized minorities and women when their employment rate in specific programs is at least 80 percent of their availability in the area. See Robert Pear, "U.S. Plans to Ease Rules for Hiring Women and Blacks," *New York Times*, April 3, 1983, p. A.1.
23. See Glazer and Kristol, eds., *The American Commonwealth*, especially Samuel Huntington, "The Democratic Distemper," pp. 9–38, for a full statement of this argument; see also Seymour Martin Lipset and William Schneider, *The Confidence Gap: Business, Labor and Government in the Public Mind* (New York: Free Press, 1983); and Beau Grosscup, "The Neoconservative State and the Politics of Terrorism," *New Political Science* 8 (Spring 1982): 39–62.
24. Kristol, *Two Cheers*, p. 14.
25. Ibid., p. 17.
26. Ibid., p. 169.
27. Ibid., p. 119.
28. Jack Meyer, "Private Sector Initiatives and Public Policy: A New Agenda," in Meyer, ed., *Meeting Human Needs* (Washington, D.C.: American Enterprise Institute for Public Policy, 1982), p. 30.
29. See Bruce Bartlett, "Coordinating Economic Policy," in Holwill, ed., *Agenda '83*, p. 11.
30. Meyer, ed., *Meeting Human Needs*, p. xiv.
31. Robert Woodson, "Investing in People: A Strategy to Combat Not Preserve Society," in Meyer, ed., *Meeting Human Needs*, p. 18.
32. Ibid., p. 19. Also see Peter Berger and Richard Neuhaus, *To Empower People* (Washington, D.C.: American Enterprise Institute for Public Policy, 1977).
33. Kristol, *Two Cheers*, p. 61.
34. Bell, *Cultural Contradictions*, p. 15.

35. Ibid., p. 55.
36. William Schambra, "From Self-Interest to Social Obligation: Local Communities v. the National Community," in Meyer, ed., Meeting Human Needs, p. 43.
37. Charles Frankel, "The New Egalitarianism and the Old," Commentary 56, no. 3 (September 1973): 56.
38. However, in his recent article "The Neo-Conservative Anguish Over Reagan's Foreign Policy," New York Times Sunday Magazine, May 2, 1982, pp. 30–97, Norman Podhoretz says he has "surrendered, more or less peaceably, to the label [neoconservative] after a period of fruitless struggle against it" (p. 30).
39. Daniel Moynihan, "The Schism in Black America," Public Interest 27 (Spring 1972), p. 3. Also see his "Equalizing Education—In Whose Benefit," Public Interest 29 (Fall 1972): 68–89, and "The Negro Family: The Case for National Action," in Lee Rainwater and William Yancey, eds., The Moynihan Report and the Politics of Controversy (Cambridge: MIT Press, 1967).
40. Kristol, Two Cheers, p. 230.
41. Michael Levin, "The Feminist Mystique," Commentary 70, no. 6 (December 1980): 25.
42. Ibid., p. 28.
43. Ibid. Also see his "Feminism and Thought Control," Commentary 73, no. 6 (June 1982): 40–44; and Keith Mano, "The Feminist Mystique," National Review 34, no. 2 (February 5, 1982): 118–20.
44. Ruth R. Wisse, "Women as Conservative Rabbis?" Commentary 68, no. 4 (October 1979): 64.
45. Carl Hoffman and John Shelton Reed, "Sex Discrimination?—The XYZ Affair," Public Interest 62 (Winter 1981): 23.
46. Ibid., p. 38.
47. Ibid., p. 23.
48. See Ellen Dubois, Feminism and Suffrage: The Emergence of an Independent Women's Movement in America, 1848–1869 (Ithaca: Cornell University Press, 1978).
49. Sara Evans, Personal Politics: The Roots of Women's Liberation in the Civil Rights Movement and the New Right (New York: Alfred A. Knopf, 1979).
50. Margaret Bonilla, "The White House and Women," in Holwill, ed., Agenda '83, p. 24.
51. Rachel Flick, "The New Feminism and the World of Work," Public Interest, no. 71 (Spring 1981): 44.
52. Allan Carlson, "Families, Sex and the Liberal Agenda," Public Interest, no. 58 (Winter 1980): 66. Also see Brigette Berger and Peter Berger, The War over the Family: Capturing the Middle Ground (New York: Anchor Doubleday, 1983); Carolyn Shaw Bell, "Should Every Job Support a Family?" Public Interest (Summer 1975): 109–18.
53. Leon R. Kass, "Making Babies—the New Biology and the 'Old' Morality," Public Interest, no. 26 (Winter 1972): 51.
54. Ibid.
55. Carlson, "Families, Sex," p. 79.
56. Ibid., p. 78.
57. Brigette Berger, "Family, Bureaucracy, and the 'Special Child,'" Public Interest, no. 40 (Summer 1975): 106.
58. Ibid., p. 107.
59. Lipset, "Social Mobility," p. 108.

60. Midge Decter, *The New Chastity and Other Arguments Against Women's Liberation* (New York: Capricorn Books, 1972), p. 43.
61. Ibid., p. 51.
62. Ibid., pp. 90–91.
63. Ibid., p. 124.
64. Jacqueline Kasun, "Turning Children into Sex Experts," *Public Interest* (Spring 1979): 9.
65. Robert Nisbet in "Letters: The Boys on the Beach," *Commentary* 70, no. 6 (December 1980): 12. Also see Midge Decter, "The Boys on the Beach," *Commentary* 70, no. 3 (September 1980): 35–48.
66. Haven Bradford Gow, "Letters," *Commentary* 70, no. 6 (December 1980): 6.
67. Samuel McCracken, "Are Homosexuals Gay?" *Commentary* 67, no. 1 (January 1979): 26.
68. Ibid., p. 27.
69. See "Letters: The Issue of Homosexuality," *Commentary* 67, no. 4 (April 1979): 4–81; Hyam Maccoby, "Sex According to the Song of Songs," *Commentary* 67, no. 6 (June 1979): 53–59; John Sisk, "Sexual Stereotypes," *Commentary* 64, no. 4 (October 1977): 58–64.
70. Bonilla, in Holwill, ed., *Agenda '83*, p. 24.
71. Ibid., p. 25.
72. Ibid., p. 24.
73. Ibid., p. 23.
74. Ibid., p. 26.
75. Ibid., p. 27.

4. The Relative Autonomy of the Capitalist Patriarchal State

The Reagan administration has successfully put the feminist movement on the defensive. It is important to remember, however, that the antifeminist focus of the New Right and the neoconservative position on "women's issues" represent a reaction to the power exercised by the women's movement through the 1970s as well as to married women's entry into the wage labor force and the changing nature of the family. It is women's potential power to transform this society that the New Right and the neoconservatives fear. Proof of this potential is the fact that the state thinks it needs to mobilize against the feminist movement and the gains made by women.

Present Reagan administration policies both reflect and exacerbate the essential conflict within liberal ideology: the conflict between individual freedom and structural inequality. The administration protects freedom for the corporate class through supply-side economics while rejecting the notion of equality, if equality is interpreted as "equality of social conditions." In the bourgeois "race of life" equality of opportunity is all that is required; one should be "free" to compete. But government, in particular, should not interfere by creating equality in the race—through welfare payments to Aid to Families with Dependent Children (AFDC), or food stamps, or affirmative action, or nutritional programs. Instead, Reagan argues that we must get government off the backs of "the people" and re-create individual freedom from government interference with people's lives. One is left with the well-worn political questions: Whose freedom are we talking about and what are the social conditions of individual freedom? How does a welfare mother or a woman of the working poor experience this freedom *from* government? Or how does the middle-class professional white or black woman, who has lost her government job because of the cutbacks, experience this freedom? Even more troubling, how does one fight *for* the social services of

87

the welfare state knowing that at the same time poor women need such aid, and all wage-earning women need day care assistance, this state involvement is part of the rearticulation and redefinition of patriarchal controls for advanced capitalist society?

In order to understand present-day state politics, we need to recognize that liberalism's ideological commitment to equality, however limited it has been, is under attack and (liberal) feminism's commitment to sexual equality is being rejected. Thus we see a rearticulation of patriarchal ideology through which the state turns away from "equality" (as equality of social conditions) and toward the more conservative notion of "equality of opportunity," given the "sexual difference" of woman from man. The attack on the welfare state reflects the pervasive rejection of liberal democracy in favor of a more authoritarian, hierarchical form, and the rejection of the ideology of liberal individualism when it is used to argue for sexual or racial equality. It is at moments like these that liberal individualism is said to be narcissistic and excessive.

The Reagan administration's hostility toward abortion, its rejection of the Equal Rights Amendment, its use of supply-side economics, its dismantling of the welfare state, all reflect an attempt to stabilize the patriarchal aspects of the state while trying to satisfy the neoconservative critique of liberalism and the New Right pseudo-populist defense of traditional family life. The particular political significance of the dismantling of the social welfare state thus must be understood within the theoretical framework of the relatively autonomous (capitalist) patriarchal state.

Conceptualizing the Capitalist Patriarchal State

How one thinks about the state matters in terms of figuring out the relationship between politics and economic class, politics and sex, politics and gender, politics and race. I understand the state to be an active participant in the struggles within society. The activism of the state grows out of the attempt to reconcile conflict: the state must create social order and political cohesion through mediating the conflicts that arise among capitalism, patriarchy, racism, and the ideology of liberalism. In this sense the state is structured by its simultaneous commitments to patriarchy, capitalism, and racism.

What does it mean to say that the state is patriarchal or that patriarchy operates on the state level?[1] Basically, it means that the distinction between public (man) and private (woman) life has been inherent in the formation of state societies. The state represents at one and the same time the *real* separation of male and female life, and an ideological cloak that defines public and private life in terms of the differentiation of woman from man.

Patriarchy enforced as a political system appears to exist nowhere. The state mystifies its patriarchal base by not only constructing but also manipulating the ideology describing public and private life. The state is said to be public (by definition) and therefore divorced from the private realm, which is the (supposed and real) realm of women's lives. The state can appear, through its own ideology, to be unrelated to the family as the private sphere, where in actuality this sphere is both *defined by and regulated in relation to* the state realm. Patriarchy becomes mystified on the state level whereas in fact it is exactly at this level that patriarchy becomes institutionalized. Unable to see how patriarchy has set itself into motion, we are left with explanations of male supremacy as natural and/or inevitable. In sum, the state by definition *reflects* the separation of public and private life as the difference of woman from man, obscuring the reality that the state actually *constructs* (and protects) this division.

The confusing issue is that the politics of assigning women a sphere different from that of men is mystified by using female biology itself. This complicated reality reflects the fact that females can bear children, but until this biological fact is distinguished from the political motivations of patriarchy, we cannot recognize the role of patriarchy in the assignment of woman to the private sphere, man to the public. Patriarchy erases the evidence of its presence on this individual level through the political and ideological manipulation of female biology. Once we understand that part of the dynamic of patriarchy is its own mystification, it becomes necessary to demystify its presence in actual everyday political activity.

Patriarchy is the process of politically differentiating the female from the male, as woman from man. Patriarchy in this sense is the politics of transforming biological sex into politicized gender, which prioritizes the man while making the woman different (unequal), less than, or the "other." This process of differentiating woman from man while establishing the privilege of men operates partially on the level of ideology that centers the phallus in the series of symbols, signs, and language while dividing the private world from the public world. And it simultaneously establishes the sexual division of labor, the distinctness of family and market, patriarchal controls within the market, and so on. Patriarchy in this sense operates both as an ideology and as a series of concrete political relations that are not separate but rather distinct realms that are dialectically related. Although the specific historical emphasis of patriarchal controls has shifted from the "father" to the "husband" to the "state" (while remaining simultaneously rooted in each), the dynamic of sexual class—the process of hierarchically differentiating woman from man—constructs the continuity of patriarchy. The understanding of patriarchy cannot be limited to either a particular family form (father, husband) or a static notion of male biological power (strength, aggression).

The relations of the state reflect and construct the relations of power in society and yet the state does not fully uncover the entirety of power relations themselves. The state, rather, condenses the relations of power in society—which are economic, sexual, and racial. The ruling class therefore is represented as a bourgeois class, which is also white and male. These specific realities become condensed within the representation of the ruling class as one and the same as the bourgeois class. The capitalist class, as the ruling class in the state, goes beyond capitalism in terms of representing and protecting the patriarchal and racist aspects of politics. Yet, on the state level, these aspects *appear* to have no (relatively) autonomous character. They are condensed as bourgeois. I will argue, however, that in actuality patriarchy operates in a relatively autonomous way within the state.

Government, as a series of institutions, further condenses these capitalist, patriarchal, and racist relations of power by mystifying the specificity of these varied loci of power, and represents the relations of power as though they were fully encompassed in

governmental institutions. Therefore, when one studies government one already has turned to the partial and legitimized institutional presentation of state conflict. Government is an actor within
state politics although it is never completely autonomous in this
activity. Constraints exist within the government realm given the
priorities of the capitalist patriarchal state.

Harold Laski wrote of the relationship between the state and the
government: "The latter is but the agent of the former; it exists to
carry out the purposes of the state. It is not itself the supreme
coercive power; it is simply the mechanism of administration
which gives effect to the purposes of that power."[2] He
oversimplifies the relationship when he says that "a state is what
its government does."[3] Although it may be true that every act of
the state is a governmental act, the activities of the state, and the
relations of power, cannot be reduced to the activity of the governmental apparatus. Neither is the government a mere reflection or
instrument of the needs of the capitalist class, or of patriarchal
society. There are different factions within the capitalist class as
there are different conceptions by this class of how best to mediate
the conflicts that presently exist between the needs of the capitalist marketplace, the traditional patriarchal family, racism, and the
ideology of liberalism. Conflict within the state itself makes its
role as a mere instrument impossible. The reason a state arises in
the first place is to mediate conflict. The activity of the state
reflects the condensation of conflicting needs arising out of (a) the
gender, racial, and economic relations of power; (2) the state's
representation of these needs; and (3) the government's further
condensation of state activity, which does not necessarily mirror
state needs because it must develop policy that necessarily requires a particularist interpretation of state need.

Ernesto Laclau correctly argues that there is no such thing as a
typical form of the state that corresponds to the capitalist relations
of production. The state, as the collection of public institutions,
appears in many different forms:

> A variety of different concentrations of power are compatible with
> the existence of capitalist relations of production. A theory of the
> capitalist state is something we cannot formulate. We can, however,
> formulate theories about the degree and forms of concentration of
> power in, let's say, advanced capitalist societies.[4]

Nicos Poulantzas also recognizes a level of relative autonomy of state activity. He writes that the "capitalist state best serves the interests of the capitalist class only, when the members of this class do not participate directly in the state apparatus, that is to say when the ruling class is not the politically governing class."[5]

The relative autonomy of the state—neither dependent nor independent—is actualized through the differentiation of the capitalist class from the state or governmental apparatus. This differentiation does not exist in the same way between patriarchal needs and the state apparatus. The governing or ruling class is made up of men who represent the sexual-class needs of men. The state itself institutionalizes patriarchy. As I have argued elsewhere:

> The formation of the state institutionalizes patriarchy; it reifies the division between public and private life as one of sexual difference. . . . The domain of the state has always signified public life, and this is distinguished in part from the private realm by differentiating men from women. . . . The state formalizes the rule by men because the division of public and private life is at one and the same time a male/female distinction. . . . The state's purpose is to enforce the separation of public and private life and with it the distinctness of male and female existence.[6]

Whereas the capitalist class functions best when it is not the governing class, patriarchal interests are not distinguished from the state through a condensed class formation that differs from the capitalist class. Rather, patriarchal interests are represented by men of the capitalist class, who enforce the sexual-class relations of patriarchy. These relations are represented as the natural differentiation of male and female, although we will see that integral to this presentation of patriarchal privilege—the hierarchal differentiation of woman from man—is the distinctness of state and economy, public and private, political and sexual, state and family.

The relative autonomy of the state is therefore expressed through the specifically capitalist nature of patriarchal needs and through the economic class differentiation of women. The actual patriarchal construction of the state serves as a constraint on its relative autonomy and necessitates state policy(ies) that utilize economic class controls. As such, the needs of patriarchal society become mystified on the state level because they are made invisible. Their presence is mystified as they seemingly become one and the same with capitalist class interests. They are represented in the state with no identity of their own.

In this sense, the relative autonomy of the state—which means that the state neither is completely dependent nor is it independent—operates more in the realm of economic class interests than patriarchal need. This is because the bourgeois class is at one and the same time a patriarchal (sexual) class. And it is also because the structuring of the relations of the state is fundamentally patriarchal. Patriarchy and sexual-class interests are not as differentiated from the state, or within the state, as are bourgeois class interests.

The state is relatively autonomous in terms of patriarchy in that factions of the bourgeois class have different conceptions of how best to protect and reconstitute patriarchy. A case in point would be the differences that exist within the state between New Rightists and neoconservatives. But these differences do not merely represent various concerns of a bourgeois class. They represent a factionalism that exists in terms of the needs of the patriarchal aspects of the state. Different commitments to patriarchy play a role in defining conflict within the state. Varied positions on abortion are not merely reflections of different factions within the bourgeoisie; they reflect different positions within the sexual class (men), within the bourgeois class, on what abortion means to them.

The relative autonomy of the state in relation to patriarchy occurs in terms of the choices made within the bourgeoisie on patriarchy. Because the bourgeoisie *is* male the state's relative autonomy is more fully constrained by its patriarchal aspects than it is by its economic class aspects.[7] Therefore, the state is relatively autonomous in that it acts as a chooser within a set of structural and ideological constraints and conflicts. The constraints emanate directly from patriarchy given the nondifferentiated state and sex-class form within the patriarchal realm; and indirectly, given the differentiation of the state and the bourgeoisie in the economic class realm. Whereas the structure and the content of the state are patriarchal, the content of the state is bourgeois. Similarly, economic class interests are represented in the bourgeois class, while patriarchal class interests are represented in the bourgeois class, which is also the patriarchal class.

Rather than accept the traditional liberal and Marxist notions that patriarchy does not operate on the state level, I argue here that present state activity is largely defined by the process of trying to mediate the conflicts arising between the needs of the capitalist marketplace for women as secondary wage-earners and the traditional patriarchal need for the "institution of motherhood," which relegates women to the private sphere. The development of the social welfare state and Reagan's dismantling of it are in part a response to this basic conflict.

Patriarchy and capitalism are relatively autonomous systems. They are differentiated in purpose. Capitalist class relations are organized around the maximization of profit and political control. Patriarchy is organized around the hierarchical differentiation of woman from man. They do not presently operate separately from each other, but rather have become mutually dependent, as well as in a conflictual relation to each other.[8] Their purposes crisscross in ways that both aid and subvert each other: woman is defined as a secondary wage-earner in capitalism given patriarchal ideology that defines motherhood as her primary purpose. But as women become wage-earners and the reality of their lives contradicts the institution of motherhood that constrains them in the market, they begin to demand equality in various ways (e.g., ERA, or pregnancy disability payments). The contradictory aspects of capitalism and patriarchy prove that they are not completely separate or "dual systems." The conflict reveals both their semi-autonomous, semi-independent nature and their semi-dependence. The dialectical relations existing within capitalist patriarchy are conflictual and synthetic. State policy reflects this.

A frequent reaction by many Marxists to the argument that capitalism and patriarchy are mutually dependent or that capitalism historically has required patriarchy is that patriarchy is not "logically pre-given as an element of the class structure that would *automatically* be reproduced by the class structure."[9] Michele Barrett clarifies this position further: "Although we may usefully argue that gender division has been built into the capitalist division of labour and is an important element of capitalist relations of production, it is more difficult to argue that gender division necessarily occupies a particular place in the class structure of capitalism."[10] This argument is troublesome because it is not clear what it means to require that patriarchy be proven to be (analytically) necessary. It has, after all, been historically necessary. What is the relationship between analytic necessity and history itself? And what does it mean to write of patriarchy as "logically pre-given"? Nothing is pre-given, because everything is constituted in its specific history. This applies also to the notion of the "automatic reproduction" of patriarchy. In terms of constituting the relations of power in society, what is ever automatic? totally determined? Barrett asks of the concept "patriarchy" what she cannot ask of capitalism or any social construction.

If the state and government are actively involved in trying to protect patriarchy, one needs to focus on how the relatively autonomous state acts. The attempt to control women's reproductive activity and limit women's choice in relation to the institution of motherhood is reflected in policies affecting day care, abortion, contraception, sterilization, the Equal Rights Amendment, and so forth. By focusing on the role of the state as an "actor," I want to show how the state is presently constrained "as a set of organizations capable of formulating distinctive goals."[11] Although the state is an active, rather than a determined locus of power, I do not agree, with Theda Skocpol, that the "state is an active force in its own right."[12] The patriarchal underpinnings of the state limit how active the state can be as a force in its own right, distinguished from patriarchal constraints. The state does not act on its own and yet it is still an actor. The concept of the state as an actor rather than merely a determined instrument of economic class interests or patriarchal needs allows us to focus on how state activity affects politics, culture, and society.

Neither the state nor the governmental apparatus is completely independent or completely determined. Reagan's activities to dismantle the welfare state confirm in part the notion of the state and government as actors that choose and decide. Because the relative autonomy of the state is not constant but rather expresses a relationship between the state apparatus (government) and the state (capitalist class and patriarchal needs), we need to study the processes that define particular aspects of the state's relative autonomy. According to Skocpol,

> "State [relative] autonomy" is not a fixed structural feature of any government system. It can come and go, not only because crises may precipitate the formulation of official strategies and policies by elites or administrators who otherwise might not mobilize their own potentials for autonomous action, but also because the very *structural potentials* for autonomous state actions change over time in any given government system.[13]

The government apparatus operates in a relatively autonomous fashion, which does not mean that the politics are disinterested or unbiased, but rather that the government apparatus has to utilize some level of choice in acting. In this sense, the Reagan administration's stance on the Equal Rights Amendment reflects the relative autonomy of the state and governmental apparatus, given that there are clear factions within the state that support ERA. The same is true for the administration's antiabortion stance.

The state as an actor seeks to mediate the conflicts among the capitalist need for wage laborers, the patriarchal needs for the institution of motherhood (which underpins the structural, institutional, and ideological differentiation of woman from man by identifying woman within the private sphere), and the ideology of liberalism and liberal feminism, which demands equal rights among men and between men and women. It is out of these contradictory needs that the welfare state developed, while the welfare state has also (subversively) heightened and intensified the conflicts. The conflict both constructs a relatively autonomous state and reflects it. The Reagan administration appears to be heightening the conflicts as it seeks to mediate between radical aspects of the New Right and the more mainstream concerns of neoconservatism. To the extent that the New Right demands state policy reinforcing the traditional heterosexual, patriarchal, two-parent family, and to the extent that the welfare state developed out of the transformations taking place in this family form, the New Right merely exacerbates the conflicts between the traditional patriarchal privilege of the man as husband and the advanced capitalist needs of the dual wage-earning family. In bringing these issues of family life to center stage within mainstream politics, the New Right has uncovered the conflicts more clearly, by demystifying the patriarchal dimensions of the state as represented in the capitalist class. These patriarchal dimensions of the state operate through the law to define the relatively autonomous status of patriarchy.

Patriarchal Law and Relative Autonomy

Once one recognizes the patriarchal aspects of the state, one needs to focus on how the law both constructs and reflects this reality. An instrumentalist view of the law as merely mirroring the patriarchal needs of the state is insufficient. The law articulates as well as reflects patriarchy; it is both real and ideal; it both constructs reality and mirrors it; it is both determined and determining. Rather than assuming the separation of the law and patriarchy, I think the appropriate framing of the problem of patriarchy requires asking how the law embodies and constructs patriarchal relations.

The state, through the law, reflects and constructs the patriarchal and liberal separation of public and private life as one of woman from man, which simultaneously constructs the differentiation of family from economy and the personal from the political. As such, the law is not merely operating in the interests of bourgeois society, but rather establishes this patriarchal division in particularly bourgeois form. Diane Polan recognizes this patriarchal essence of the law. "The whole structure of law—its hierarchal organization; its combative, adversarial format; and its undeviating bias in favor of rationality over all other values—defines it as a fundamentally patriarchal institution."[14] She also argues somewhat contradictorily that "it is not so much that laws must be changed; it is patriarchy that must be changed."[15] But Polan herself acknowledges that the structure of law is patriarchal. Why, then, separate these realms and argue that it is patriarchy that needs changing rather than the law?

Part of the relations of patriarchy—its dynamic force, which is always in flux—is embodied in the law. Changing the law changes patriarchy as it presently exists. Although the relative autonomy of the bourgeois state is actualized through the differentiation of the capitalist class from the state or governmental apparatus, this differentiation does not exist in the same way between patriarchal needs and the state apparatus because the sexual class of men *is* the governing or ruling class. And yet this ruling class is identified not in terms of its patriarchal aspects but rather as bourgeois. The law both structures these relations and reflects them. As such, although the dynamic life force of patriarchy is not completely embodied within the law, important aspects of patriarchal relations are constructed in the law, as it defines the contours of public and private life, state and family, man and woman.

The law may, as Polan asserts, play a much different role in maintaining patriarchy than it does in perpetuating capitalism, but I do not think that it plays a less significant role. Again, it matters how one is defining the patriarchal aspects of the law and the way they structure the state and the law itself in terms of the *relations between public and private life*. The patriarchal aspects of the law are used to perpetuate the relations necessary to capitalism. Yet the economic aspects of the law are more explicit, the patriarchal aspects more implicit.

> The legal system has also used the public/private dichotomy in another, more subtle fashion that has further reinforced patriarchy. By placing the operation of law squarely in the public realm and, at least rhetorically, removing itself from the "private realm" of personal life and the family, the legal system created a distinction between a public realm of life, which is a proper arena for legal or social regulation, and another, fundamentally different, personal sphere, which is somehow outside the law's or society's authority to regulate. Thus, the legal system has functioned to legitimate that very distinction by asserting it as a natural, rather than socially imposed, ground for different treatment.[16]

If the state and the law are as structured by patriarchy as they are by the relations of capital, then challenges to the law challenge the actual relations of patriarchy. This is not to reduce patriarchy to its embodiment in the law, because much patriarchal privilege is not contained within the law. Many of the privileges of patriarchy are not to be found in the law, and yet its very structure (as well as its substance) defines the relations of patriarchy: the differentiation of public from private, state from economy, reason from passion, fact from value. Challenges to "the" law as such become the basis for a challenge to the state itself. The patriarchal aspects of the law more intimately construct the relations of the state than do its specifically capitalist aspects. This clearly is not to say that reforms of the patriarchal aspects of the law are the equivalent of revolution but it is to argue that such reforms have the *potential* to revolutionize the state. The moment one begins to question the categorization of woman as a sexual class within the law—or her absence as a sexual class in the law—one begins to challenge the most intimate foundations of the state because the law is not merely an instrument of patriarchy. It is patriarchal.

This leads to the concern about the role of law as an ideological force: the law, as ideology, comes to have a "material" identity. It structures choices, options, and so on, and in this sense has a real, material presence that at one and the same time mystifies other concrete relations of power. Because the law operates in this ambiguous fashion—and does so particularly in terms of its patriarchal aspects in that it both constructs public and private life as an ideological construction *and* actually delineates spheres that *are* public and private—the neat division between ideology (as superstructure and determined) and material life (as structure and determining) is not helpful.

It is important to distinguish between two different ways of conceptualizing the relationship between law and ideology. One can assume that the law operates as ideology and as such mystifies the "real." I believe instead that the law constructs the real while also mystifying reality. Accepting the traditional dichotomization of the real and the ideal often implies acceptance of the related dichotomy between reformist (ideal) and revolutionary (real) politics.[17] However, both of these dichotomies, which are inaccurate for studying the relationship between liberal ideology and capitalist class relations, are even more problematic when one recognizes the patriarchal constructions within the law. The particular way that patriarchal ideology becomes real through the law negates the dichotomy between ideal and material. Changing the law, although not sufficient unto itself, does begin to challenge and erode *real, material* aspects of patriarchal privilege.

In order for "women's rights" to be fully acknowledged within the law, the law will have to be transformed. However, in the process of challenging the patriarchal aspects of the law, the law itself becomes challenged. The demand for women's rights does move beyond liberal individualist claims because the demands are based in a recognition of the denial to women of their rights as a sexual class. It is just too simplistic, and somewhat mechanistic, to say, as Janet Rifkin does, that "litigation and other forms of formal legal relief, however, cannot lead to social changes, because in upholding and relying on the paradigm of law, the paradigm of patriarchy is upheld and reinforced."[18] My difference with Rifkin on this issue is not with her assessment that challenges to the law are insufficient for attacking the relation of patriarchy in society but rather with her denial of the import of law within the realm of the real. In this sense the law does have relative autonomy, and struggles within the law are *part of the process* of challenging patriarchal privilege. And although this challenge is not sufficient, I do believe it is a *necessary* element of feminist struggle. The law can be a crucial arena of feminist political struggle where concrete gains and losses affecting patriarchal privilege can occur. But this can only be recognized once we grant patriarchal ideology its material content; recognize the ideological content within the realm of material life; view the state as structuring and delineating patriarchal social relations; and reject the dichotomization of reform and revolution. Most discussions of the state do not work from this perspective, however; instead they either conceptualize the state as the arena of capitalist class struggle or reduce the patriarchal aspects of the state to a psychoanalytic dynamic.

State Activity as Economic Class Struggle

Piven and Cloward's recent book *New Class War* examines the Reagan state and the dismantling of the welfare state as reflecting the conflict between labor and capital. According to Piven and Cloward, the welfare state, defined as the social programs that aid in income maintenance, reflects the struggle between employer and employee rights. The present attempts to dismantle the welfare state are therefore seen as part of "the recurring conflict between property rights and subsistence rights," since employers understand that "subsistence resources interfere with wage-labor."[19] This interpretation of the welfare state leads Piven and Cloward to conclude that "the income-maintenance programs have weakened capital's ability to depress wages by means of economic security especially by means of manipulating the relative numbers of people searching for work."[20] As such, the welfare state has "altered the struggle between business and labor."

The social programs—income-maintenance policies—of the welfare state have begun to redefine the dynamics of the labor market by "augmenting the power of workers," which is why the programs are under special attack by the Reagan administration. The state has now finally become the main arena of class conflict, according to Piven and Cloward.[21] The state's role as an active participant in economic class struggle has become more obvious. The interdependence of the state and the economy, which has been increasing in scale and visibility, "will continue to nourish popular convictions that government has a great deal to do with the economic circumstances of people," and people will therefore "continue to produce demands that government enact policies of economic reform."[22] The criticism about "big government" is really a warning against this continual tendency of the state to move into the realm of the market while collapsing the distinction between politics and economics. After all, liberal democratic government is based on the differentiation (although not the separation) of the governing (political) and economic classes, and the welfare state has played a part in exposing the interrelations that exist between the state and the market, politics and economics. The welfare state has been subversive, then, by making more visible the interrelationship between government (politics) and economics. In terms of liberal ideology, these realms are supposed to be separate.

The state itself has become more vulnerable through its welfare state apparatus (unemployment insurance, public welfare, retirement benefits, food stamps, Medicaid, and so forth) because it has created what Piven and Cloward call a "new moral economy" in which the unemployed or underemployed blame themselves less and government more. Much as the neoconservatives argue, people expect more from government. The liberal ideology of the welfare state has legitimized a whole set of new expectations.

Piven and Cloward argue that the welfare state has become vulnerable to democratic influences because its growth and development are dependent on popular constituencies. The welfare state reflects positive gains made by the working class on their own behalf.

Piven and Cloward overstate the power of the working class, however. They also cut short their own analysis by not recognizing that the state not only is an arena of economic class conflict but also represents the conflict between the state and family life that is ultimately a struggle to stabilize the patriarchal foundation of capitalism. Present crises within the welfare state reflect the fight over the state's appropriate domain in relation to family life as much as they reflect the state's relationship to the economy. The relationship between the state and family life is as much at the heart of the welfare state as is the relationship between employee and employer; economic class and social class are both at issue here. Piven and Cloward need to see the "struggle for subsistence needs from the welfare state" as a part of the changing nature of family life and the shifting of power from the husband in particular family forms to the (patriarchal) state.

In their recent article "The American Road to Democratic Socialism," Piven and Cloward recognize that "the social welfare state is altering power relations in the family."[23] But they regard the family as an institution within the complex of capitalist class relations; patriarchy has no relatively autonomous status:

> These shifts of power in private spheres have helped provoke the contemporary countermobilization by capital and the New Right against the welfare state. The attack is assuredly intended to restore traditional economic and familial power relations. But if, as orthodox critics assert, the welfare state poses no challenge to capitalism, why has it become the focus of so concerted an assault by corporate interests and their right-wing allies?[24]

They see the welfare state as a challenge to capitalism rather than a simultaneous challenge to and reconstitution of patriarchal relations within the capitalist patriarchal state.

In the same way that Piven and Cloward envision the state as a representation of the capitalist class (who are only *incidentally* male and white) and not as representing patriarchal needs and priorities, they do not distinguish the unemployed and underemployed as disproportionately female. Nor do they analyze the fact that women are the major recipients of welfare in terms of the patriarchal aspects of capitalist society. They need to recognize that women's poverty, which is largely due to changes in family structure, high divorce rates, and disproportionate underemployment, reflects the problem of women as a "sexual class" within patriarchy as much as it reflects the capitalist nature of poverty. Women form a main constituency within the welfare state because patriarchy defines them *as women* with an assigned place in the economy as such. No matter how differentiated their lives may be along economic class or racial lines, the fact that they are women is never irrelevant. This is not to say that the concept of a sexual class denies the economic or racial differences that exist among women. But in relation to the welfare-state apparatus, poor and welfare women, who need assistance, form a particular constituency *as women who are* poor. Given the present upheaval in family structure, neat economic class categories do not hold for women. The economic class identity of women today is complex, but they clearly do constitute a major presence as welfare recipients *and* they predominate the low-pay "employee" category. Whether one wants to term them working class is another issue. However, it is really quite unacceptable for Piven and Cloward to treat women as *absent* when they write of the "underemployed and unemployed," as this statement illustrates: "There is reason to believe that women will *also* become a significant oppositional force. Female political values tip to the side of peace, greater equality, and economic security."[25] To say that women will *also* become a force, together with the working class, is to deny that the working class—however one chooses to define it—is made up in large part of women. More important, such a conceptualization gives little recognition to the fact that women are the major recipients of the social programs of the welfare state and are thus a class that is more ideologically pro-peace and pro-equality; it is a class with a material commonality of interests.

Once one recognizes that women have a particular relationship to the welfare state, it becomes imperative to examine the historical roots of this relationship. How does women's relationship to the state uncover the welfare state as an arena of patriarchal struggle as well as capitalist class conflict? How does the welfare state reflect a particular and changing relationship to family life? And how does the development of the welfare state reflect new and needed developments within the advanced capitalist patriarchal state? In the same way that Piven and Cloward argue that the welfare state further erodes the distinctness between the state and the economy, and hence political and economic life, they need to recognize that it has also challenged the distinctness between "the" state and "the" family that is as necessary to patriarchy as the distinctness between politics and economics is necessary to capitalism. The social welfare state has uncovered the particular interests that the state has in affirming specific family forms and functions. Although the state has always been active in defining the family realm, the social welfare state has made this involvement explicit. And this reality—the state's involvement in the family—stands counter to the (liberal) ideology of public/private life, which presumes the separateness of state/family: if the state is viewed as actively involved in family life, the politics of family life is revealed. However, the notion of the separateness of the family from the state underlines the ideology of the capitalist patriarchal state.

The social welfare state has made the state's interest in family life more obvious as it has sought to reconstitute the patriarchal aspects of society and family. Rather than challenging the distinctness of family from state, the social welfare state has redefined the relationship, and in such a way that exposes state involvement more directly than earlier state family policy has done, particularly in terms of policies directed to single-parent families. The welfare state reflects the needs created by multiple family forms (besides the traditional nuclear family) for a rearticulation of patriarchal authority on the state level. In such a statement, the patriarchal aspects of the state become exposed and vulnerable because the distinctness between state and family, public and private, is further eroded in this process of reconstituting patriarchy. Although the state has always been active in defining family life, the welfare state makes this clearer than before and thereby more directly challenges the ideological vision of the separateness of family life. Actually, the breakdown of the ideological distinctness between family and state is more subversive in terms of people's understanding the relations of power

than the breakdown between the state and the economy because it
affects people's everyday life more directly.

The State vs. the Family

Christopher Lasch views the welfare state less as an arena for
economic class conflict and more as the arena that has displaced
the power of "the" family. He is critical of the welfare state for
having eroded the autonomy of family life. The individual and the
family have supposedly lost power to "the" state. The "helping
professions," characterized as health, education, and welfare services that developed in the first three decades of the twentieth
century, have invaded the family and destroyed its capacities to
provide as a unit for the private emotional needs of its members.
Assuming that the family was at one time a haven in a heartless
world, Lasch bemoans its loss.[26]
Lasch believes that the "transfer of functions" from the family to
the state has eroded the family and supplanted it by the state.[27] He
terms the transfer of functions from the family to "doctors, psy-
chiatrists, child development experts, spokesmen for the juvenile
courts, marriage counselors," the "socialization of reproduction."[28] Lasch is primarily concerned with the erosion of parental
authority, which parallels the delegation of discipline to other
agencies. "The history of modern society, from one point of view,
is the assertion of social control over activities once left to individuals or their families."[29] He is critical of these developments,
and what he calls welfare liberalism, in that it absolves individuals of moral responsibility.[30] He is also critical of what he terms
the new ruling class of administrators and experts who represent
the ascendance of the helping professions.
It is interesting that although Lasch is a Marxist (about questions concerning the economy), he criticizes the welfare state from
a neoconservative and psychoanalytic perspective. He shares the
neoconservative outlook that the welfare state has eroded the autonomy of the family and the father. The autonomy of the family,
which is rooted in the authority of the father, has been undermined by the state through the "socialization of reproduction"

which "expropriates parental functions."[31] Although it is true that there are more and more agencies that are supposedly responsible for particular functions that used to be defined within the home, these agencies do not "expropriate" the functions of the family. They at best supplement them. The family, and particularly the mother, is still ultimately responsible for organizing the needs of its members. Women are still responsible for the rearing of children, even if this is defined differently from the way it was in the eighteenth or nineteenth century. This is actually becoming more and more true under the Reagan administration, as government cuts back social welfare programs and assumes that families will take up the slack.

In reaction to criticism of his work as defensive of patriarchal family life, Lasch has responded "that society without the father is not utopia."[32] He argues that the New Left and feminist criticism of the patriarchal family is wrongheaded. "It has deflected criticism from the real problem to a pseudo-problem, from the corporation and the state to the family." He does not think that the worst features of society are to be found in "the despotism of the authoritarian father, much eroded in any case, but from the regressive psychology of industrialism, which reduces the citizen to a consumer and bombards him with images of immediate and total gratification."[33] By defining things in this way he erases the relationship between patriarchal society and state activity. The family becomes a "pseudo" issue because real politics is about the state and corporate needs. In this sense his analysis is similar to that of Piven and Cloward. None of them recognizes patriarchal power as part of the politics of state. Whereas Piven and Cloward view the welfare state as representing gains for the working class, Lasch criticizes the welfare state (broadly defined as the "helping professions") for eroding family life and creating a crisis of (patriarchal) authority. He becomes an apologist for the traditional patriarchal family against the advanced capitalist form of the patriarchal state. Although he states that real politics is about the state and corporate needs, and the family is a pseudo-issue, his own criticism of the welfare state seems to prove the place of the family in a discussion of the politics of the state.

Actually Lasch's stand on the state's relationship to the family never acknowledges the important point that the state is and has always been a partner to the family on the most basic possible level: given that the family is not just a private voluntary arrangement but an institution, the socially prescribed arrangement for conducting sexual relations, child rearing, and domestic life, it could hardly exist under modern conditions without the state to reinforce its social requirements with legal sanctions. Marriage is a legal contract, whose provisions (some of which are more enforced and enforceable than others) are determined by a complex of domestic relations laws regulating the rights and obligations that go with marriage, divorce, and parenthood. Married people and their legitimate children have a host of legally sanctioned discriminatory privileges. So the issue is conceived wrongly by Lasch. The issue has never been whether there should be state intervention in the family, but rather whether (that) state intervention reinforces or undercuts familialism (the hegemonic status of households consisting of those related by birth or marriage) and male or parental authority.[34]

The Paternalistic Welfare State

Unlike Lasch, Isaac Balbus sees the growth of the welfare state as a particular historical and psychoanalytic development that cannot be fully understood in terms of the needs of the capitalist mode of production.[35] He believes that the growth of the welfare state "demands an appreciation of the transformations in the form of childrearing that both underlie and [have been] reinforced by it," arguing that in the second half of the twentieth century a more indulgent form of childrearing developed that "has intensified the child's early identification with an increasingly nurturant mother."[36] The tendency toward father-absent families has increased through suburbanization and other twentieth-century family transformations. While the father has become less available to the child, the child has developed more of a need to escape maternal authority. According to Balbus, the state fills the gap by taking over "compensatory authority functions."

The welfare state becomes the missing father and therefore sets up a particularly oppressive relationship to women. "The pater-

nalism of the father is supplanted by the paternalism of the welfare state."[37] The increasing scope of state authority is supposedly
rooted "in the intensification of mother-related emotional needs
that with the increasing absence of the father, can no longer be
even partly satisfied with the family."[38] The state comes to represent the reaffirmation and the repudiation of the child's dependence on the mother.

Balbus accepts and works from the psychoanalytic premise that
hatred of the mother defines the unconscious and is critical of the
state's role in reaffirming this hatred:

> The state does not merely impose needs on the individual but rather
> fulfills unconscious needs that have developed in the course of the
> individual's now transformed relationship with his or her mother. In
> the process of fulfilling these dependency and mother-hating needs,
> of course, the state reinforces them and encourages their prolifera-
> tion.[39]

The present welfare state is seen by Balbus as both responding to
and reaffirming "mother-controlled child rearing." And he argues
that the intensity of the love/hate relationship of the child to the
mother is reflected in the state's authoritarianism. A more democratic state would correlate with more shared parenting.

Defining the patriarchal aspects of the state on the level of the
unconscious raises as many questions as it answers. Even if one
does not reject the premise of "mother hatred," which I do, it is
not at all clear whether Balbus's discussion of the state represents
an accurate social and historical picture. How are the present
moves of the Reagan state away from liberal democracy (the
"rights" of the individual) toward authoritarian democracy (the
"rights" of the state) to be understood in terms of the prevalence of
"mother-monopolized" child care? First, "mother-monopolized"
child care is a somewhat troublesome phrase. It is usually assumed that monopoly means power and control, and power and
control are usually chosen and fought for. Women have rather
been assigned child care. The welfare state has not reaffirmed
"mother-monopolized" child care because this particular state
form controls female parenting while at the same time it assigns
women this work. The state defines the contours and context of
childrearing: whether there is day care available, or abortion on

demand, or Medicaid payments for abortion, or supplemental nutritional food programs, and so on.

One also needs to rethink the meaning of mother-defined childrearing when a majority of married women are in the labor force.
What happens to the dynamic of "mother hatred"? Suburban
housewives make up a small minority of the population today.
Does the intensity of the hatred of the mother-child relationship
remain as intense as it (supposedly) was even as the mother becomes more "absent"? Is the unconscious a static, unchanging
form? And how well does this notion of mother-monopolized
child care apply to black women who have never experienced the
notion of femininity and exclusive childrearing rights in the same
way it is assumed white women have? Balbus' picture of the "increasingly indulgent socialization" by the mother just does not
ring true for a majority of women in the 1970s and 1980s.

Balbus assumes that the state is *determined* by mother hatred,
which is an example of the instrumentalist interpretation of the
patriarchal state that sees patriarchy as predetermined via the
unconscious. Patriarchy rather operates in a relatively autonomous manner on the state level. Therefore the understanding of
patriarchy as a static construction (1) either rooted in a dynamic
hidden in the unconscious or (2) derived from the notion of men
(as biological beings) as the sole transmitters of patriarchy blunts
the understanding of the dynamic, changing, historical force of
patriarchy. The unconscious and the biological male (body) are
not unimportant or irrelevant to the study of patriarchal privilege.
But they cannot be understood without seeing how the state relates to them given particular historical needs.

The state, as patriarchal, represents all men as more valued than
women. Although all men become privileged by this presentation,
an individual male as father or husband or brother retains his
privilege in relation to the way in which the state formulates his
position as a man, which is partially defined by his (biological)
maleness. In other words, just as the phallus—the symbol of male
power—is not one and the same as the penis—the actual biological "thing"—the man as political construction is not one and the
same as the male, which is a biological reality although all men
are male. Patriarchy is then not one and the same as male (privi-

lege). And yet they are intimately interrelated. The biological male is as constant and unchanging as nature. Patriarchy, however, as a system of power, is always changing and in flux, although its presentation of self—the male or the phallus—is presented as a static thing. To understand the politics of patriarchy one therefore has to focus as much on the state level as on the level of individual (biological) male life.

Part of the force of patriarchal power has been rooted in the specific way the state mystifies its relation to patriarchy, most particularly through the ideological distinction between public and private life as represented in the differentiation of family and state. The more the social welfare state has uncovered the state's interest in family life, the more the ideological distinctions between family and state, public and private, sexual and political life seem to crisscross. And ideology is not assumed to be completely separate from reality in this instance. It rather constructs, reflects, defines, distorts reality. As a result, the terrain of political struggle has moved into realms once considered private. It is true that the social welfare state is partially responsible for this, and as such is subversive to its own (patriarchal) needs; that is, the separateness of public/private, family/state, man/woman, has been challenged by the welfare state's open involvement in these realms.

What happens when the redefinition of distinct lines between family and state within capitalist patriarchal society is challenged? Does the loss of male power as it is located in the father or the husband and transferred to or supplanted by the state mean more power for women? The state realm means the domain of men, the realm of public life, the activity of politics. And all of these notions are differentiated from the domain of women, the realm of private life, the activity of the family. These distinctions, which have always contained an ideological purpose and have never simply described reality, have lost much of their potency today because the state has exposed its relations to the family, to patriarchal power, to the economy. The social welfare state has played a progressive role in exposing the state for what it is, particularly in terms of its patriarchal dimensions. Hence the Reagan administration's attack against it.

NOTES

1. See Zillah Eisenstein, *The Radical Future of Liberal Feminism* (New York: Longman, 1981), chaps. 2 and 10, for a more complete development of this point.
2. Harold J. Laski, *The State in Theory and Practice* (New York: Viking Press, 1935), p. 11.
3. Ibid., p. 57.
4. "Recasting Marxism: Hegemony and New Political Movements," interview with Ernesto Laclau and Chantal Mouffe, *Socialist Review* 12, no. 6 (November–December 1982): 107.
5. Nicos Poulantzas, "The Problem of the Capitalist State," revised and reproduced in Robin Blackburn, ed., *Ideology in Social Science* (New York: Vintage Books, 1973). For a discussion of the relatively autonomous state, see Nicos Poulantzas, *Classes in Contemporary Capitalism* (London: Verso, 1974); *State, Power, Socialism* (London: New Left Books, 1978); *Political Power and Social Classes*, trans. Timothy O'Hagan (London: New Left Books, 1973); and Ralph Miliband, *Marxism and Politics* (Oxford: Oxford University Press, 1977). For clarification of the neoinstrumentalist view of the state, as an instrument of the capitalist class, see Louis Althusser, *Lenin and Philosophy and Other Essays* (New York: Monthly Review Press, 1971); Sally Hibbin et al., *Politics, Ideology, and the State* (London: Lawrence and Wishart, 1978); Gary Littlejohn et al., *Power and the State* (London: Croom Helm, 1978); Ralph Miliband, "The Capitalist State: Reply to Nicos Poulantzas," *New Left Review* 59 (January–February 1970): 53–60; idem, "Poulantzas and the Capitalist State," *New Left Review* 82 (November–December 1973): 83–92; Eric Nordlinger, *On the Autonomy of the Democratic State* (Cambridge, Mass.: Harvard University Press, 1981); Nicos Poulantzas, "The Problem of the Capitalist State," *New Left Review* 58 (November–December 1969): 67–78; and idem, "The Capitalist State: A Reply to Miliband and Laclau," *New Left Review* 95 (January–February 1976).
6. Eisenstein, *The Radical Future of Liberal Feminism*, pp. 25–26.
7. Catharine MacKinnon in "Feminism, Marxism, Method and the State: Toward Feminist Jurisprudence," *Signs* 9, no. 4 (Summer 1983): 635–59, argues that the state is not autonomous of patriarchy, whereas I think it is *relatively* autonomous.
8. See Zillah Eisenstein, "Developing a Theory of Capitalist Patriarchy and Socialist Feminism," in *Capitalist Patriarchy and the Case for Socialist Feminism* (New York: Monthly Review Press, 1979).
9. Michele Barrett, *Women's Oppression Today: Problems in Marxist Feminist Analysis* (London: NLB, 1980), p. 138.
10. Ibid.
11. Theda Skocpol, "Bringing the State Back In: False Leads and Promising Starts in Current Theories and Research," working paper presented at a Conference on States and Social Structures, Seven Springs Conference Center, Mount Kisco, New York, February 25–27, 1982, p. 37. Also see Skocpol, *States and Social Revolutions* (Cambridge: Cambridge University Press, 1979).
12. Skocpol, "Bringing the State Back In," p. 38.
13. Ibid., pp. 25–26.
14. Diane Polan, "Toward a Theory of Law and Patriarchy," in David Kairys, ed.,

The Politics of Law: A Progressive Critique (New York: Pantheon Books, 1982), p. 301.

15. Ibid.

16. Ibid., p. 298.

17. For important discussions of the Marxist meaning of ideology and its relation to material life see Louis Althusser, Lenin and Philosophy and Other Essays; Antonio Gramsci, Selections from the Prison Notebooks (New York: International Publishers, 1971); Douglas Kellner, "Ideology, Marxism, and Advanced Capitalism," Socialist Review 8, no. 42 (November–December 1978): 37–67; and idem, "T.V., Ideology and Emancipatory Popular Culture," Socialist Review 9, no. 45 (May–June 1977): 13–54. Also see Stephen Resnick and Richard Wolff, "Marxist Epistemology: The Critique of Economic Determinism," Social Text 2, no. 3 (1982): 31–72, for an intriguing argument about the relationship between the real and ideal in Marxist epistemology.

18. Janet Rifkin, "Toward a Theory of Law and Patriarchy," in Piers Beirne and Richard Quinney, eds., Marxism and Law (New York: John Wiley & Sons, 1982), p. 297.

19. Frances Fox Piven and Richard Cloward, The New Class War: Reagan's Attack on the Welfare State and Its Consequences (New York: Pantheon Books, 1982), pp. 41–42.

20. Ibid., p. 31.

21. Ibid., p. 124.

22. Ibid., p. 135.

23. Frances Fox Piven and Richard Cloward, "The American Road to Democratic Socialism," Democracy 3, no. 3 (Summer 1983): 64.

24. Ibid., pp. 64–65. This conception of the state as an arena of capitalist class conflict has a long history within Marxist thought. See V. I. Lenin, "State and Revolution," in Selected Works, vol. 2 (Moscow: Progress, 1970); Frederick Engels, The Origin of the Family, Private Property, and the State, ed. Eleanor Burke Leacock (New York: International Publishers, 1972); Alan Hunt, ed., Class and Class Structure (London: Lawrence and Wishart, 1977); Karl Marx, The Eighteenth Brumaire of Louis Bonaparte (New York: International Publishers, 1963); Karl Marx and Frederick Engels, The Communist Manifesto (New York: International Publishers, 1948); Goran Therborn, What Does the Ruling Class Do When It Rules? (London: New Left Books, 1978); and Erik Olin Wright, Class, Crisis and the State (London: New Left Books, 1978).

25. Piven and Cloward, New Class War, p. 140.

26. See Christopher Lasch, Haven in a Heartless World (New York: Basic Books, 1977).

27. Christopher Lasch, The Culture of Narcissism (New York: W. W. Norton, 1979), p. 320.

28. Ibid., p. 268; and Haven in a Heartless World, p. xv.

29. Lasch, Haven in a Heartless World, p. xiv.

30. Lasch, Culture of Narcissism, p. 369.

31. Lasch, Haven in a Heartless World, p. 25.

32. Christopher Lasch, "The Freudian Left and Cultural Revolution," New Left Review 129 (September–October 1981): 33.

33. Ibid.

34. I am grateful for discussions with Ellen Willis about this point.

35. Isaac Balbus, *Marxism and Domination* (Princeton: Princeton University Press, 1982).
36. Ibid., p. 332.
37. Ibid.
38. Ibid., p. 333.
39. Ibid.

5. The Reagan Administration: Changes in Family Life and the Redefinition of the Welfare State

The Reagan administration's attempts to deal with the growing crisis of the welfare state reveal an ongoing effort to reconstitute the patriarchal aspects of the state in the light of changes in family forms, central to which is a'rolling back of gains made by middle-class white and black women and black men, as well as a redefinition of the state's relationship to poor women, particularly in single-parent families. Because conflict exists within the state on how best to reformulate the patriarchal aspects of the state for advanced capitalist society, a coherent state policy does not yet exist for the 1980s. But, to the extent both the New Right and neoconservatives blame the social welfare state for creating excessive demands for equality, as well as creating a crisis of patriarchal authority, the dismantling of social services remains a core element of the state's resolve to address the "crisis of liberalism." While doing this the Reagan administration must try to articulate a politics that does not appear completely hostile to (liberal) feminist demands.

The Welfare State and Changing Family Forms

The welfare state has arisen in part out of changing patterns of family life and has also created intended and unintended consequences for family life. White married women's entry into the labor force, increased divorce rates, changes in sexual mores, changes in the structure of the economy, and the growth of a feminist movement have all served to reveal the outmoded aspects of the traditional (white) patriarchal family. The state is therefore being forced to reformulate a dynamic of patriarchal privilege that no longer rests solely on the traditional family model.

There are several forms of the advanced capitalist patriarchal family. The largest number of families are made up of dual wage-earners. The fastest growing family form is the single-parent type, headed by a woman. A small minority of families adhere to the traditional capitalist patriarchal model of the heterosexual couple with the man earning the income and the woman at home with the children. State policies related to family life have yet to deal sufficiently with these changes. The social programs of the welfare state were meant to be a step in this direction. The dismantling of the welfare state by the Reagan administration, initiated under Carter, is another step in this same direction.

The relations of patriarchal privilege have become more differentiated, given the multiple family forms that presently exist. There has been a "transfer of power" from the father and/or husband to the welfare state for the woman heading a single-parent poor family. The reformulation of woman as dependent on the state, as replacing the "absent" husband, redefines the locus of patriarchal power for the single-parent poor family. Given the poverty of the single-parent family, many of these women become directly dependent on the social programs of the state. This conflicts with the ideology of the privacy of the family, which is still adhered to by the state.

In the dual wage-earning family, where both husband and wife work in the labor force, the husband's power is under challenge as well, tied as it has been to the ideological notion that he is the sole economic provider. As women have entered the labor force in greater numbers and have continued to challenge the neat division between home and market, economy and family, private and public life, they have also become a challenge to existing patriarchal authority rooted in the ideological separation of home and market. The state operates as the missing father in relation to the dual wage-earning family in a more indirect form than it does for the single-parent family headed by a woman.

The patriarchal controls on the woman in the dual wage-earning family operate predominantly in the market. There, women are segregated in the low-paying service sector and are disproportionately relegated to underemployment (part-time work) as secondary workers. The market becomes an active participant in redefining the control systems of patriarchal privilege for women who are in the labor force.[1] The market in this sense bolsters the privilege of the man, even if he is not the sole economic provider; when he is not the economic provider (as husband), as in the single-parent family headed by a woman, the state directly steps in.

This discussion about the relations between state activity and family life needs to be qualified in terms of the black family. Much of the concern of the state with changes in family life occurs because these changes—particularly the increase in married wage-earning women—now affect the white family. Black married women have always worked outside the home disproportionately to white women.[2] This particular reality, that a majority of black married women have never been solely supported by their husbands, sets up a particular dynamic between racism and patriarchy. The racist dynamic expresses itself in the fact that black men have never been allowed to be the sole economic support of black women, which differentiates black men from white men, black women from white women. And yet the state has always stepped in as patriarch to extend direct controls over the black woman.[3]

There is a particular and specific dynamic to be understood here between racism and patriarchy that cuts across social lines but should not allow one to simplistically parallel white and black women's experience of patriarchy. Racism is used to deflect patriarchal privilege. Patriarchal privilege is used to mediate racism, which may explain why the wage gains by white women in the labor force (in relation to white men) are smaller than the gains that have been made by black women in relation to black men.[4]

Patriarchal privilege, which has been located in the white man as father and/or husband as sole economic provider and now seems to be located more (although not exclusively) in a series of economic inequalities found in the market with either no man present in the family or a shared, though unequal, economic relationship between husband and wife, must be reformulated on the state level. This requires a more active state, both in the realm of family life and in the market. As family forms have become more differentiated and diverse, patriarchal power has become more actively administered by the state. This is a real problem for a

state that has been bound by liberal patriarchal ideology that is
hostile to a collapse of state/family, public/private, sexual/
political dichotomies.

Reorganizing the Welfare State and Reconstituting Patriarchy

There are two fundamental aspects to the dismantling of the
social programs of the welfare state. First, it is an attempt to revitalize the unchallenged ideological division between public and
private life, the government and the economy, family and political
life, while keeping intact a full series of patriarchal controls on
family life. This attack on the welfare state does not apply to
welfare militarism or corporatism but targets only welfare state
familialism. At the very same time that the dismantling of the
welfare state is said to be a way of getting government off the
backs of the "people" (and the family), the state is *reformulating*
the policies of the state to family life in the hopes of increasing the
state's authority in family life.

Second, the dismantling of the welfare state is supposed to
eliminate the "new class"—those who administer the welfare
state. The people of the supposed new class are disproportionately white and black women and black men. The expansion of
government services of the welfare state increased the job opportunities for middle-class educated black and white women. In
1976 government employed 21 percent of all women, 25 percent
of all blacks, 15 percent of all people of Spanish origin, and 16
percent of all men.[5] More particularly, government employed 49.9
percent of all female professionals and 34.5 percent of all male
professionals. Therefore, government cutbacks in hiring at these
levels will affect (middle-class) professional women at a higher
rate than men. The dismantling of the welfare state and its personnel is directed against the gains made by these women, and by
black men as well.

The effects of these cutbacks are staggering:

> Minority employees of the federal agencies have been laid off at a
> rate 50% greater than non-minority employees. Women adminis-
> trators have been laid off at a rate 150% higher than male adminis-

trators. Minorities in administrative positions have been laid off at a rate about 220% higher than non-minority employees in similar positions.[6]

The Reagan administration's reduction of federal employees further discriminates against women because every woman in the federal workforce is subject to veteran's preference laws unless she is a political appointee.[7] One might need to be reminded that during the Carter administration the Supreme Court decided that veteran's preference laws were not discriminatory against women; they merely discriminate against non-veterans. Therefore, the discriminatory practices involved here are not recognized as such.

The Reagan administration argues that cutbacks of federal jobs will be offset by an increase in private-sector employment, particularly in the defense industry. But the people who have lost their jobs in these cutbacks are not the ones who will be hired in the private sector. Private industry does not have a good record of hiring professional black and white women or black men. It is the public sector that does. "Government employment primarily benefits professional women (both white and black) and professional minority men (about 50% of these two groups worked at all levels of government in the 1970's). Indeed, since 1950, increased public spending has been the single most important impetus behind the greater economic mobility of women and minorites."[8] In 1980, about 20 percent of black men and 28 percent of black women were classified as government wage and salary workers. Both sexes were more than 50 percent more likely to be employed in the government sector than whites.[9]

Dismantling the welfare state and attacking the new class ends up being a direct assault on the gains made by black men and black and white women, particularly in the professional middle class. The gains of the middle-class professional woman are under attack while the state tries to reaffirm patriarchal privilege through the sexual hierarchy of the market. The welfare state itself had become subversive, as liberal democracy has, in challenging the patriarchal ordering of the marketplace, to the degree that it played an active role in providing opportunities to women.

Besides firing those who administer the welfare state, the dismantling of the welfare state has meant cutting back drastically on social programs. These cutbacks are particularly aimed at underemployed, poor, and welfare women, whereas the dismantling of the new class is aimed at the middle-class white and black woman and black man. The patriarchal and racist aspects of the Reagan state are differentiated along economic class lines. A major problem for the state, however, is that a woman's economic class is partially defined by the family form in which she lives. The fastest growing population in the United States is the poverty population: 3.2 million people were added to the poverty population from 1979 to 1980, with 13.0 percent living below the poverty level.[10] Black and white women are disproportionately represented in this population. In 1979 many of these poor women were to be found amidst the 5.3 million woman-headed families. Between 1970 and 1978 the unemployment rate among these women rose sharply, from 5.6 percent to 9 percent.[11]

The dismantling of the social welfare state, which is outlined in the budget cuts of 1981–84, implicitly expresses a sexual politics. To say that the politics of the economy is implicitly a sexual politics is more than saying that the budget cuts have particular effect on women, which they do. It says that at the base of economic policy is a policy on the family and patriarchal society. In this sense, the Reagan budgets seek to realign the relationship between the (welfare) state and the family, men and women, and public and private life as much as they attempt to deal with inflation. The relationship between the state and the family has been undergoing basic changes since World War II with the entry of large numbers of white, married (middle-class conscious) women into the labor force. The expansion of the social service sector of the state and the development of the welfare state itself parallel the entry of women into the labor force. One can argue that the reaction against state policies that developed through the 1960s and 1970s is in part a reaction against the need for them, and this partially reflects the redefinition of responsibilities of the family and the state as women have entered the labor force. Seen as such, the reaction against state involvement in social services is a statement against the transformations taking place in the family and the relationship between the state and the family. The Reagan budgets attempt to limit and curtail the responsibilities of the (welfare) state and to increase the responsibilities (and supposed freedom) of the family.

Dismantling the Social Welfare State

Most of the major cutbacks affect Aid to Families with Dependent Children (AFDC), Medicaid, Legal Services, the Comprehensive Employment and Training Act (CETA), and food stamps. The family is supposed to be the social unit now responsible for all these aspects of health and welfare. Medicaid, a joint federal and state program, was designed to provide medical assistance to low-income persons who cannot afford medical care. In 1979, 61 percent of all Medicaid recipients—11 million people—were women. Thirty-four percent of all Medicaid recipients were under the age of fifteen. Thirty-six percent of all households covered by Medicaid were headed by females with no spouse present. And about 40 percent of all Medicaid expenditures went for nursing-home care.[12] The cuts in Medicaid hit women and children directly, specifically those women heading households. The cuts also made nursing-home care inaccessible to many, and therefore the care of the aged has been forced back onto women in the family.

Food stamps subsidize food purchases for households that have a net income below the poverty level and assets of less than $1,500. By 1983 some 203 million people (400,000–600,000 families) had been dropped from food stamp rolls. Six out of ten food stamp households are headed by women.

Child nutrition programs include the national school lunch program, the breakfast program, the special milk program, the child care and summer feeding program, and the special nutrition program. As many as 200,000 women have been eliminated from the Women, Infant and Child (WIC) program, which provides food packages to pregnant low-income women, infants, and children.[13]

Aid to Families with Dependent Children provides cash benefits to needy families with dependent children. Over 90 percent of the AFDC recipients are women and their children. Over 80 percent of all single-parent households are headed by women, and one-third of these households are in poverty. According to administration estimates, the cutbacks and changes in AFDC have affected benefits to 400,000 families and reduced benefits to 250,000. Presumably persons who are forced off AFDC rolls will enter the workforce, even though 40 percent of all poverty-level women heading families alone already had some work experience in 1979.[14] These are precisely the women who need training in order to get jobs, and the Comprehensive Employment and Training Act (CETA) program, designed for this purpose, has also been all but destroyed.

These budget cuts take on even more significance when one sees that the fastest-growing form of the family today is the single-parent, woman-headed family. Whereas the total number of families increased by 12 percent between 1970 and 1979, the number maintained by female householders grew by 51 percent.[15] In 1981, 18.8 percent of all families with children under eighteen years of age were headed by women; 47.3 percent of black families of this kind were headed by women. The median income in 1978 of families maintained by a woman was $8,540, or slightly less than one-half (48 percent) of the $17,640 median income of families overall.[16] Almost one female-headed family in three is poor; about one in eighteen families headed by a man is poor.[17]

Overall, women headed about half of all poor families in 1981. Families headed by women with no husband present constituted 47 percent of all families below the poverty line in 1981. This is a rise of 54 percent from 1960 to 1981. Whereas a two-spouse family with a working wife had a median income of $29,247 in 1981, a female householder's income was $10,960 compared with the male householder's $19,889.[18]

Over one-third of those defined as poor in the United States are children. It is the programs to aid them and their mothers that have been cut. By 1982 the school breakfast program had been cut by 20 percent; further, restrictions were instituted for the food stamp program; the school lunch program was cut by 30 percent; the summer feeding program was cut by 50 percent; the special milk program was cut by 80 percent; and the child care food program was cut by 30 percent.[19] At the time of this writing the proposed 1984 budget projects another 14 percent decrease (or a 19 percent real decline) in programs directed at the poor.

Food stamps are to be cut another 9 percent and child nutrition funds are to be cut by 8 percent. It is expected that there will be a six-month delay in cost-of-living adjustments for those receiving food stamps. Special supplemental food programs for women, infants, and children are undergoing stringent revision. A 42 percent cut is projected for the special milk program. Block grants are to be totally abolished. Military spending, however, is expected to rise to $238.6 billion in 1984, which accounts for three-quarters of the increase in government spending. It does seem bizarre that the administration that has instituted these policies has been identified as "pro-family" and "pro-life." One has to wonder just what kind of family the sponsors of such politics are interested in instituting.

The paradoxes are endless. The Reagan administration, despite its "pro-motherhood" stance, provided the single U.N. vote in favor of instant baby formula (instead of mother's milk) for third world countries. Although Reagan says he is committed to the housewife, he has proposed a decrease in the percentage of benefits paid to dependent spouses at age 62 from 37.5 percent to 27.5 percent and has proposed a change in retirement age from 65 to 68.[20] Reagan speaks of work incentives for the poor while at the same time the above-mentioned social program cuts have forced many poor but employed women to give up their jobs and go onto welfare. The new eligibility rules on day care, food stamps, and Medicaid are forcing women onto welfare. One could call these actions a program of disincentives for poor women to continue working.[21]

Rather than setting the poor to work, these new poor laws are "forcing women heading families to choose welfare over work."[22] The U.S. Commission on Civil Rights report *A Growing Crisis: Disadvantaged Women and Their Children* finds that the cutbacks and new eligibility requirements are having "adverse effects on the working poor."[23] The report also finds that "the biggest factor in reducing their [women's] poverty rate is welfare programs."[24] The commission argues that long-term dependency on welfare is the exception but that women do not obtain labor market benefits comparable to men with similar education and training. Therefore, the government needs to provide "alternative sources of skill training for poor women unable to gain access to currently available resources. If not, they may find themselves trapped in poverty in spite of their best efforts to avoid or overcome their dependency."[25]

All CETA workers who were former welfare recipients have

been forced to reapply for public assistance because of the Reconciliation Act of 1981, which dismantled the CETA program. Women displaced by this act have a better chance of receiving AFDC aid if their husbands are not present. These women who are being forced onto welfare and qualify for it because of an absent spouse reflect the consequences of the state's contradictory policies on the family. On the one hand, the state is destroying family life as a locus of patriarchal relations between poor men and women, and on the other hand, it argues in defense of the family form organized around husband and wife. This latter form seems to be reserved for the non-poor, dual wage-earning, or traditional nuclear family. For the white poor the state is becoming the father and husband, as it has been for the black poor.

Women's poverty can be seen more readily today because of the changing nature of the family. Divorce can easily leave a formerly middle-class woman on welfare. "For some women marital status matters more than labor market status as an indicator of financial well being."[26] For unmarried women—divorced, separated, lesbian, never married, widowed—economic class and sexual class seem to merge under advanced capitalism. One might argue that these women are increasingly visible as an economic class through the "feminization of poverty," which is more a reflection of the changing structure of family life than it is a change in individual economic status. Three out of every five persons with incomes below the poverty level are women. Two out of every three older persons living in poverty are women. Female-headed families with no husband present comprise only 15 percent of all families but 48 percent of all poverty-level families. The median income of all women age fourteen and above is well below half that of their male counterparts.[27] This reality is accentuated when a woman's economic inequality and dependence are not mediated through a husband and her family's needs increasingly have to be met by the state.

It has been found that divorced women lose 29 percent in real income while divorced men lose 11 percent. Over a seven-year period following divorce, the economic position of men, when assessed in terms of need, improved 17 percent while the position of women declined by 29 percent.[28] The point is that the economic class reality of women's lives is very much in flux today because family forms are themselves in flux. Serious rethinking and study remain to be done in this area, given the changing nature of the family and the impact this has on understanding women's economic class. Although economic class differences exist among women, their similar economic vulnerability due to their secondary sexual-class status is more readily identifiable when it is not mediated through a husband's wages or salary.

Women as a sexual class share an economic vulnerability due to their status as secondary wage-earners. "At the moment, the earnings differences for wives of high-earnings husbands and wives of low-earnings husbands are not substantial. Working wives contribute to equality since their earnings are much more equally distributed than those of their husbands."[29] As secondary wage-earners, women earned approximately 59 percent as much as men in 1981. Thirteen percent of fully employed women had earnings of $7,000 or less compared with 4 percent of fully employed men. Forty-seven percent of fully employed men earned over $20,000 a year compared with 10 percent of women. The Commission on Civil Rights found that 61 percent of black, 51 percent of Hispanic, and 45 percent of white women in the labor force in 1980 were either unemployed or underemployed compared with 35 percent of white men.[30]

In the dismantling of the social programs of the welfare state, the multiple forms of family life are being uncovered along with their needs. Two points stand out clearly. The dual wage-earning family has become the most common family form in the society. Fifty-seven percent of two-parent families today have two wage earners.[31] The single-parent, woman-headed family is now as common as the traditional patriarchal family. The former presently accounts for 15 percent of the families today, whereas the latter comprises 14 percent.[32] Neither the dual wage-earning family nor the single-parent, female-headed family fits the model of the "pro-family" policy of the New Right. The budget cuts and their attack on the welfare state presume to protect the traditional patriarchal family from intrusion by the state, but by protecting this form of the family, the Reagan administration merely exacerbates the conflicts that exist between the state and other family forms.

In essence, then, the Reagan administration budgets try to re-stabilize patriarchy by reestablishing the so-called privacy of the traditional nuclear family as much as they try to fight inflation and stabilize capitalism. The government's cutbacks in the social ser-vices budget while the military budget is increased are an attempt to redefine the responsibilities and purview of the state. Individu-als and hence the family are supposed to be responsible for their health, education, and welfare. The state will be responsible for defense. Social services have been labeled the "excesses of de-mocracy" and therefore must be curtailed. Neoconservatives want people to understand that the state cannot and should not create equality of conditions for them. They say little about what family life should look like and instead merely assume that it will be rooted in heterosexual marriage while enjoying "privacy" from the state. The New Right more directly attempts to reestablish the traditional patriarchal power of the father in the family by assert-ing the private role and purpose of the family *against* the public duties of the state.

The Reagan administration is faced with the dilemma of trying to redefine the relationship between family life and the state when no one policy for all family forms will do. At present, the state seems to be articulating a differentiated series of patriarchal policies that may well construct and exacerbate economic class divisions among women as they are defined through the familial forms of which they are a part. To the extent that economic class divisions among women are mediated through their secondary sexual-class status and family forms themselves, the state is ac-tively trying to devise a new policy accounting for this. Economic class differences are more readily found among women occupying different types of family life—divorced, married, single—than among individual women in the market. State policy has yet to absorb this in terms of redefining patriarchal controls within the state. So far, the dismantling of the welfare state has attacked the gains made by the wage-earning woman *and* the middle-class woman of the "new class." The two major aspects of the Reagan administrations's attempt to redefine the relationship between the state and the family, the state and the economy, and patriarchy and the state have been the removal of subsidies for the single-

parent poor family and the firing of disproportionate numbers of
women from government jobs. Both curtail real gains made by
women toward economic equality of opportunity.

The New Right, Feminism, and the State

Neoconservatives and the New Right believe that state intervention must be decreased in order to protect the privacy of the family and to limit inflation. But their support for state spending in
the military realm only increases the possibility of further inflation. According to Lester Thurow, Reagan's military build-up will
be the largest in American history, three times as large as the one
that took place during the Vietnam war.[33] At the same time,
Reagan proposes to cut taxes 30 percent. It is important to remember that Johnson's refusal to raise taxes to pay for the Vietnam war
was largely responsible for the increased inflation rate in this
country.

If Thurow's analysis is correct, the present cuts in social services and taxes will not limit inflation but rather increase it. In
terms of the New Right's analysis of inflation's impact on the
family, this will further increase the burdens on married wage-
earning women and families, particularly on the families of the
working and nonworking poor. In the end, the New Right and
neoconservative attack on the welfare state appears contradictory
at best. First, it criticizes state expenditures only in the social
service realm, not in the military and defense sector of the welfare
state. Second, its support for cuts in the social service budget only
increases the need for social services, particularly for the working
poor. Finally, the demand to get government "off our backs" is
completely contradicted by New Right "pro-family" legislation.
Basically, when the New Right argues against state intervention in
the family, it is criticizing economic aid to the family. It actively
supports state involvement in legislating sexual matters such as
abortion and teenage pregnancy counseling, in limiting venereal
disease programs, and in curtailing sex education. The Family
Protection Act and the "Human Life" Bill have been two cases of
such legislation.

This contradiction in New Right policy between a noninterventionist state (cutting social services) and an interventionist state (legislating family morality) poses serious problems for its profamily program and has slowed enactment of much of its legislation.[34] First of all, 72 percent of the American public rejects the idea of a human life bill that would consider the fetus a person and make abortion and some forms of birth control illegal.[35] A majority of the American public does not believe that this issue should be regulated by government or that anyone but the woman and her doctor should decide whether she should have an abortion. Second, to the extent that a majority of Americans do not live in the family form that will benefit from the New Right's profamily policies, the New Right will have difficulty enacting its legislation, providing a politics rooted in the other family forms can be articulated and politically mobilized.

The welfare state has its problems, given its own contradictory nature. Irving Howe has defined at least two functions of the welfare state: "It steps in to modulate the excesses of the economy, helping to create rationality and order, and thereby to save capitalism from its own tendency to destruction. And it steps in to provide humanizing reforms, as a response to insurgent groups and communities."[36] The problem, however, is not the welfare state, although it poses significant problems. The problem is rather the kind of society we live in, which is both patriarchal and capitalist, which would return individuals to self-reliance while maintaining structural barriers related to economic class, sexual class, and racism that limit and curtail the individual. It is up to feminists of all political persuasions, left-liberals, and leftists to shift the critique from the welfare state to the patriarchal society that creates it. As feminists we need to marshal the liberal demands for individual self-determination, freedom of choice, individual autonomy, and equality before the law to indict capitalist patriarchal society. This use of liberal ideology by feminists will permit us to direct the public's consciousness to a critique of capitalist patriarchy, not merely a critique of the welfare state.

The New Right assault is aimed against feminism precisely because women's (liberal) feminist consciousness about their rights to equality is the major radicalizing force of the 1980s. Liberalism is in crisis today not merely because the welfare state is in crisis as the New Right believes, or because liberalism contains cultural contradictions as the neoconservatives argue, or because capitalism itself is in crisis, as Marxists and left-liberals contend. The "crisis of liberalism" is a result of the conflict between the traditional white patriarchal family, advanced capitalism, and the ideology of liberalism. The married wage-earning woman, black or white, and the potential of her feminist consciousness demonstrate this reality; hence the assault by the state against the feminist movement in general and the ERA in particular.

The Patriarchal State and the ERA

The attack on women, which is somewhat masked within the politics of the Reagan budget, becomes blatantly clear with the defeat of the Equal Rights Amendment. The patriarchal bias of the state is made explicit in its anti-ERA stance even though there is little agreement within the state on the ERA. Although New Right forces, headed by Jerry Falwell and Phyllis Schlafly, fought for the defeat of the ERA and in defense of the rights of the housewife, some neoconservatives and center forces within the Democratic and Republican parties believe the ERA is a necessary revision of the law, given the prevalence of the dual wage-earning family and the needs of the working mother. Senators Durenberger and Hatfield recognize the need for the state (at least on the level of ideology and the law) to deal with the conflicts between the reality of the dual wage-earning family and the ideology of the traditional patriarchal family. The ERA does not challenge the patriarchal aspects of the home or the patriarchal division between public and private life, but rather recognizes, in advanced capitalist patriarchal form, that a majority of women need legal rights within the market. In this sense, as we shall see later, Phyllis Schlafly is right. The ERA is a recognition of the wage-earning woman, not the traditional housewife, and therefore is seen by the New Right as a challenge to the traditional patriarchal family.

Reagan's New Right anti-ERA stance creates as many problems

as it solves, possibly more. It signifies that the relations of power of the state in 1984 remain patriarchal—that those in government today think that the political system of capitalist patriarchy cannot abide women's (legal) equality. The state, by protecting its interests in an outmoded form, draws attention to its patriarchal needs. With a majority of Americans supporting the ERA, it becomes apparent that factions within the state rule in their own interest. The bluntness of this contradiction—between majority opinion in favor of the ERA and its legislative defeats—can only be subversive to the state in the long run. Whereas 66 percent of anti-ERA women voted for Reagan, only 32 percent of pro-ERA women did.

This pro-ERA consciousness has already begun to materialize politically with the newly announced strategy by the National Organization for Women (NOW) for a continued ERA campaign calling for the election of women to state and federal legislatures. Such a strategy, which is clearly reformist, also points to what George Gilder has called the revolutionary aspects of (liberal) feminism, namely, that the role of men as the primary operatives in the public sector is under attack. Among women, a subversive consciousness is developing about the Reagan administration, which is being termed the "gender gap": women seem to support Reagan less than men do. Even as early as the 1980 election, this gap (though small) was evident. At the end of 1982, 53 percent of the women polled said they were inclined to vote Democratic; 35 percent said they would vote Republican.

The Reagan administration is increasingly concerned about the gender gap, as we shall see in the next chapter. Before discussing this issue in detail, it is important to examine how Reagan has been trying to mediate some of the conflict his own policies have created, as well as the conflicts that exist within the state between the radical right and the neoconservatives over how best to reformulate and bolster the patriarchal aspects of the state. The state operates within the constraints of its patriarchal needs. Exactly how the state chooses between alternatives, how it adopts particular positions on abortion and the ERA, why two women were recently appointed to cabinet positions, are all part of explicating the relatively autonomous character of patriarchy within the state.

Intrastate Conflict in the Patriarchal State

The conflicts within the state over what to do about the changing nature of the family and the issues of feminism are quite real. Intrastate conflict appeared during the Carter administration over the issues of the working mother, the Equal Rights Amendment, the threat to draft women, abortion legislation, and pregnancy disability payments. These issues continue to be significant areas of controversy.

The Reagan administration has sought to mediate the conflicts between the radical right, which gained a stronghold with his election, and the neoconservative factions of the state, which gained ascendancy under Carter. The 1978 report of the Commission on Families and Public Policies in the United States compiled during Carter's term argues, in somewhat liberal feminist fashion, that social services for the family should be upgraded; that income maintenance programs are needed, given the economic needs of families; and that a pluralistic view of family life should structure policymaking.[37] In this view, state involvement in the family was seen as necessary to enable the family to fulfill its responsibilities.

The commission specifically recommended a national employment policy that would legally enforce everyone's right to a job; the greater use of flextime, shared work, and other arrangements for full-time jobs; the support of part-time work arrangements to make possible the care of children and the elderly; and increased career counseling with special emphasis on programs for women.[38] These policy guidelines clearly recognize the changing nature of the family, particularly in relation to the dual wage-earning family.

More recent legislation introduced by David Durenberger, Mark Hatfield, and Bob Packwood and endorsed by Patrick Moynihan attempts to follow through on some of these recommendations related to the dual wage-earning family. Their Economic Equity Act (S. 888) tries to counter "policies in the public and private sector that are completely at odds with work patterns determined by the realities of women's dual wage-earning and parenting" by proposing tax credits to employers who hire women entering the workforce after divorce or death of a spouse, equal tax status for heads of households and for married couples, employer-sponsored child care that would be provided as a tax-free fringe benefit similar to health insurance, and tax credits to offset the cost of child care.

Both the Commission Report of 1978 and the Economic Equity Act recognize the changing nature of the family and the unresolved conflicts between capitalism and patriarchy that these changes embody. Although this proposed legislation in and of itself cannot resolve the contradictions in the married wage-earning woman's life, it can begin to initiate necessary policy changes. As such, it is a beginning in the process of utilizing liberal feminist reforms to instigate progressive change. By virtue of the nature of the problem—the irresolvable conflict between liberalism and patriarchal society—we must move beyond such legislation. But it is through the struggle to pass such legislation that we can build a consciousness of the need for more progressive changes.

The importance of such legislation as the Economic Equity Act becomes clear when it is compared with policy proposals of the New Right that seek to enforce the model of the traditional male-headed household. The Laxalt-Jepsen Family Protection Act and its recent revisions in the Economic Recovery Tax Act, Senate Bill 1378, Section 206, as one example of New Right legislation, recommends that textbooks belittling the traditional role of women in society not be purchased with federal money; that tax exemptions of $1,000 be extended to households with dependents over the age of sixty-five; that a wage-earner's contributions to a savings account for his or her nonworking spouse be tax deductible, up to $1,500 per year; that the current marriage tax penalizing married couples with two incomes be eliminated; that legal services corporation money be denied for abortions, school desegregation, divorce, or homosexual rights litigation.

Whereas Carter's administration endorsed ERA (although it did nothing to aid its ratification), the Reagan administration's position is "against the amendment but for equal rights." Reagan has tried to walk this tightrope; he supports the New Right position against the Equal Rights Amendment and yet he tries to appear supportive of equal rights for women. This particular position adopts the neoconservative position that supports equality of opportunity, but not equality of conditions. In this sense Reagan's position on the ERA straddles both neoconservative and New Right politics. To the extent the liberal feminist position demands "opportunity" but logically leads to a more progressive position, (liberal) feminists cannot abide the Reagan administration's present policy of rejecting the amendment. The gender gap suggests that this is in fact the case. The gender gap reflects a consciousness among women that rejects present Reagan administration polices affecting women, in either their New Right or neoconservative guise. It is interesting that the Reagan state has had an easier time rejecting welfare-state liberalism than liberal feminist ideology in terms of the ERA and abortion rights. The state appears to be caught between its patriarchal constraints and liberalism's promise of equality of opportunity for women, and cannot abide equality (of opportunity or conditions) for women. New Right and neoconservative fears about sexual equality are in fact valid if one seeks to protect the capitalist patriarchal order.

The appointment of Sandra O'Connor to the Supreme Court is a case in point of how the Reagan administration has tried to disassociate the question of "women's rights" (and their equality of opportunity even to become Supreme Court justices) from the issue of the amendment itself, which supposedly will make men and women the same and create equality of conditions. Reagan argues that the amendment would be harmful to women because it will treat men and women as though they were the same (equal?). On the other hand, the appointment of O'Connor was supposed to prove that a woman is free to be anything she wants to be. All women supposedly need is freedom of choice—not equality.

O'Connor's appointment to the Supreme Court reflects the constraints within which the state operates as it attempts to re-stabilize the relationship between family forms, advanced capitalist market needs, and the state. Reagan's administration is not fully free to reject the ideology of women's equality without enlarging the gender gap and further heightening the conflicts within the dual wage-earning family. These pose real problems, both in the electoral arena and in family life itself.

Because the Reagan administration is caught among the conflicts of the antifeminist stance of the New Right and the liberal feminist (pro-ERA, pro-abortion) stance of the American public, Reagan appointed O'Connor, who was not readily identified with the New Right antiabortion position. In fact, the New Right initially opposed her appointment. A Supreme Court appointee who was clearly a part of the antifeminist New Right would have counted for little among feminist or pro-abortion men and women. But the nomination of O'Connor could be seen as a recognition of mainstream feminist demands. Whether it continues to do so remains unlikely now that O'Connor has made her antiabortion stance clear. Whereas the Supreme Court has reaffirmed the constitutional right to obtain an abortion and has struck down a series of local legislative restrictions on access to abortions, O'Connor has dissented along with Justices Byron White and William Rehnquist. She dissented because she believes that the state has a legitimate interest in protecting the fetus' health through the entire pregnancy.[39]

Whatever the motives of Reagan were, it is significant that a woman has been appointed to the Supreme Court. It is an open recognition, no matter how limited, of the changing nature of women's lives. Exactly how significant O'Connor's nomination is to feminists remains to be seen in the way she sits on the court. Even though O'Connor has turned out not to be supportive of abortion, her nomination was an attempt to meet liberal feminist demands, albeit within their narrowest context, in the hopes of deradicalizing feminist demands as part of reasserting and redefining the patriarchal aspects of the state.

One last interesting point to be considered about the appointment of O'Connor: Reagan possibly used the O'Connor appointment to delegitimize the radical right factions of the pro-life movement in hopes of directing them away from their purist positions on abortion and the ERA. The Reagan administration may have realized that the radical factions of the right wing radicalize the feminist movement and increase the "gender gap." After all, more than two out of every three Americans oppose any law that would make abortion murder. The Reagan administration has never had a mandate for the antifeminist politics of the New Right that is anti-ERA and antiabortion. The appointment of O'Connor is proof that the Reagan administration may be partially conceding this.

Conflict over policies affecting women and feminism in general is evident in several other recent firings and appointments within the Reagan administration. Reagan fired Wendy Borscherdt after she removed Joy Simonson as executive director of the National Advisory Council on Women's Educational Programs for supposedly recommending that left-wing feminist organizations be funded by the Women's Educational Equity Act program (WEEA). Borscherdt replaced Simonson with Rosemary Thomson, a former director of the Illinois Eagle Forum, the largest anti-ERA group in the country, run by Phyllis Schlafly. This appears to be another loss for the radical right antifeminist forces. However, contradictory policies abound.

Reagan has abolished the Presidential Advisory Committee for Women and has instead set up the Task Force on Legal Equity for Women (Executive Order 12336). This task force will merely report on the progress made in implementing the president's directives rather than advise on issues of sexual discrimination. And as of June 1, 1982, of 679 administrative appointments, only 51 were women, which is 7.5 percent of the total. Six percent of judicial appointments have been women. At this time there were no women in the cabinet, although Jeane Kirkpatrick, as permanent representative for the United Nations, held a cabinet-level position. Judith Whittaker, a Republican, was dropped as a nominee for the Eighth Circuit Court of Appeals because the New Right branded her a "liberal democrat." In February 1982 Reagan dismissed leading Republican feminist Jill Ruckleshaus from the U.S. Civil Rights Commission.

Shortly after the 1982 elections, which seemed to reaffirm the reality of the "gender gap" between men and women's voting preferences, Reagan appointed two women to the cabinet. Presidential liaison Elizabeth Dole replaced Drew Lewis, who resigned as Secretary of Transportation, and defeated Congresswoman Margaret Heckler replaced Richard Schweiker, who resigned as Secretary of Health and Human Services. Dole is considered to be a moderate Republican and Heckler, although she is antiabortion, did not support Schweiker's (squeal) rule that federally funded family planning agencies when providing teenagers with contraceptives must notify their families. She has recently changed her stance on this. Heckler also supported the endorsement of the

ERA at the 1980 Republican convention.[40] Both of these cabinet appointments are aimed at women's disaffection with Reagan.

In terms of understanding how the state is attempting to re-stabilize patriarchy, it is significant to note that these two recent cabinet appointments are women and that neither of the women is of the radical right antifeminist spectrum of the New Right. The administration's support of the sexual-discrimination lawsuit against the insurance industry (the Spirt Case) is another example of how the administration has to defer at times to the constraints of liberal feminism in the hopes of deradicalizing it. The administration has submitted a brief to the Supreme Court taking the position that the Court of Appeals in New York correctly concluded that the use of sex-segregated actuarial tables to calculate employees' retirement benefits violated Title VII of the Civil Rights Act, which forbids the treatment of individuals as groups. The government's position, in this instance, reaffirms the fact that Reagan is not completely free to act on behalf of New Right antifeminism, nor completely free to ignore liberal feminist concerns if the state is to succeed in remystifying the patriarchal aspects of liberalism by extending a limited notion of equality of opportunity to women.

As a result of many of these policy decisions, conflicts between the New Right and the Reagan administration continue to develop. Members of the New Right, like Richard Viguerie, argue that Reagan is no longer a Reaganite or that he has not implemented a truly "conservative" government.[41] They think that James Baker, Reagan's chief of staff, asserts too liberal an influence in the administration. They actually consider Baker a foe of Reaganism, since he masterminded Jerry Ford's successful campaign for the Republican presidential nomination in 1976, beating Reagan, and plotted George Bush's unsuccessful bid against Reagan in the Republican primary. The New Right is much more partial to Edwin Meese III, President Reagan's counselor, and William Clark, former national security advisor, who they think are much more committed to a truly conservative program.[42]

Whereas liberalism, as an ideology justifying the welfare state, has been largely rejected by the Reagan administration, the administration remains caught within the constraints of liberal feminism as an ideology and a public consciousness. This creates problems for reasserting and redefining patriarchal controls, particularly when the policies of the state mean the disproportionate firing of black and white professional women and the disproportionate suffering of poor women, whether they are on welfare or are part of the working poor heading single-parent families. Affirmative action, CETA programs, the right to abortion, the right to equal pay, are the policies of (liberal) feminism. To the extent that Reagan opposes these policies, he may find his opposition increasing among women. Hence his attention to the much publicized "gender gap"—the difference in the way men and women perceive and judge the Reagan administration. Although the Reagan administration assesses the "gender gap" as a series of self-interested policy stances, I think that it reflects the developing consciousness among women of their identity as a sexual class with particular economic vulnerabilities.

NOTES

1. See Heidi Hartmann, "Capitalism, Patriarchy, and Job Segregation by Sex," in Zillah Eisenstein, *Capitalist Patriarchy and the Case for Socialist Feminism* (New York: Monthly Review Press, 1978), pp. 206–47; Emma Rothschild, "Reagan and the Real America," *New York Review of Books*, February 5, 1981.
2. See Philip S. Foner, *Women and the American Labor Movement: From World War I to the Present* (New York: Free Press, 1980); Eugene Genovese, *Roll, Jordan, Roll* (New York: Pantheon, 1974); Herbert G. Gutman, *The Black Family in Slavery and Freedom, 1750–1925* (New York: Pantheon, 1976); Patrick Moynihan, "The Negro Family: The Case for National Action," in Lee Rainwater and William Yancey, eds., *The Moynihan Report and the Politics of Controversy* (Cambridge: MIT Press, 1967).
3. James D. Williams, ed., *The State of Black America 1983* (Washington, D.C.: National Urban League, 1983). Also see Angela Davis, *Women, Race and Class* (New York: Random House, 1981); Bell Hooks, *Ain't I a Woman: Black Women and Feminism* (Boston: South End Press, 1981); Gloria Joseph and Hill Lewis, *Common Differences: Conflicts in Black and White Feminist Perspectives* (New York: Anchor Books, 1981); Gloria Hull, Patricia Bell Scott, and Barbara Smith, eds., *All the Women Are White, All the Blacks Are Men, but Some of Us Are Brave* (New York: Feminist Press, 1982).
4. Lester Thurow, *The Zero-Sum Society* (New York: Penguin, 1970), p. 187.
5. Ibid., p. 163.
6. Augustus F. Hawkins, "Minorities and Unemployment," in Alan Gartner, Colin Greer, and Frank Riessman, eds., *What Reagan Is Doing to Us* (New York: Harper & Row, 1982), p. 134. For further discussion of the Reagan administration's fiscal policies, see Frank Ackerman, *Reaganomics, Rhetoric vs.*

Reality (Boston: South End Press, 1982); and Robert Lekachman, Greed Is Not Enough: Reaganomics (New York: Pantheon, 1982).

7. Lynn Hecht Schafran, "Women: Reversing a Decade of Progress," in Gartner et al., eds, What Reagan Is Doing to Us, p. 167.

8. Martin Carnoy and Derek Shearer, "The Supply Side of the Street," The Nation 233, no. 15 (November 7, 1981): 464.

9. Williams, ed., The State of Black America, p. 64.

10. Ruth Sidel, "The Family: A Dream Deferred," in Gartner et al., eds., What Reagan Is Doing to Us, p. 54.

11. Steven Erie and Martin Rein, "Welfare: The New Poor Laws," in ibid., p. 77.

12. Families and Public Policies in the United States: Final Report on the Commission (Washington, D.C.: National Conference on Social Welfare, 1978), p. 2. (Available from National Conference on Social Welfare, 1730 M Street N.W., Suite 914, Washington, D.C. 20036.)

13. Ibid.

14. Ibid., p. 1.

15. U.S. Bureau of the Census, "Families Maintained by Female Householders, 1970–79," Current Population Reports, Series P-23, no. 107 (October 1980), p. 5.

16. Ibid., p. 33.

17. "Facts We Dare Not Forget—Excerpts from a Neglected Government Report on Poverty and Unemployment to Which the New Administration Will Surely Pay No Attention," Dissent 28, no. 2 (Spring 1981): 166. Also see "Families Maintained by Female Householders, 1970–79."

18. A Growing Crisis: Disadvantaged Women and Their Children (Washington, D.C.: U.S. Commission on Civil Rights; Clearinghouse Publication 78, May 1983), p. 7. Also see "Families Maintained by Female Householders, 1970–79."

19. Sidel, "The Family," p. 60. Also see Mimi Abramovitz, "The Conservative Program Is a Women's Issue," Journal of Sociology and Social Welfare 14, no. 3 (September 1982): 399–424; and Kristine Nelson and Arnold Kahn, "Conservative Policies and Women's Power," ibid., pp. 435–49.

20. Schafran, "Women." p. 178.

21. Ibid., p. 180.

22. Erie and Rein, "Welfare," p. 76. The Reagan administration denies that this is happening. Margaret Heckler, quoting a study commissioned by the administration, has stated "that people removed from the welfare rolls in the last 18 months have generally stayed off the rolls and have not quit their jobs to get public assistance payments." See Robert Pear, "Most of Those Taken Off Welfare Are Said Not to Leave Their Jobs," New York Times, April 29, 1983, p. A1.

23. Disadvantaged Women and Their Children, p. 63.

24. Ibid., p. 62.

25. Ibid. p. 35.

26. Ibid., p. 5. In a study done by Janet Kohen, Carol Brown, and Roslyn Feldberg, "Divorced Mothers: The Costs and Benefits of Female Family Control," in George Levinger and Oliver Moles, eds., Divorce and Separation: Context, Causes and Consequences (New York: Basic Books, 1979), pp. 228–45, it was found that after divorce, sixteen of the thirty women interviewed turned to AFDC either immediately or within a year. "AFDC must be seen as an equivalent of unemployment insurance for mothers" (p. 234). It was also found that "from an average pre-divorce family income of $12,500, the women in the sample fell to a post-divorce average of $6,100, a drop of just one-half. This

overall average obscures an important class difference—the higher they start, the farther they fall" (p. 234).

27. "Impact on Women of the Administration's Proposed Budget," prepared by the Women's Research and Education Institute for the Congresswomen's Caucus, April 1981, p. 5. (Available from WREI, 400 South Capital Street S.E., Washington, D.C. 20003.)

28. *Disadvantaged Women and Their Children*, p. 12.

29. Thurow, *Zero-Sum*, p. 161.

30. *Disadvantaged Women and Their Children*, p. 63.

31. *Families and Public Policies in the United States*, p. 14.

32. This information comes from the March 1982 *Current Population Survey*. Also see "Impact on Women of . . . Proposed Budget," p. 5.

33. Lester Thurow, "How to Wreck the Economy," *New York Review of Books*, May 14, 1981, pp. 3–8, esp. p. 3.

34. See Allen Hunter, "In the Wings: New Right Organization and Ideology," *Radical America* 15, nos. 1–2 (Spring 1981): 113–40, for a similar discussion that he terms selective antistatism.

35. Documented in a February 1981 *Newsday* poll that was conducted nationwide and reported in *The National NOW Times*, April 1981, p. 2. See also Frederick Jaffe, Barbara Lindheim, and Philip Lee, *Abortion Politics, Private Morality and Public Policy* (New York: McGraw Hill, 1981), for a full discussion of public opinion about abortion.

36. Irving Howe, "The Right Menace," published in *Dissent* pamphlet no. 1, *The Threat of Conservatism*, p. 29. (Available from *Dissent*, 505 Fifth Avenue, New York, NY 10017.)

37. See *Families and Public Policies in the United States*.

38. Ibid., pp. 22–23.

39. See Linda Greenhouse, "Court Reaffirms Right to Abortion and Bars Variety of Local Curbs," *New York Times*, June 16, 1983, p. A1; and Francis Clines, "Reagan Urges Congress to Nullify Supreme Court's Abortion Rulings," *New York Times*, June 17, 1983, p. A16.

40. Judith Paterson and Lavinia Edmunds, "Cabinet Member Margaret Heckler: Reagan's Answer to the Gender Gap?" *Ms.* 12, no. 1 (July 1983): 61–66.

41. The *Conservative Digest* repeatedly states that "we have Reagan without Reaganism." See David Broder, "Nixon-Ford Retreads Return," *Conservative Digest* 9, no. 5 (May 1983): 6–7.

42. John Seiles "Dungeons and Dragons—Washington Style," *Conservative Digest* 9, no. 1 (January 1983): 6.

6. Sexual-Class Consciousness and the Gender Gap

Conflicts exist among the relations of traditional patriarchy and advanced capitalism, the ideology of liberalism, and the welfare state. Whereas welfare-state liberalism is in crisis today, liberal feminism, meaning woman's right to equality of opportunity, is not. Therefore, although the Reagan administration has had a somewhat free hand in dismantling the social welfare state, it has not been free to ignore the ideological constraints set up by liberal feminism. Liberal feminism, defined as support for ERA, abortion rights, and economic equity in the market, underlines the consciousness of a majority of women (and men) today as witnessed by polls on these issues. This (liberal) feminist consciousness creates problems for the state in its attempt to mediate the conflicts between traditional patriarchy and the promise of equality of opportunity for women. As the Reagan state pushes back the gains made by women by dismantling the "new class" and social welfare programs, it must contend with a sexual class coming to consciousness of itself. It may be that Reagan's attack on the welfare state is as subversive for women in their development as feminists (i.e., coming to consciousness of their needs as a sexual class) as feminism was/is subversive of liberalism.

Sexual Politics and the Gender Gap

"Gender gap" is the phrase used to describe the fact that men and women voted somewhat differently from each other in the 1980 presidential and 1982 congressional elections and that women seem to be more critical of the Reagan administration than are men. Whereas 55 percent of the men who voted in the 1980 election voted for Reagan, only 47 percent of the women did. This is a spread of 3.3 million votes. This election was also the first

139

time in a decade that fewer women than men voted; it had the lowest overall turnout since 1948. In this same election 35 percent of the men compared with 32 percent of the women identified themselves as Republican.

In a 1981 CBS/New York Times news poll, 61 percent of the men polled approved of Reagan's presidency, compared with 46 percent of the women. This gender gap grew from 8 percent in November 1980 to twice that, 16 percent, by August 1981. At this same time a series of other polls found that only 23 percent of women said that the Republican party best served their needs; 48 percent said the Democratic party did. When asked whether they were better off economically under Reagan, only 27 percent of the women polled said that they were better off; 42 percent of the men said they were. Forty percent of the men voiced strong approval for Reagan, compared with 29 percent of the women.[1]

By May 1982 an Associated Press/NBC News Poll found that only 37 percent of women favored Reagan's running for a second term; 49 percent of the men did. By 1983, 33 percent of the women polled approved of the job that Reagan was doing as president, compared with 40 percent of men. Such findings are discussed in great detail in a White House twelve-page memorandum compiled by Ronald H. Hinckley for the White House Coordinating Council on Women. It is interesting to note that when I called the White House in order to get a copy of this memorandum, I was told that no such memo existed. I was finally able to obtain a copy from a feminist group in Washington. The memorandum, dated November 5, 1982, is premised on the notion that "the continued growth of the 'gender gap' in its current form could cause serious trouble for Republicans in 1984."[2] The gender gap, according to the memo, is a multifaceted, complex reality. First, it reflects the differences between men and women in "the way they judge political morality, their economic vulnerabilities, their levels of political awareness, variations in the impact of education on them, and their perceived self-interests."[3] Second, it reflects the changes in population characteristics, particularly the rise of single-parent families headed by women, many of which are dependent on government subsidies. Third, it reflects the president's policies on the budget and foreign defense. In sum, the memorandum argues that the gender gap is a reflection "of differences between men and women in terms of their issue awareness, their way of judging political actions, their changing lifestyle characteristics, and the varying impact that education has on each in confluence with the images, policies and programs of this President and Administration."[4]

The above description of the gender gap characterizes it in a somewhat ambivalent way. On the one hand gender differences are assumed to reflect differences between men and women because they are men and women—that women think about things differently from men. In instances like this, gender is assumed to override other identities, as though it were an independent factor. "Let's not forget that another likely factor in the gender gap is that the President has many traits and policies that are very popular with men."[5] Women are said to be more likely to favor a "caring" candidate and are more likely to be concerned with inflation, unemployment, and poverty, whereas men are more likely to be concerned with welfare cheaters, taxes, and government spending.[6] Women are more likely to fear nuclear war, less likely to desire an aggressive foreign policy, more likely to be concerned with preserving the environment. "Women focus more on issues that have an immediate impact on their lives or the lives of their families (micro-level). Men tend to focus more on problems at a societal (macro) level."[7] Such descriptions characterize women as women and as different from men. These differences are assumed to reflect the given (static, natural, unquestioned) predispositions of women. In this sense, the gender gap is viewed as reflecting the "feminine" aspects of women (peaceableness, caring, and so on), their particular sexual-class status as mothers and nurturers.

On the other hand, the gender gap is assumed to be as much a reflection of "a very rational process based on self-interest differences between women and men," due to economic self-interest (rather than their sexual-class identity).[8] Given this view, the memorandum presents gender as though it were dependent on, or overridden by, the more traditional political concerns: income, education, age, and the like. In this vein, the gender gap is analyzed in terms of factors *other than* one's sexual identity or sexual-class status. It appears to be the largest among women between twenty-five and fifty-four years of age, and largest among women who are clerical and blue-collar workers, even though professional women are not likely to be as conservative as professional men. The gender gap appears to be the greatest for women who are separated and/or divorced. In the memo unmarried women are described as more liberal, more Democratic, and less well educated than married women. They are also more pessimistic about their future. Many of these women fear losing government benefits and therefore oppose the administration. Single and separated/divorced women are said to form the core of the gender gap. The report advises that this part of the gender gap will be the most difficult to close because of its particular makeup. "The extreme vulnerability present among these women will make them suspicious of anyone, even more so of someone like President Reagan whose image and policies they find personally threatening."[9]

The analysis of the gender gap in terms of traditional political categories becomes the most problematic when education is discussed. Education does not appear to have the same conservative impact for married women as for married men.[10] The same is true of single women. Single women do not become as pro-Reagan as single men when education increases. Yet the memorandum states that "sex alone is generally not as strong a predictor of an anti-Reagan stance as some of the more traditional predictors of political attitudes."[11] The memo asks the question: "At what point does sex become a significant contributing factor in combination with other influences?" but it prefers to discuss the "other influences." Gender (the political aspect of sex or one's sexual class) becomes incidental for a political explanation of the gap; gender is not recognized as an autonomous or semiautonomous factor.

The White House analysis of the gender gap assumes that gender is the dependent or nonautonomous factor. The idea that women form a sexual class, as an identifiable assemblage with particular needs, *as women,* and have a gender identity that is constructed through this reality is never discussed as such. By treating the gender gap not as a difference reflecting the particular needs of a sexual class, but rather as a series of differences related to income, education, age, and so on, the relationship that exists between gender and these realms is not recognized. Although the Reagan administration tries to keep the gender and economic realms distinct, in the hopes of using economic class differences

to destroy a consciousness of "sex class," women's lives crisscross
these realms. Findings like the fact that there is not a gender gap
among high-income married men and women on how the president has handled the federal budget are used to support the idea
that it is special interests that determine the gender gap. "The
gender gap is largest in each group in the particular areas of greatest self-interest to the women in the group."[12]

The memorandum assumes that "the size of the gender gap
varies from issue to issue and image perception to image perception."[13] The memo concludes that the different views are largely
due to different perceptions about what is happening in many of
these areas: inflation, unemployment, and national defense. In the
end, a large aspect of the gender gap is defined as a problem of
perception. The gender gap is largest (-15) on the issue of inflation. Women are more likely to think that prices have stayed the
same or risen, whereas men recognize that prices have increased
more slowly. This gender difference is assumed to be a problem of
gender perception. Women have interpreted the facts wrongly and
hence a campaign that targets women in order to educate them
about Reagan's success with inflation is recommended in the report. "A carefully planned and executed communication program
regarding inflation could contribute to the reduction of the gender
gap on economic issues."[14]

The gender gap is smallest on the issue of unemployment.
"Both men and women are equally (-6) aware of the rise in unemployment and more equally critical of the President in this
area."[15] Hence in this area the report recommends making progress
by lowering unemployment in order to gain support from both
men and women.

The third major issue of the gender gap—that of Reagan's pro-
pensity toward war—is also discussed as reflecting a communications problem between Reagan and women. "How something is
said is as important as what is said, particularly for the gender
gap."[16] Aggressive statements increase the gap. The report once
again recommends a carefully executed communications program
to correct women's misperceptions of Reagan. "There is a continual need to carefully spell out for the public as a whole Reagan
policies and accomplishments and to target women specifically."[17] The report refers to earlier successful attempts to lessen

the gender gap by launching specially targeted communications toward women.

Recommendations to lessen the gender gap center around developing better communications with women and changing their perceptions. The memorandum documents the importance of the ideological role of the state: affecting the way people think about reality becomes as important or more important than doing something about the reality itself. But the problem is not merely one of perception. Rather, many women who are primarily responsible for shopping for their families do not in fact experience a decrease in inflation. Inflation does not go down for those women who are underemployed, unemployed, or on welfare. It seems irrelevant to them that inflation is rising more slowly than it was in 1980. Instead of asking *why* women view inflation differently from men, or *how* their particular situations as single parents or working mothers affect their perceptions, the memorandum merely seeks an ideological campaign to change women's views. Implicit in this campaign is a denial of the *real* differences that exist between men and women because of the way patriarchy differentiates woman from man. Although one's gender (one's political sexual-class identity) is mediated through differences in income, economic class, race, age, and so on, sex class underlines the specific meaning these other factors have on one's life. I argue that the gender gap is a reflection of and reaction to women's sexual-class position, particularly in terms of the way one's economic status is defined in terms of it.

As much as it tries to deny it, the memo is forced to recognize the problem of women's assignment to a sexual class differentiated from men without ever acknowledging it as such. The report advised that while trying to close the gender gap, care must be taken not to alienate men, who are more favorable toward the president. "Efforts to close the gap that come at the expense of some of the reasons for which men are more favorable toward the President might prove to be very counter productive."[18] The report also advised against appearing to favor one section of the populace against another. In trying to deal with single, poor women, the program "must not lead to further growth in the numbers of the group or appear to be unfair to other women and men—single or married—or else the gap will widen."[19]

The political significance of the gender gap has yet to be defined for the 1984 presidential election. It is therefore important to understand the meaning of the gender gap in the hope of building a politics out of this political reality. How does the fact that women are members of a sexual class—differentiated from men— particularly through developing economic controls in the market and the state affect the way women think about the Reagan administration? Whereas the White House memo assumes that the gender gap reflects the "feminine" (female) characteristics of antimilitarism and pro-social welfare policies it can also be argued that these views reflect the developing consciousness of women as a sexual (gendered) class that identifies its own needs as antimilitarist and pro-social welfare. As such these so-called feminine values become feminist as women identify them with their need for equality. This turns the focus beyond the ERA and abortion rights toward economic equity in the market, equality of opportunity in professional work, support of economic policies that subsidize women who head families. And it creates criticism of the expanded military budget.

Pro-ERA women disproportionately voted for Carter. Anti-ERA women voted for Reagan in 1980. Wage-earning women are more critical of Reagan administration policies than are housewives who do not work in the labor force.[20] Low-income women are the single most critical group opposing Reagan.[21] Given these realities, and the changing nature of women's place in the economy due to the multiple forms of family life, the particular economic reality(ies) of women as sharing a (secondary) sexual-class status becomes more visible. A decision like the one made by New Jersey's NOW chapter to endorse Frank Lautenberg rather than Millicent Fenwick reflects this possible shifting of emphasis among (liberal) feminists toward concerns with the economy; Lautenberg's criticism of Reaganomics took precedence over supporting Fenwick and electing a woman. A (liberal) feminist politics that focuses on the problems of poverty, unemployment, and underemployment has long been overdue. Because women are increasingly represented among the poor this emphasis has become a necessity. The highlighting of women's economic secondary status is part of the process of understanding the political meaning of women's identity as a sexual class for the 1980s. However, we need to make sure that the understanding of the sexual-class oppression of women is not reduced to its economic dimension because in the end sexual equality means more than economic equality; it means sexual freedom as well. Before entering this discussion, let us further clarify the meaning of women as a sexual class.

Women as a Sexual Class

The meaning of sexual class is to be found within the dynamic relations of patriarchy in society and in the state. It is necessary to recognize that women constitute a sexual class of political struggle in order to fully understand the politics of gender and family.[22] Because patriarchal society is organized and structured through sexual classes, the state operates to mediate the conflicts that exist between sexual classes that constitute females as women, males as men. The capitalist patriarchal state must mediate the intra-economic and intereconomic class and racial conflict along with intrasexual and intersexual class conflict. The gender gap may reflect the fact that women are coming to understand their dissatisfaction with the state's present attempts to mediate conflict in terms of its patriarchal interests.

To identify women as a sexual class does not mean that women are a class, like the proletariat, for example, defined by their similar relationship to the mode of production. They rather are a sexual class in that they constitute the basic and necessary activities of society: reproduction, childrearing, nurturing, consuming, domestic laboring, and wage-earning. Their sexual-class identity is initially defined in terms of their being female but is fully revealed in the identification of females as women, that is, as nurturers, mothers, secondary wage-earners, and so on. Women are a sexual class because *what they do as women*—the activities they are responsible for in society, the labor that they perform—is essential and necessary to the operation of society as it presently exists. Women as a sexual class do much more than the working class in the maintenance and reproduction of society because a majority of women labor for wages as well as perform the duties of

womanhood, wifehood, motherhood. They mother and do domestic labor and more than 50 percent of women do wage labor besides. I therefore use the term "sexual class" to represent the fact
that women's activities as women in reproducing and sustaining
society are fundamental and necessary to the present social order.

In this sense, I draw on the Marxist notion of class, which recognizes the individuals who do the series of activities that are socially necessary to society as constituting a class. For Marxists this
vision defines the proletariat as the revolutionary class because
they perform the necessary labor of society. For me, the view of a
socially necessary class applies to women, as a sexual class, as
well as to the proletariat as an economic class. It is also true that
some women are part of the proletariat (or working class) and that
all women as members of a sexual class have a secondary status
within the economic class structure. And this is further specified
for third world women. Some may argue that my use of "sexual
class" makes no sense: that the Marxist use of the term is too
specific, and the non-Marxist use of it is too general, not much
better, in fact, than group. But language has political meaning.
Class, in this case "sexual class," highlights the uniqueness of the
set of activities done by a particular assemblage of persons. Along
with this centrality and necessity of what they do goes the possibility of revolutionary activity.

Marxist-feminist Michele Barrett rejects the idea that women
form a social class because she argues that this view conflicts with
the Marxist notion of class; although certain categories of women
share occupational roles that might be said to form a class, this is
not what Marx meant by class. "Marxist categories of class, however, are not descriptive of occupation in this way; they operate
according to specified relations within a mode of production."[23]
But the real problem is the narrow conception of class that Barrett
chooses to work from. She argues that "the oppression of women
differs significantly from class to class."[24] I would agree. But this
does not negate the fact that women constitute a sexual class at the
same time that this (sexual) class identity is differentiated along
economic class and racial lines on specific issues. This does not
necessarily mean that a white middle-class woman and a white
working-class woman or a third world and white woman will
differ on their position on the ERA or abortion. If one looks care-

fully at the changing structure of family life, the secondary wage status of women, their underemployment or unemployment, it becomes clear that large numbers of women share an economic identity as poor and that this is connected with their sexual-class status. So why keep writing of the economic class differences of women as though their sexual-class status did not define their economic class positions in significant ways? This, however, is not to say that economic class differences do not exist *within* the secondary economic class status of women defined as a sexual class. Nor is it to ignore the fact that racial differences continue to exist within women's economic secondary class status and economic class differences.

Marxist-feminists such as Barrett not only reject the notion of sexual class because they consider economic class as primary but they also disagree with the conflation of "the capitalists" as male. "It is not, in fact, adequate to address the question of class and gender by posing a unity of interest between capitalists and men, since the capitalist class is composed of both men and women."[25] One should not assume a unity between capitalists and men, but for reasons different from those Barrett gives. Clearly not all men are capitalists. But it is appropriate to conflate the capitalist class with white men. Capitalist class interests are represented and fought for by white men, with few exceptions. Patriarchal class interests are represented and fought for by the capitalist class. False parallels are being drawn here. Even though not all white men are in the capitalist class, the capitalist class represents male privilege and patriarchal class interests. And the fact that a few women are capitalists does little to alter this.

Even if one wants to say that some women are in the capitalist class, what does this say about the relationship between capitalism and patriarchy or sexual-class relations themselves? It says nothing because it talks around the issue. To ask the question of what Margaret Thatcher or Indira Gandhi or Jacqueline Onassis has in common with a poor working-class woman is not really to ask much. After all, does the fact that an individual can achieve upward mobility in the economic class structure negate the reality of economic class structure? The fact that not all women share the reality of sexual-class identity in a similar manner does not negate the fact that a majority do so. Nor is it necessary to mobilize the

at some point, yes.

entire class of women in order to struggle for equality or liberation. Feminism and feminist political struggle have never
mobilized all women as a sexual class, even though today more
than 70 percent of women, when polled, support the major feminist demands of abortion and the ERA.

My use of the term "class" is therefore neither Marxist nor non-
Marxist. It instead further specifies the Marxist notion of class.
Women are not a class meaning an economic class. They are a
sexual class with a particular status that cuts through economic
class lines and is differentiated by these lines. Women as a sexual
class are also racially differentiated. But through these differences, the fact that they are women—a sexual class differentiated
from men—is never irrelevant or politically unimportant. Although I have argued in the previous chapter that the economic
reality of women as poor is increasing today, and that traditional
economic class categories need rethinking given the changing
structures of family life, this does not mean that women as a
sexual class are an economic class. Rather, the particular economic reality of sexual-class identity is making it more possible to
see the secondary class status of women through and in economic
class divisions. These economic class divisions have yet to be
carefully defined in terms of women's positioning in family structures and the racist order. Economic class divisions among
women do not invalidate the notion of sexual class; they just
require that the economic class differentiations within sexual
class be recognized. Therefore, one can argue that the liberal
democratic gains made by women affect all women (no matter
how differently). Recognizing this fact requires an understanding
of the importance of ideology in constituting women as a sexual
class and its relation to the "real" sexual, racial, and economic
class dynamics of patriarchy.

Much of the way the unity of sexual class is constituted is
through ideology, though the structural relations of patriarchy,
racism, and capitalism are as present and vital as the ideological.
However, it is misleading to completely separate the ideological
and the real. The dialectical relationship that exists between these
realms defies a neat distinction because there are moments in
which ideological life has as much impact on constructing life as
the so-called concrete realm does. After all, which is more power-

ful, the phallus (as symbol) or the penis (as real)? Ideology can operate with a material content and ideology can be material. This has particular importance for understanding the construction of sexual class when a female is defined as a woman and is acted upon as such, whether or not she acts on this definition.

Materializing Sex Class

Women constitute a class by definition of the biological sexual self, which is at one and the same time as political (socially and economically constructed) as it is biological. Their political nature as a class reflects the way in which patriarchal society defines a particular place and purpose for the female as a woman and it also points to the potential of women becoming a class in political struggle. The politics of sexual class has two aspects here. First, the sexual class of women descriptively refers to the fact that it is a construction of patriarchal relations: the biological female is transformed through a series of political relations into a woman, differentiated from man. The only natural thing about the sexual class of women is that they are biologically female, but nature in this instance remains an unknown "thing." It is in this first sense, as female, that women are a class in themselves. The second sense of the term "sexual class" points to the development of a consciousness of being women (and not merely being female). This consciousness reflects the development of a sexual class for itself.[26] It is in this sense that women come to recognize that as women (and female) they are set apart and denied equality, in terms of both racist and patriarchal social relations. Therefore, part of coming to consciousness as a sexual class is the process of understanding how white privilege has separated white and third world women from each other, and how patriarchal sexual class identity cuts through this.

Woman's biological sexual self is never just that because of the gendered (socialized, culturalized, economized, politicized) relations of patriarchy, which continuously seek to hierarchically differentiate woman from man. Woman's biological and sexual self is always defined within the relations of patriarchal society, which invert her capacity for childbirth into a liability and seek to control her sexuality. Women share a similar relationship to their bodies and to society through the depiction of women in patriarchal ideology and its representation in society, however differently racist ideology and practice specify this.

By focusing on the biological aspect of sexual class, namely, woman's capacity for childbearing, we further specify the political relations of society, allowing us to correct the abstractness of Marx's notion of economic class. As Mary O'Brien writes: "A compromise is impossible in any theory where the individual is constituted abstractly without ever getting born."[27] One must rather address the question of how the relations of power and sexual class are constituted in terms of the dynamic they express about sexual reproduction and sexuality. "The low social and philosophical value given to reproduction and to birth is not ontological, not immanent, but socio-historical, and the sturdiest plank in the platform of male supremacy."[28] According to O'Brien, the "biological process of reproduction is a material substructure of history" out of which a "reproductive consciousness" develops that begins to define a specific class consciousness of women. She believes that this consciousness is a universal consciousness common to all women because of the material, historical reality of childbirth. One need not bear a child to know oneself a woman because "women's reproductive consciousness is culturally transmitted."[29] Catharine MacKinnon argues this point as well: "Consciousness raising has revealed gender relations to be a collective fact, no more simply personal than class relations."[30]

It is in these realms of human reproduction and sexuality that sexual-class identity is constructed, although it is reinforced through the economy. Sexuality needs to be understood as a "complex unity of physicality, emotionality, identity, and status affirmation."[31] MacKinnon argues that sexuality determines gender and that it is not the other way around:

> Sexuality, then, is a form of power. Gender, as socially constructed embodies it, not the reverse. Women and men are divided by gender, made into the sexes as we know them, by the social requirements of heterosexuality, which institutionalize male sexual dominance and female sexual submission. If this is true, sexuality is the linchpin of gender inequality.[32]

Although sexuality is absolutely fundamental to an understanding of sexual class, it is not helpful to set up a causal relation between sexuality and gender. The intricate relationship between sex and gender is that gender is made out of sex, and yet sex has never been defined (historically) outside of gender. There is really no such thing as sex or gender. They are both constructed out of a series of social relations that constitute each other's meanings. Once you assume there is such a thing as sex, or sexuality (in some natural—presocial—form), you sidestep the real issue of how sexual class is constructed.

Sexuality itself is defined in ways that ensure that the female becomes a woman. Part of understanding the meaning of sexual class is understanding how a female becomes a woman, how her sexual distinctness is politically constituted and constructed in terms of the patriarchal need to differentiate woman from man as a mother, a secondary wage-earner, a whore, as the "other," or as "absent," or as "lacking." Whereas the female is sexually distinct from the male, the woman is hierarchically differentiated from the man. She is less than: not a man.[33] Although there is a biological content to sexual distinctness, the political differentiation of woman from man through the construction of sexual classes makes it impossible to delineate the contours of biology other than the fact that women can sexually reproduce.

There is nothing "natural" about sexual class—rather it is a patriarchal-political construction that uses racist and economic class relations. But this is different from stating that biological distinctness does not play a part in defining women as a sexual class. Biology, that is, woman's capacity to sexually reproduce (which is assumed to be "natural"), is defined in particular political terms in relation to the needs of patriarchal society. In this sense, the sexual class of women is politically constructed and defined in order to meet the social needs of the state and society. The sexual class of women is consciously organized by the state apparatus in order to be able to guarantee and sustain women's particular relations to reproduction. Some of the proof of the politics of sexual class is to be found in the laws surrounding marriage, abortion, sexuality, contraception, sexual practices, and so on. These are examples of the patriarchal role of the state, through the law, as it constructs the controls on the sexual class of women. This is true in China today as the state seeks to enforce particular birth control practices. It is also true in France and Spain, as their socialist parties try to articulate an "acceptable" position on abortion. And the New Right, in the United States, has brought the patriarchal interests of the state to the center stage of politics.

If women did not have power as women—even within existing patriarchal controls—there would be no need for the elaborate systems that seek to enforce the hierarchical differentiation of woman from man. The other side of oppression is potential power. This brings us to the issue of women's becoming conscious of their power, conscious of their position within patriarchal society, conscious of themselves as a sexual class. Because patriarchal ideology does its best to intervene and stunt a conscious realization of woman's particular place within patriarchal relations, the struggle for this consciousness is part of the process of constituting women as a sexual class for itself. The fact that (feminist) consciousness is not full blown hardly invalidates the fact that women are or form a sexual class in political struggle. It rather speaks to the fact that patriarchal ideology intervenes successfully to limit feminist consciousness. Nevertheless, there is as much consciousness of sex class among women as there is of economic class among men and women, although one should not parallel these realities.

Patriarchal ideology that denies women their individuality and rather relegates them to a sexual-class status both highlights the sexual-class nature of women's lives and cloaks it. Ideologically women are treated as though they were all the same, and as such patriarchal ideology constructs a certain kind of sexual-class unity. Materially, women are constituted as a sexual class in terms of their sexual and reproductive selves, and this also provides a form of unity in developing sexual-class consciousness. But women are also concretely differentiated from one another in terms of economic class and racial differences, and this affects the white privileged identity of womanhood. It is on this basis, in particular, that Marxists argue that women cannot constitute a sexual class (which is semiautonomous from their economic class or racial identity).

Sex-Class Consciousness

Once one recognizes the importance of feminist consciousness in actualizing the potential of women as a sexual class it becomes as important to study liberal, racist, and patriarchal ideology as it is to study the capitalist patriarchal relations of family life, the economy, and the state. These realms impact on consciousness and the development of sexual-class identity. It is the conflicts arising within and between the ideologies of liberalism, racism, and phallocratism and the capitalist patriarchal relations of society that lay the basis for a consciousness that embodies a sexual class's becoming conscious "for itself." The question of how women become a self-conscious political sexual class and how they work through political struggle to develop themselves as a sexual class politically is the concern of feminism. Although women constitute a sexual class by virtue of the gendered relations of their biological sexual selves, women become a class through feminist struggle. They become a class in actual struggle against patriarchal privilege. In some sense, one could argue that in the United States the struggle from 1848 to 1920 and then the struggle again from 1969 to the present demonstrates the development, the process of a sexual class coming to a consciousness for itself. Women continue to emerge as a sexual class through political struggle in the United States over abortion and the ERA. As I have elsewhere stated:

> There is greater potential today than ever before for women to become more fully conscious of themselves as a sexual class, given the post-World War II phenomena of the married wage earner and the "working mother" alongside the subsequent struggles with the state on abortion, the ERA, etc. These struggles have begun to uncover the way patriarchy functions through the law, through ideology, and through woman's assignment to the double day of work. Out of these struggles for greater equality, the mystified form of patriarchal rule is uncovered. It is in this sense that women's identity as a sexual class reflects political and historical processes and cannot be predefined statically as merely a biological class.[34]

The sexual class of women embodies political process. It is not merely a thing—the female—that can be abstractly or statistically identified. It is rather a process that is always in flux and changes in relation to the meaning of women that derives from being female. As E. P. Thompson has written of economic classes:

> Classes do not exist as separate entities, look around, find an enemy class, and then start to struggle. On the contrary, people find themselves in a society structured in predetermined ways . . . they identify points of antagonistic interest, they commence to struggle around these issues and in the process of struggling they discover themselves as classes, they come to know this discovery as class consciousness.[35]

As women have entered into struggles with the state over abortion and have fought for equal pay in the economy and the right to day care, and other essential services, they have uncovered different sites and locations of patriarchal power.

It is both too abstract and too simplistic to say that men are the enemy class. There is a difference between patriarchy—which reflects all the political and economic relations that differentiate women from men—and the power of men as biological beings. Although the two—men and patriarchy—are never separate, they are not one and the same thing. The phallus as the symbol of the (biological) male *derives its power from the penis as the penis is defined in patriarchal society*. The phallus has power because the penis represents power in phallocratic society; and the penis has power because of the way the phallus is centered in patriarchal ideology. They are completely dependent on each other and yet they are not the same.

It is therefore similarly inadequate to define the enemy or opposing patriarchal class as simply white males. There is no *organized*, relatively autonomous male class as there is a capitalist ruling class. Individual men enjoy sexual privilege by virtue of belonging to the sex class: men. But the struggle against patriarchal privilege is not merely a struggle by the sexual class women against men. It is rather a struggle by women against the different locations—in the market, the family, the state—of patriarchal and white privilege, which is only partially located in the class men.

One of the problems with the notion of sex class as it was first developed by radical feminist Shulamith Firestone was that sex class was made parallel to economic class. A similar dynamic was assumed to exist between the proletariat and bourgeoisie as that which exists between woman and man. But the dynamics of power are different. Patriarchal privilege is more disparate and is not concentrated in a (ruling) class in the same way that capitalist class interests are condensed. The exchange of labor between proletariat and bourgeoisie is different from the exchange of women among men. Once again some may ask: if the dynamic is different then why call women a sexual class?

It is important to recognize that women constitute a sexual class and are developing as a political sexual class. The concept "class" focuses on the vital positioning of a woman within the political relations of society. However, there is no automatic relationship between being a member of the sexual class women and becoming progressive and/or revolutionary as one comes to consciousness. In the United States, New Right women are a clear example of how sex-class consciousness can be used for reactionary political purposes.

Given this possibility, it becomes all the more important to better understand how to build feminist consciousness out of sex-class consciousness. This becomes necessary if we are to utilize the gender gap to fight for feminist demands. The gender gap reflects two contradictory realities simultaneously. First, it reflects the gendered reality of women's lives: the tendency for females to think "like" women because they are the nurturers of society and thereby are often (though not always) more caring or peace-loving than men. On this basis they reject the militarism of Reagan. Second, the gender gap reflects the fact that women believe in their right to equality (of opportunity), which requires the rejection of their assignment as females to the sex class women. The gender gap simultaneously mirrors and rejects aspects of the sexual class system; it reflects the positioning of women within patriarchy and critiques the patriarchal organization of sexual classes.

The gender gap also represents the fact that women as a sexual class have economic class needs defined by their secondary sexual-class status in the economy and the family realm. Assessments of the gender gap as being merely economically self-interested, rather than feminist in orientation, distort the above reality. Women's upset with Reagan reflects the reality that their economic, political, and sexual lives are all of one piece. The

ERA, abortion rights, AFDC payments, and economic equity are not separate issues. They are the issues that reflect the fact that women as a sexual class share a secondary economic class status as women and that this status is further differentiated along economic class and racial lines.

The gender gap embodies the developing consciousness of a sexual class coming into consciousness of itself. This consciousness may be uneven, and even contradictory at points, but it is in process. Whether the Reagan administration will be able to contain this process remains to be seen. But it will not be able to do so while simultaneously trying to mediate the conflicts between the New Right and the neoconservative elements of the state. The question that remains is whether feminists can act on the gender gap and organize a politics based on this developing consciousness of women as a sexual class. The 1984 election holds out an opportunity for women to organize as a sexual class for the removal of the Reagan administration. The really fearful possibility is that Reagan will run against a neoconservative Democrat, in which case women's choices will be seriously curtailed. Whatever the options are, it is important for women to try to articulate the gender gap electorally in 1984, more as a first attempt at constituting ourselves as a political class than in the naive hope that we can fundamentally change society through the electoral process. Nevertheless, if the state is relatively autonomous, then it does matter on some level who is in office. And because it does not matter enough to send us to the polls enthusiastically, we also must continue to challenge patriarchy from outside the electoral arena. We should have learned the lesson from the New Right in 1980 that feminists cannot give over the electoral arena to reactionary forces. We must struggle within and outside the state because patriarchal privilege is defind and reflected in both realms. The gender gap provides us with a beginning step in creating a feminist politics that challenges the state, and governmental arena, directly.

NOTES

1. For a full accounting of these data see *N.O.W. Times* 14, no. 9 (October 1981): 8.
2. *Memorandum for White House Coordinating Council on Women and Working Group Members* from Emily Rock, subject: Gender Gap, Ronald Hinckley Report, November 9, 1982, p. 3. The memo was first revealed by Adam Clymer in "Warning on 'Gender Gap' from the White House," *New York Times*, December 3, 1982, p. 18.
3. Ibid., Introduction, p. 1.
4. Ibid., p. 12.
5. Ibid.
6. Ibid., p. 3.
7. Ibid., p. 2.
8. Ibid., p. 10. But Arthur Miller and Oksana Malanchuk, in an unpublished paper, "The Gender Gap in the 1982 Elections," presented at the 38th Annual Conference of the American Association for Public Opinion Research, Buck Hill Falls, Pa., May 19–22, 1983, argue that the gender gap reflects more than the issue of economic self-interest. It also reflects the fact that women have distinct concerns about human rights, war, and peace.
9. *White House Memorandum*, p. 11.
10. Ibid., p. 19.
11. Ibid., p. 8.
12. Ibid., p. 7.
13. Ibid., p. 4. See Kurt Schlichting and Peter Tuckel, "Beyond the Gender Gap: Working Women and the 1982 Election," unpublished paper presented at the American Association for Public Opinion Research, Buck Hill Falls, Pennsylvania, May 19–22, 1983.
14. Ibid., p. 2.
15. Ibid., p. 3.
16. Ibid., p. 4.
17. Ibid.
18. Ibid., p. 2.
19. Ibid., p. 6.
20. See Adam Clymer, "Gap Between Sexes in Voting Seen as Outlasting Recession," *New York Times*, May 22, 1983, p. 5; Kathleen Frankovic, "Sex and Politics: New Alignments and Issues," *D/S* 15, no. 3 (Summer 1982): 439–48; Howell Raines, "President Is Assailed by Women's Leader; 2d Term Is Opposed," *New York Times*, July 10, 1983, p. 1.
21. See Ted Goertzel, "The Gender Gap: Sex, Family Income and Political Attitudes in the 1980s," unpublished paper, 1983.
22. I wish to move beyond the biological (male/female) focus of sex class as developed within radical feminism. For the radical feminist view, see Shulamith Firestone, *The Dialectic of Sex* (New York: Bantam, 1970); Germaine Greer, *The Female Eunuch* (New York: McGraw-Hill, 1970); Susan Griffin, *Woman and Nature* (New York: Harper & Row, 1978); Kate Millett, *Sexual Politics* (New York: Avon, 1971).
23. Michele Barrett, *Women's Oppression Today: Problems in Marxist Feminist Analysis* (London: New Left Books, 1980), pp. 127–28.
24. Ibid., p. 131.
25. Ibid., p. 133.
26. See Karl Marx, *The Eighteenth Brumaire of Louis Bonaparte* (New York: Inter-

national Publishers, 1969) and *The Poverty of Philosophy* (New York: International Publishers, 1963) for a discussion of a class in and for itself.

27. Mary O'Brien, *The Politics of Reproduction* (London: Routledge & Kegan Paul, 1981), p. 184.
28. Ibid., p. 75.
29. Ibid., p. 50.
30. Catharine MacKinnon, "Feminism, Marxism, Method, and the State: An Agenda for Theory," *Signs* 7, no. 3 (Spring 1982): 543.
31. Ibid., p. 531.
32. Ibid., p. 533.
33. See Elaine Marks and Isabelle de Courtivron, eds., *New French Feminisms* (Amherst: University of Massachusetts Press, 1980). Also see the proceedings of *The Second Sex: Thirty Years Later*, Conference on Feminist Theory, New York University, September 27–29, 1979; Julia Kristeva, *Desire in Language*, ed. Leon Rondiez (New York: Columbia University Press, 1980); and Jane Gallop, *The Daughter's Seduction: Feminism and Psychoanalysis* (Ithaca: Cornell University Press, 1982).
34. Zillah Eisenstein, *The Radical Future of Liberal Feminism* (New York: Longman, 1981), p. 8.
35. E. P. Thompson, "Eighteenth-Century English Society: Class Struggle Without Class?" *Social History* 3, no. 2 (May 1978): 149.

Part II
Revisionist Feminism

The first part of this book documents the New Right and neoconservative rejection of feminism's quest for sexual equality. These conservative forces argue that the liberal feminist demand for equality (of opportunity) escalates to a demand for equality (of conditions) that does not recognize the sexual differences between men and women. They therefore defend and use the concept "sexual difference" in an attempt to resolve the crisis of liberalism by limiting the demands for sexual equality. Although liberal feminism has often argued only for equality of opportunity—as in the ERA, which recognizes women's equality before the law—the demand for equality of opportunity for individual women becomes subversive in and of itself, uncovering as it does the sexual-class bias of the patriarchal liberal race of life that defines females as women, not as individuals. The liberal feminist commitment to equality of opportunity carried to its logical conclusion requires an attack on the sexual-class nature of the race, *if* women are to be treated as individuals. This is exactly what the New Right and neoconservatives attempt to contain: the radical potential of liberal feminism to move beyond the limits of patriarchal liberalism.

This concern with containing the radical aspects of liberal feminism as well as radical feminism has found allies within feminism itself. It is to this troubling development that we now turn: the development of what I term revisionist feminism.[1] Although this revisionism takes several different forms, it is basically an attempt to reassert the notion of sexual difference over that of sexual equality. And although these revisions are not appropriately termed antifeminist, they are attempts at deradicalizing feminism.

Over the past decade the feminist landscape has come to include many forms: liberal, radical, socialist, third world, lesbian, and anarchist. Revisionist feminism is a new form, which recently has been gaining currency. It rejects feminism's commitment to sexual egalitarianism, characterized as meaning sexual sameness between men and women, and argues instead for an equality that protects "sexual difference." In essence, this rejection attempts to redirect feminism away from its radical critique of sexual difference by defining feminism itself as the enemy.

The exact meaning of "sexual difference" within this discussion is often not clear, as we shall see. There is also no one consistent meaning attributed to the phrase, although one can outline several usages. Often sexual difference is assumed to reflect the biological, innate, bodily differences between men and women. Biological can mean anything from hormones, to brain cells, to vaginas and breasts. Radical feminists assume that these differences create a different woman's "essence" that is rooted in woman's body. In this sense a woman's essence is somewhat predefined, outside of cultural relations. Others, like socialist feminists, argue that the differences reflect culture more than nature. I assume that the only (politically) relevant biological difference between men and women is that of childbearing and that the other differences that exist between the sexes derive from the way this difference is culturally defined.

The purpose of these chapters is to examine notions of sexual difference and to place these discussions within the political context in which the women's movement presently exists. As the Reagan administration seeks to enforce antifeminist and neoconservative policies on women by utilizing the well-worn patriarchal notions of woman's difference from man, particularly in terms of motherhood (witnessed in the fight against abortion) and housewifery (articulated in the fight against the Equal Rights Amendment), we need to be careful about how we think about this issue of the sexual difference between men and women.

The concern with protecting sexual difference defines revisionist feminism within the women's movement as well as antifeminism. Feminists, therefore, need to think carefully about the similar sexual and moral views that exist between the Moral Majority and some elements of the antipornography movement; between Betty Friedan and Phyllis Schlafly on the question of sexual egalitarianism; and between revisionist left feminist Jean Elshtain and New Right economist George Gilder, both of whom believe that sexual distinctness between male and female is utterly necessary for human and moral development.[2] Although feminist revisionists do not accept Gilder's defense of the patriarchal family

or the neoconservative rejection of affirmative action, the notion
of sexual difference that the revisionists defend is used on behalf
of these patriarchal concerns. Even more troubling is that this
neoconservative mood can be found in Betty Friedan's most recent critiques of feminism. Friedan was a leading spokesperson
for liberal feminism in the 1960s. In her recent book *The Second
Stage*, she rejects her earlier vision of sexual equality and becomes
a major spokesperson for revisionist liberal feminism.

I argue here that the notion of sexual difference is being used by
feminist revisionists to reject feminism's radical potential to
transform the sex-gender system toward sexual egalitarianism. My
use of the term "feminism," as though it were a unified whole, is
purposeful, even though problematic. Although not all feminism
is committed to a sexual egalitarianism in terms of sexual, racial,
and economic relations, all feminism has the *potential* for this.
This is true of even liberal feminism.

> Liberal feminism involves more than simply achieving the bourgeois
> male rights earlier denied women, although it includes this. Liberal
> feminism is not feminism merely added onto liberalism. Rather,
> there is a real difference between liberalism and liberal feminism in
> that feminism requires a recognition, however implicit and
> undefined, of the sexual-class identification of women as women. . . .
> This recognition of women as a sexual class lays the subversive
> quality of feminism.[3]

The identification of women as a sexual class, which is the first
(even if implicit) tenet of any form of feminism, lays the basis for
the challenge against the patriarchal differentiation of woman
from man. Radical feminists in the late 1960s took this previously
underdeveloped notion of sexual class and elaborated it further.
They argued that there is a politics to sex; that nature itself has
been politicized; that personal life is defined by political life; that
the family is a political institution.

Given the history of the way women have been differentiated
from men, the argument for sameness, whatever its meaning and
oversimplifications, has revolutionary implications for the sex-
gender system, the family, and, in the end, the state. George Gilder
has recognized this radical potential of even the moderate wing of
feminism. The fact that male legislators defeated the popularly
supported ERA proves the point that feminist reform politics has a

radical aspect to it. Although ERA in and of itself cannot create sexual egalitarianism between men and women—no liberal law can do that—it does *begin* to erode the legal aspects of the patriarchal differentiation of woman from man. This differentiation is at the heart of the politics of the traditional patriarchal family and the advanced capitalist patriarchal state. As this differentiation has been challenged by feminism, sexual equality has been called into fundamental question by feminist revisionists who believe this attack on the sex-gender system goes too far.

Feminist revisionism is a part of the larger neoconservative political climate that rejects liberalism for its excesses, particularly in its quest for "equality." Both seek to curtail the radical potential inherent in the quest for sexual equality within feminism. One must therefore examine the relationship of "neofemininity" (woman's sexual difference)—the celebration of woman's different moral voice, her capacity for maternal thinking, her supportive, loving, caring "nature"—with the rise of neoconservatism.

Because feminist revisionism defines egalitarianism as sexual sameness, the important feminist question is never asked: that is, what does sexual equality mean and how does one try to create truly egalitarian relations—sexually, racially, economically, and politically—while recognizing biological difference constituted by women's ability to bear children? This issue of equality is the crux of the problem. What can sexual equality mean in the revisionist context that differentiates women from men with the intent of rejecting sexual sameness? And what does the revisionist rejection of sameness mean? After all, revisionist feminists do not mean to deny that : (l) men and women are similar in that they eat, sleep, want sex, and need creative work, companionship, intellectual activity; that they both are human, or (2) that women should be politically the same as men, having the same rights and opportunities. It would therefore seem as important to stress the likeness between men and women as the difference.

I wish to avoid making simple-minded parallels of different forms of revisionist feminism or their equation with right-wing antifeminism, seeking rather to direct readers to the question of how divergent political viewpoints (traditionally defined) agree on questions of sexuality and sexual difference. This very statement shows that such questions stand outside traditional political categories. When one addresses the issue of sexual difference, political traditions that are usually understood as distinctly separate from each other begin to merge: liberalism begins to contain conservative views; neoconservatism contains a difficult mix of liberalism and conservatism; antifeminism and revisionist feminisms produce aspects of each of these traditions.

The revisionists raise an important problem within feminism that warrants careful consideration. By rejecting a sexual egalitarianism that defines men and women as the same, they uncover the inadequacy of existing feminist visions of sexual egalitarianism, thus forcing further consideration of this issue. The following discussion is not meant to sidestep the questions feminist revisionists pose about sexual difference and sexual equality, but rather to take issue with their answers, which repudiate the radicalism of feminism. It is clear that on many points feminist revisionists find themselves in agreement with much of the feminist movement and yet they define this movement as the enemy.

The problem with embracing the notion of sexual difference is that it is often done with little recognition of its connection to the history of patriarchal relations. Indeed, Simone de Beauvoir argued in *The Second Sex* that antifeminists have never had any trouble showing that women "simply *are not* men."[4] This is the argument used by antifeminists such as Phyllis Schlafly against the Equal Rights Amendment: men and women are not the same and the ERA will treat them as though they are. There are important differences between antifeminists and feminist revisionists on the economy, family life, abortion rights, and the ERA; yet the failure of the revisionists to deal with the patriarchal politics involved in the concept "sexual difference" places their arguments in close proximity with those of the conservative antifeminist camp on this issue.

The following chapters highlight how discussions of sexual difference are being used to argue against sexual egalitarianism. This analysis should alert feminists to the difficulties inherent in the political fact that women's differences from men have been used to oppress women—and at the same time, that that difference can be the source of strength and creativity. This double-edged reality must be recognized. Idealizing the positive side of this reality will only reconstruct women's oppression. Negating the reality entirely will not allow us to recognize its positive aspects.

The question of sexual difference has particular political import right now, given the presence of the gender gap. If we are to try to mobilize women as a sexual class, as feminists, we need to address several political questions: Does the gender gap reflect the "gendered" (cultural) differences between women and men? What do these differences mean for trying to reorganize society without gendered lines? Do we mean to destroy sexual class (gender) or do we mean to preserve aspects of it?

I will discuss Betty Friedan as the example of revisionist liberal feminism, or what can also be termed neoconservative feminism, and Jean Elshtain as representative of revisionist left feminism, and will discuss troublesome similarities between these revisionist feminists and radical feminism. Before beginning these discussions we need to examine and clarify the antifeminist position on women's equality. For this we turn to a discussion of New Rightist Phyllis Schlafly.

NOTES

1. For another and somewhat different discussion of this notion "revisionism" see Benjamin Barber, "Beyond the Feminist Mystique," New Republic, July 11, 1983, pp. 26–32.
2. Michael Levin, "The Feminist Mystique," Commentary 70, no. 6 (December 1980): 25.
3. Zillah Eisenstein, The Radical Future of Liberal Feminism (New York: Longman, 1981), p. 10.
4. Simone de Beauvoir, The Second Sex (New York: Bantam, 1952), p. xiv.

7. New Right Antifeminism: Justice vs. Equality

New Right antifeminist politics is a reaction to the feminist challenge to patriarchy within liberal America. Phyllis Schlafly, much like George Gilder and Jerry Falwell, argues that women should not presume their equality with men, which assumes their likeness with men, but rather should fight for what is rightly theirs: their protection from working in the marketplace in exchange for their services as housewives and mothers. Women are different from men, according to Schlafly, and should be protected as such. She believes that a just society will recognize the difference between men and women, and protect women as a sexual class differentiated from men. In essence this is the point that distinguishes antifeminism from different forms of revisionist feminism. Antifeminists want to protect the sexual-class system. They believe that the differentiation of woman from man is not problematic, and therefore they argue against sexual equality and for "justice," that is, difference and protection. Although revisionist feminists may inadvertently protect the sexual-class system, they do not explicitly do so, nor do they accept the ascribed status of women as part of the natural order of things.

In explicating her antifeminist stance, Schlafly calls upon a contradictory set of positions: she argues as a religious conservative in defense of the ascribed status of women; utilizes a rugged individualist approach that assumes the importance of individual achievement; adopts an antistatist position against the ERA; and supports a statist position on a constitutional amendment against abortion. Within this somewhat mixed bag of Old Right, New Right, conservative, and liberal individualistic assumptions Schlafly attempts to justify the traditional forms of patriarchal family life. She argues in defense of the housewife and the woman as economic dependent. She is the spokesperson for New Right women: the women still defined in terms of housewifery in a society where a majority of married women now work in the labor force.

169

According to Schlafly and the New Right, the challenge to traditional forms of patriarchy, which underline the hierarchical relations of the market and the home, is one of the main factors
creating the crisis of capitalism and liberal ideology that promises
individuals freedom of choice and equality of opportunity. It then
follows that a resolution of the crisis will initially be sought in
trying to restrengthen and/or reformulate traditional patriarchal
family life. The conflict between the needs of traditional patriarchy and those of advanced capitalism is demonstrated by the
contrast between patriarchal images of women and the reality of
the married wage-earning women, the "working mother," the single mother in the labor force, and the professional woman. Attempts to resolve this conflict show how profoundly changing
roles for women challenge the social structure. The radical potential represented by the wage-earning mother and her feminist demands for sexual equality in the labor force and reproductive
rights has provoked the New Right antifeminist response that tries
to redirect and contain feminism's potential to radically transform
the meaning of (sexual) equality.

Phyllis Schlafly: The Old and New Right

Phyllis Schlafly was born in 1924 in Alton, Illinois. She was
educated in private Catholic schools. Her mother worked outside
the home after Phyllis' father became ill. Schlafly graduated Phi
Beta Kappa from Washington University and received an M.A. in
political science from Radcliffe. Her politics through the 1950s
can be defined as cold war anticommunist. She identified with the
Old Right within the Republican party. In the 1950s she was national defense chairperson of the Republican party and Illinois
state officer of the Daughters of the American Revolution. In the
early 1960s she did speaking for the Cardinal Mindszenty Foundation, which was headed by her sister-in-law, Eleanor Schlafly.
The foundation was dedicated to uncovering and exposing the
threat of "atheistic communism."[1] In 1963 she devoted much of
her time to fighting against the Nuclear Test Ban Treaty. During all
this time she was actively involved in Republican party national

conventions and was a delegate to several. She was, and remains, very critical of the eastern wing of the Republican party, specifically the J. P. Morgans and the Rockefellers, whom she believes dominate the Republican party and are responsible for the party's "America last—procommunist foreign policy." She makes this argument in her book *A Choice, Not an Echo*, written in 1964, in which she supports Goldwater against Rockefeller for the presidential nomination. It is one of many books she has written that argue for the necessity of a strong military and defense system, including nuclear arsenals, and a strong traditional Republican party dedicated to anticommunism.[2] She was preoccupied with issues of foreign policy, military strategy, and the nuclear arms race throughout the 1950s and 1960s.

In 1967 she ran and lost the election for president of the National Federation of Republican Women; several leaders of the Republican party lobbied against her because they thought she was too conservative. Shortly after this defeat, she started *The Phyllis Schlafly Report*. In 1972 Schlafly's focus shifted to the issues of family life: abortion, homosexuality, the ERA, sex education, the drafting of women into the military, and she used her newsletter to launch her "stop ERA" campaign. It was not until 1977 that Schlafly wrote *The Power of the Positive Woman*, her critique of the women's liberation movement. The positive woman is a woman who is proud of her femininity, and the feminist is the negative woman who wants to deny her womanhood.

It is significant that Schlafly was a cold war anticommunist in the 1950s and 1960s and only in the 1970s redefined and redirected this world view in a "pro-family," antifeminist direction. This shift of emphasis reflects an important development in conservative politics, which involves the recognition that the traditional patriarchal family is in crisis. This crisis has been developing in America since World War II; in response, some members of the Old Right, such as Schlafly, have focused on the importance of family life to a strong national defense, arguing that stable families make stable citizens. In this sense, the New Right's emphasis on the crisis of the family and the moral order of society distinguishes it from Old Right politics. Schlafly's pro-family, antifeminist politics is not merely a cover for her anticommunism. Rather, in the 1980s the politics of the family and the anticommunist state are completely related in her mind. Therefore, her antifeminism serves as the cutting edge in the fight against communism and evil. Antifeminism has become central to the anticommunist world view of the New Right because the moral woman, if she can be saved as housewife and mother, will help keep America strong.

One might easily wonder what antifeminism means to Schlafly, a woman who has had six children, written nine books, been active in Republican party politics since the 1950s, received a law degree at the age of fifty-four, run for Congress twice, and at present heads the Eagle Forum— a pro-family lobbying group claiming a membership of 30,000.[3] In practical political terms, it means she is against the Equal Rights Amendment and the drafting of women, and she is for a constitutional amendment banning abortion. We need to examine the theoretical underpinnings of this antifeminist politics: that she views woman's sexual-class identity as a biological reality that needs protection and that she argues in defense of sexual difference and against equality.

Conservatism and Antifeminism

Schlafly holds many traditional (Old Right) conservative views, while she is also a leading member of the New Right. Her conservative world view is primarily religious.[4] She sees society as organized in accordance with God's will. The religion favored by conservatives reflects the Catholic view of original sin and the corruptibility of the individual. God's authority, embodied in tradition and custom, is necessary to guide individuals away from evil. Traditional institutions establish God's order in the natural hierarchy among men and between men and women. Schlafly and conservatives in general view the traditional patriarchal family as central to establishing this natural and necessary hierarchy, which underpins the authority of the state.

As a conservative, Schlafly believes the family is "the soil from which moral duty, natural affection and society grows. Unless all of us say no to the forces destroying the family, there will be no future."[5] Schlafly has a very particular view of the family in mind:

the traditional patriarchal family with the woman as a housewife and economic dependent and the man as the income provider. Her vision is of the white, upper-middle-class, heterosexual patriarchal family. She takes this traditional family structure as the natural God-given form that reflects the natural order of things.

The traditional patriarchal family reflects the natural differences between men and women. The major distinction between men and women in Schlafly's mind is the fact that women bear children. The female body, which has been designed by "the Divine architect of the human race," has given woman a functional role to perform. A woman who is at peace with herself "looks upon her femaleness and her fertility as part of her purpose, her potential, and her power."[6] This capacity for creating new life distinguishes woman from man, and the positive woman is one who accepts and rejoices in this difference instead of believing that the female body was designed by a male conspiracy, as feminists would have it.[7]

Schlafly believes that if women recognize and utilize their capacity to bear children, men will do their part and take care of them. If this is the natural order of things, society must establish "woman's right to be a full-time wife and mother, to have this right recognized by laws that obligate her husband to provide the primary financial support and a home for her and their children."[8] Schlafly's New Right conservatism assumes human inequality and rearticulates the necessity of patriarchal authority as God-given.

It is Schlafly's religious stance that leads to her criticism of what she calls "humanism." She rejects the humanist secular world view and its attempt to justify the separation of church and state. According to her, ethics comes from God, not from human experience.[9] One must therefore follow custom and tradition in the hopes of protecting God's natural order. Schlafly continually invokes tradition when she argues about women's proper place, as for example, when she argues against drafting women: "It is contrary to American traditions, laws, morals, and the wishes of the majority of the American people. It is contrary to the Judeo-Christian culture which honors and respects women in their role as wives and mothers."[10]

In Schlafly's view, which she shares with New Right leaders

Viguerie, Weyrich, and Falwell, any denial of the importance of the "religious viewpoint of family life" and women's place within it only contributes to the destruction of the moral order. On this basis, she criticizes sex education in the schools which does not teach moral standards of right and wrong, eliminates all guilt for sin, and omits mention of "the spiritual, psychological, emotional, and physical benefits of premarital chastity, marital fidelity, and traditional family life."[11] Without religious guidance the individual will be corrupted by evil. If homosexuality is presented as normal and abortion as acceptable, students will not learn the truth, as Schlafly sees it, that the moral, satisfying sexual life depends on marriage.

Schlafly also views the ERA as a religious issue, in fact, a war. When asked in an interview whose side she thought God was on, she answered: "Well, I think he's on the side of right and goodness and justice, all those things. And I think that's the side antiERA is on."[12] Her religious view of the world sees things in terms of good or evil, where goodness means "justice" and evil means (sexual) equality.

This view of the ERA as a religious issue stems from Schlafly's belief that the relations between men and women are God-given in the first place. The natural order that exists between men and women should not be tampered with: "I've always known that there really are differences between the sexes—innate differences—which we ignore only at peril to the family and civilization as we now know it."[13] These differences that Schlafly wants to protect "are in substantial measure biological and are most obvious with regard to physical size, physical strength, and the psychological quality called aggressiveness."[14] But Schlafly extends her description of the sexual differences between men and women: men are supposedly discursive, logical, abstract, and philosophical; women are emotional, personal, practical, and mystical.[15]

She contradictorily argues, however, that women are as smart as men or, rather, that there are as many smart women as there are smart men. Maybe this is why she believes that the differences between boys and girls, men and women, must be maintained. Otherwise we will create a massive "leveling" process between men and women that will endanger the natural ordering of family and political life. If the differentiation between femininity and masculinity is not protected, Schlafly believes women will strive for what men have "rather than strive for more recognition and greater reward for what women are and contribute to society."[16] They will thus tend to deny their homemaking function and marriage.

The differentiation of women from men is absolutely central to Schlafly's world view, and is one reason why she is so against the drafting of women. According to her, the military functions as a public reinforcement for family life in that it distinguishes between the spheres of men and women. Her argument reminds one of Jean-Jacques Rousseau: in her words, let women do what they can do best, and they can "produce better warriors than they themselves can ever become."[17] Schlafly never explains why the "natural order" must be enforced or reinforced by society. After all, if the relations between men and women, and particularly woman's specific role as mother, are natural, will not nature assert itself? And if the differences are essentially biological, won't physical difference always asert itself? Schlafly obviously does not think so because she fears that women will choose to be like men if the chance to do so exists. She must think that they can be "like" men if she fears it so much. And she must also believe that most women would prefer to be men, which is a strange position for her to take as protector of true "womanhood."

Schlafly never poses the feminist question, which asks at what point sexual difference becomes sexual inequality. Her vision of the natural difference between men and women is at the base of her criticism of the women's liberation movement, which she says wants to replace the distinction between men and women with uniformity. Schlafly, interestingly enough, does not criticize feminists for trying to replace inequality with equality but instead says they try to level society to a common denominator: they try to make men and women the same. They try to replace difference with sameness. As a conservative, Schlafly sees the differences between men and women as reflecting the *natural* hierarchy that is part of the just ordering of society. Women are different from men, and this is both natural and good. Sexual difference is therefore never a problem for Schlafly as an antifeminist. She views the different treatment of men and women as natural and hence not a political problem of inequality. Yet Schlafly does seem to recognize that the sexual differentiation of the feminine from the masculine is not completely natural and needs societal reinforcement. In this case one is left to ponder how natural the sexual hierarchy can be if it must be taught in the schools, reinforced by the law, and protected through a total devotion to custom and tradition, as Schlafly argues it must.

There is yet another sense in which Schlafly seems to know that the differentiation of women from men does create a problem of inequality, which emerges specifically in her discussion of the economic dependence of the housewife. Schlafly tries to "protect" women within this unequal situation in the hopes that protecting a woman's right as a dependent being will make her able or willing to remain a housewife and mother. She claims the Equal Rights Amendment will deny women the right to be housewives, but she is in fact concerned that the ERA will recognize the wage-earning woman and her rights within the marketplace at the expense of the housewife's "rights" as an economic dependent. In actuality, the ERA will neither enhance nor limit a woman's option to be a housewife. The patriarchal and economic needs of the family of which she is a part will define her choices in this realm. Schlafly, however, is partially right. The women that she speaks for, the women who are defined as and define themselves as housewives within the institutions of marriage and motherhood, have little vested in the ERA. But the question Schlafly must still answer is why women need to be protected if they are only different and not unequal, and what it is that women need protection from if the relations between men and women are natural and God-given. Protection involves relations of power and assumes that those who need protection have less power or are unequal to another's power. Sexual difference, defined by and in the institutions of motherhood, marriage, and housewifery, does make "difference" a political problem reflecting inequality even though Schlafly does not discuss or recognize it as such.

Antifeminism and the Equal Rights Amendment

As a conservative, Schlafly is concerned with creating what she views as a just society. Justice does not require equality, and society cannot legislate equality at the expense of justice. Schlafly argues: "The fact is that equality cannot always be equated with justice, and may sometimes even be highly unjust."[18] Schlafly distinguishes the feminist from what she terms the "positive woman" on this basis. The positive woman recognizes her worth as a woman (housewife and mother) and therefore believes in her own differential treatment. The feminist does not believe in such differential treatment because it constitutes a dependent and unequal relation. According to Schlafly, equality assumes the sexes are the same, whereas *justice is premised on sexual difference.*

It is the protection of the housewife's economic dependence with which Schlafly's Eagle Forum is primarily concerned. The Eagle Forum, "a national organization of women and men who believe in God, Home, and Country," believes that it is the responsibility of society to honor the career of motherhood by recognizing the right of woman to be a full-time wife and mother and to have laws that obligate her husband to provide the primary financial support and a home for her and their children.[19] Schlafly identifies the housewife's enemy as the (liberal) feminist ERA, rather than the economy, which requires women to enter the labor force, and blames the feminist movement for the changing structure of the family, which leaves many women heading households by themselves.

The Equal Rights Amendment simply states that (1) equality of rights under the law shall not be denied or abridged by the United States or by any state on account of sex, (2) Congress will be given the power to enforce it, and (3) it will take effect two years after the date of ratification. This is the document that Schlafly has pitted her political energy against. She says she is against the ERA because she objects to state involvement in private life.[20] The federal government steps outside its boundaries when it enters into issues of family life, although Schlafly is not consistent on this issue; after all, she supports a constitutional amendment banning abortion. She also argues that laws allowing equality of opportunity for women are already on the books: the Equal Employment Opportunity Act of 1972 and the Equal Credit Opportunity Act of 1974 are sufficient guarantees of women's equality. "The legislative, administrative, and judicial machinery to give women a fair opportunity to reap life's economic rewards are all in place."[21]

Schlafly believes that it is already possible for a woman to be anything she might like to choose—"a coal miner, a truck driver, an architectural engineer, a stockbroker; she can follow whatever career avenue her imagination and ambition lead her to select."[22] She is quick to point out, however, that this does not mean that *every* woman will be paid as much as she is worth or be educated to her full potential, because this is not the case for men either: "Most women and men believe they are underpaid and that their real worth is underrecognized."[23] In her mind, the ERA cannot and should not change this. After all, the disparities among men and between men and women are "just," specifically because they reflect natural inequalities. What really is at issue in Schlafly's rejection of the ERA is the notion of sexual equality. For her, men and women are not equal *because* they are (sexually) different: sexual equality assumes that men and women are the same, and they are not. The "ERA will prevent us forever from making reasonable differences between men and women based on factual differences in childbearing and physical strength."[24]

The ERA means sexual equality, which means "a reduction of rights that women formerly possessed" as women, as members of a sexual class. These so-called rights are the distinguishing characteristics that differentiate women from men. Schlafly argues that the ERA would deny the "obligation to support" and therefore challenges the legal right of a woman to be a full-time homemaker, provided with a home, child support, alimony, and so on. However, the "choice" to be a homemaker today is not protected as a legal right, and therefore Schlafly is wrong in arguing that the ERA will challenge such a right. The ERA will not require women to take a job; economic necessity will do that. But this is really beside the point. What is to the point is that Schlafly believes that ERA fails to *protect* the status of women as a sexual class—as sexually differentiated from men. The ERA makes the category of sexual class suspect, whereas Schlafly argues for the protection of women as a sexual class.[25]

Schlafly rejects the (liberal) feminist position, which assumes that equality before the law will create a just society for men and women. She believes instead that women are (sexually) different from men, that they are economically dependent on men, and that they have the "right" to be protected and provided for as wives and mothers. Equality before the law will ignore this reality of the housewife and is therefore unjust. In the end, her defense of tradi-

tional patriarchal family relations is a defense of the economic
dependence of the housewife and her right to be different from
men.

Schlafly's depiction of the ERA as an endorsement of the wage-
earning woman is accurate. And her assessment that it has little
directly to offer the woman homemaker is also true. However,
ERA does not destroy the housewife role; it merely recognizes that
liberal individualism must be extended to women specifically in
the market. In doing so, the ERA helps to recognize the economic
rights of women in the marketplace. Schlafly, as a conservative,
opposes the way that liberalism undermines woman's ascribed
status in the home. She rejects both the idea that women should
be wage earners and the feminist defense of wage-earning women.
Feminism, defined in terms of the ERA, represents the excesses of
liberalism: the demand for sexual equality before the law. As a
conservative, Schlaflly believes in sexual hierarchy, not sexual
equality. Women need to be free to choose the institutions of
motherhood and housewifery, and their freedom to do so requires
that their economic dependence on men be protected. Dependence rather than equality should define woman's relation to
man. Hence the single-minded attack against the ERA.

Although Schlafly is credited with the defeat of the ERA by
many inside and outside the New Right, this misrepresents the
complexity of the issues involved. First one needs to recognize
that the ERA, in demanding equal rights before the law for
women, reflects the minimum vision of women's equality enter-
tained by feminists today. This is not to say that it is an irrelevant
or inconsequential demand, but that it is understood by most
feminists, including liberal feminists, to be necessary but not
sufficient for creating real sexual, economic, and racial equality
for women. It is true that ERA would make it illegal to pay women
60 percent of a man's wage for doing the same work. But the ERA
would not by itself *enforce* economic equality or destroy the sexual or racial ghetto of which woman is a part. It would simply
make unequal pay illegal while doing little about the structural
relations of inequality.

Feminists by now know that a law in and of itself cannot create
sexual equality. But they also know that it can lay the basis for
further assaults against patriarchal privileges, and is therefore im-

portant. In this same vein, feminists also know that, although it will affect them, ERA does not legislate relations in the home between husband and wife, even though Schlafly argues that it would. The ERA applies directly to the public, not the private sphere.

To the degree that feminists understand that sexual equality requires changes in the private *and* public realms, and changes in the way these realms are defined in relation to each other, they also understand the limits of liberal legislation that focuses on the public realm. Hence, although feminists, especially liberal feminists who are committed to creating legal equality between men and women, believe the ERA is utterly important to American women, they also know that it is more symbolic than substantive. Abortion law would be an example of legislation that has a *real*, *direct* effect. Interestingly enough, legislators like Laxalt seem to be backtracking on their antiabortion stands, whereas Senators Hatch and Hatfield cannot seem to agree on how to demobilize this aspect of the women's movement. It is much simpler to attempt to delegitimize the women's movement by defeating the ERA because of the ambiguities it reflects and because it is limited in terms of its direct effect.

The ERA clearly reflects the contradictory nature of liberal (and liberal feminist) reform legislation. It may be more symbolic than real, but it does affect consciousness. It also constructs ideology, which never reflects a true or full picture of reality and yet defines reality. And it operates in a semiautonomous fashion from our real sexual, economic, and racial identities. This contradictory nature of the ERA has limited its effectiveness as a rallying point for the women's movement because it is so clearly insufficient for creating woman's real sexual equality. As a demand, it does not encompass the politics of feminism, which in some sense has moved beyond it. Yet the ERA remains a necessary element in the struggle toward equality in a liberal democratic society. It is because the ERA does not represent the feminism of the 1980s adequately, and because it does represent the antifeminist politics of the New Right sufficiently, that the New Right was able to mobilize against the ERA so effectively. The New Right sought to curtail the radical potential of the ERA to go beyond its own liberal-legalistic framework.

The problem with the ERA is that it seems to be, and is, insufficient to feminists, and it is also radical in its *potential* to redefine patriarchal law. The ERA is not enough for feminists, and it is too much for antifeminists. Schlafly has therefore been more singly committed to the defeat of the ERA than feminists have been singly committed to its ratification. It remains to be seen whether feminists will be able to build a pro-ERA politics that more directly encompasses the radical potential of feminism itself by focusing on the private as well as the public realm. This is really the crucial dilemma facing the women's movement today: to decipher how it can utilize the radical potential of liberal feminist reform that challenges the legal basis of patriarchal privilege while not being limited to liberal feminist reforms of the public arena.

The ERA was defeated by state legislators, not the incapacity of the women's movement or the skill of Phyllis Schlafly. A simple lesson can be uncovered here: legislators effectively protect the interests of the patriarchal state, even when there is popular support for legislation supporting sexual equality. With a majority of Americans supporting the ERA, the only explanation for its defeat is that those in positions of power rule in their own patriarchal interest. The defeat of the ERA only proves the state's commitment to patriarchal politics, and its desire to fight it out in this arena because it has the upper hand. The bluntness of this contradiction—between majority opinion in favor of the ERA and its legislative defeats—has radicalized feminists in the pro-ERA struggle.

New Right antifeminism and anti-ERA politics is a partial reaction to the changing structure of family life and feminist demands in the 1960s and 1970s. Arguing that a renewal of sexual difference is essential to reestablishing the necessary hierarchial order of society, the New Right utilizes much of the traditional Old Right conservative's outlook, while redefining its focus as antifeminist and anti-ERA. The New Right conservative view that wishes to restrict woman to a sexually defined ascribed status creates problems for Schlafly, however, because she is also wedded to the liberal values of individual achievement, which are present even within conservatism. Let us take a closer look at this dimension of her antifeminist position.

Liberal Individualism and Antifeminism

At the same time that Schlafly argues that there are sexual differences between men and women that must be protected, she
also believes that a woman can become anything she wants to be:
"I've achieved my goals in life and I did it without sex-neutral
laws."[26] She argues that "if you're willing to work hard, there's no
barrier you can't jump."[27] Her daughter Liza Schlafly sums up her
mother's position on the necessity of hard work: "You go out and
do what you want to do. You don't sit around complaining and
expecting the government to do it for you. . . . It [women's liberation movement] did a lot of good, but also a lot of harm because it
blames society instead of placing responsibility on the individual."[28] This view of the self-achieving individual mixes uneas-
ily with Schlafly's position about the divinely ordained sexual
hierarchy of ascribed status. Schlafly nevertheless remains committed to the view that any woman who wishes to be other than,
or more than, a housewife can be so. If a woman does not choose
to be otherwise, it is her own fault. It is not a problem of an unfair
status derived from an ascribed sexual class.

Critics of Schlafly often interpret her position as prescribing
housewifery for other women but not for herself. This is not quite
accurate. She applauds Margaret Thatcher and Golda Meir. In this
limited sense, Schlafly does not confine her vision of the "positive
woman" to the housewife or mother, but extends this vision to
women at the top of business or political life. The positive woman
is a woman who has succeeded: "They did it by competing, not
complaining. They've had the personal satisfaction of achievement. Because they are positive women, they are not defensive
about their womanhood."[29]

Schlafly's elitism, however, is clear: she believes that women
like herself, who are capable, will achieve. The others, who do not
achieve, fail because they lack ability, since there are no structural
constraints to keep them from the possibility of success. The natural hierarchy between the sexes will be reinforced by the incapacity of the majority of women to be successful. Somewhat
reminiscent of John Stuart Mill, she thinks that women who are
able and want to compete in the professional world should do so.
However, most women will not be professionals; most women

will find themselves in the labor force doing boring, monotonous work. She therefore believes that most women will do better to stay with housewifery. Schlafly does not criticize the ghettoization of women into the low-pay, low-skill jobs. She rather takes the capitalist marketplace as given and the position of women in the labor force as the natural result of marketplace forces in determining individual work. But given the risks, she wonders why a woman would choose to leave the home. "If you think diapers and dishes are a never-ending, repetitive routine, just remember that most of the jobs outside the home are just as repetitive, tiresome, and boring."[30]

Her argument runs something like this: women are basically as intelligent and gifted as men, although most men and women are unable to achieve real distinction. Those of us who can, will. Outside intervention by the state through legislation creates a false equality that will only lead to greater mediocrity. Given the mediocrity of most women (and men), women are better off as mothers and housewives because when most women enter the male world of the market they will be faced with the same demeaning jobs that a majority of men have. The jobs that await women in the labor force are no more "self-fulfilling than the daily duties of a wife and mother in the home." She uses this somewhat accurate description of the labor force to conclude that "the plain fact is that most women would rather cuddle a baby than a typewriter or factory machine."[31]

Schlafly supposedly opens up the race of life to women: "In business, professional, intellectual, and academic pursuits, women can compete equally with men because they are just as smart."[32] But she then shuts them out of the race on the grounds that most women won't achieve such distinction. Why not? Not because the patriarchal definition of woman as dependent wife and mother precludes her winning the race, and not because the capitalist marketplace is dominated by menial, boring jobs that limit the number of winners, but because most women will not have the innate ability to succeed. Schlafly's thinking thus emphasizes the elitist view of freedom that underpins conservatism and can be found implicit in liberalism. Within liberalism one should be free to choose whether one wishes to compete in the race of life, but the race itself implies winners and losers.

Schlafly's liberal vision of individual achievement is structured by her religious conservative vision of sexual ascription and by the patriarchal attitudes she derives from both traditions. It is on this contradictory view—that women constitute a sexual class differentiated from men and yet free to compete as individuals with men—that Schlafly constructs her vision of a "just" society. Justice for her means the freedom to experience differential treatment or protection rather than sexual equality. Women should have the opportunity to compete with men but only if the competition is not based on egalitarianism, which treats men and women as though they were the same.

Schlafly cannot resolve the conflict between her liberal commitment to individual equality of opportunity and the explicit conservative commitment to sexual-class differentiation. The liberal theory of equality of opportunity does not require that individuals be equal to one another in order to compete but merely allows them the opportunity to compete. It allows for inequality but does not explicitly root this hierarchy in terms of the sexual differentiation of woman from man. Schlafly's conservatism, by contrast, sees competition as limited by a static, ascribed sexual hierarchy. She asserts both views even though they contradict each other.

One begins to see why the definition of woman in terms of her differentiation from man is so central to the conservative outlook. Schlafly uses biology, and nature itself, to justify the elitism of sexual hierarchy and to curtail the progressive spirit of liberal ideology. She sees sexual egalitarianism—treating men and women as though sexual difference were of no importance—as an excess of liberalism.

The differentiation of woman from man is the basis for distinguishing between equality and justice and between equality of opportunity and egalitarianism. As Rosalyn Yalow, winner of the 1977 Nobel Prize in Physiology or Medicine, has stated: "The essential feature of democracy is not that all people are the same but rather that opportunities not be denied nor discrimination practiced because of differences among people." But she also believes that "males and females are distinguishable, and it is not unexpected or undesirable to treat them differently from birth."[33] The distinguishing characteristic is the biological fact that only a woman can bear children. This is an example of the conservative

position on women's equality: women should enjoy equality of
opportunity, as limited by the differences that exist between men
and women. Egalitarianism, as distinguished from equality of opportunity, is a problem because it assumes the sameness of the
sexes.

Schlafly's conservatism is in clear contradiction with the
rhetoric of the New Right, which is much more populist than it is
elitist. Populism has a democratic vision of equal rights for all and
therefore conflicts with Schlafly's religious negativism about the
human soul and the necessity of hierarchy.[34] Nevertheless,
Schlafly presents herself as the champion of the common woman
and disguises her elitist ideas by defending the housewife and the
blue-collar woman worker. The rhetoric she uses focuses on the
"ordinary" person and the dreariness of people's everyday lives.
Hence her descriptions of people's limited options: "The big percentage of jobs in the world—both male and female—fulfill a need
for money, but little else."[35]

When Schlafly discusses the woman in the labor force she focuses on the blue-collar working woman. Her model of the economy is the somewhat outmoded industrial economy rather than
the service sector economy, which employs a majority of women
workers.[36] Her focus on the blue-collar working woman allows her
to argue against women's employment in manual labor: women
are weaker than men and therefore must be protected from physical strain. "There are thousands of jobs in industry that are strenu-
ous, hard, unpleasant, dirty, and dangerous that men can and will
do, and for which they receive good wages, but which women
don't want to do and should not be compelled to do."[37] By utilizing this vision of the blue-collar worker, Schlafly distinguishes
the "common" woman from the feminist. Feminists support the
ERA and reject protective legislation because they are professional women who sit at desks all day in clean and spacious
offices and never lift anything heavier than a few books and
papers.[38] She constructs an image of the common woman as a
housewife or a blue-collar worker and defends her against feminists and the ERA. Her rhetoric obscures the elitist position of
many economically privileged housewives and the fact that a
minority of women in the labor force are blue-collar workers. In
reality, the majority of women work in the service sector and are

sexually segregated in the labor market, which means that women aren't doing "men's jobs" at all but rather continue to do women's work in a different setting: food service, health service, business service.

Schlafly is partially correct in arguing that the new options for women, particularly their entry into the labor force, hardly constitute a better alternative to housewifery, since the wage-earning mother may in fact be no freer than the housewife. However, the wage-earning mother is more equal to her husband than the housewife if one defines equality in terms of sameness, as Schlafly does. This explains Schlafly's hostility to her. Her real objection to the wage-earning mother lies in the confusion such a mother causes for identifying woman as housewife as different from man as income earner. For Schlafly, the wage-earning mother creates the kind of "unjust" equality between men and women that undermines the traditional patriarchal family: women become more like men.

To the extent that Schlafly is committed to conservatism, while also holding certain liberal values, her outlook coincides with some aspects of Friedan's revisionist liberal feminism. But while Friedan seeks to redefine the distinction between egalitarianism and equality of opportunity from a liberal feminist viewpoint, Schlafly does so from a conservative antifeminist one. Friedan attempts to redefine liberal feminism while Schlafly, as an antifeminist, rejects it. As a result they construct New Right antifeminism and revisionist liberal feminism, or neoconservative feminism, respectively. Schlafly therefore seeks to protect the economic dependence of women in order to protect the sexual differentiation of woman from man in terms of childbearing and childrearing, whereas Friedan argues against protection and for equality. Nevertheless, Friedan and Schlafly have come to share some disturbing similarities. In The Power of the Positive Woman (1977), Schlafly defended the same woman (housewife) that Friedan rejected in The Feminine Mystique (1963). In 1982, however, Schlafly and Friedan agree that women must reject the "feminist mystique." Friedan and Schlafly share the same enemy today: the egalitarian impulse of feminism, particularly contained within liberal feminism.

Schlafly and Friedan have different politics, although theoretical continuities exist between them. Whereas Schlafly is opposed to the Equal Rights Amendment and to abortion, Friedan is a strong supporter of the ERA and believes in a woman's right to abortion; whereas Schlafly rejects the ideology of sexual equality in favor of sexual difference, Friedan redefines sexual equality to mean freedom to choose difference. But neither accepts sexual egalitarianism, and this is the key to the similarity of their theoretical views, which transcend their different politics.

NOTES

1. Carol Felsenthal, *The Sweetheart of the Silent Majority: The Biography of Phyllis Schlafly* (New York: Doubleday, 1981), p. 168.
2. Schlafly's books on this topic include *A Choice, Not an Echo* (1964); *The Gravediggers* (1964), written with Rear Admiral Chester Ward; *Strike from Space* (1965), with Ward; *Safe—Not Sorry* (1967); *The Betrayers* (1968), with Ward; *Kissinger on the Couch* (1972), with Ward; *Ambush at Vladivostok* (1976), with Ward. These books are available from Pere Marquette Press, Box 495, Alton, Ill. 62002.
3. Frances Fitzgerald, "The Triumphs of the New Right," *New York Review of Books* 28, no. 18 (November 19, 1981): 19–26.
4. See Isaac Kramnick, *The Rage of Edmund Burke: Portrait of an Ambivalent Conservative* (New York: Basic Books, 1977), for an important analysis and definition of conservative theory.
5. *The Phyllis Schlafly Report* 13, no. 8 (March 1980), sec. 2, p. 3.
6. Phyllis Schlafly, *The Power of the Positive Woman* (New York: Jove/HBJ Books, 1977), p. 11.
7. Ibid., p. 9.
8. Ibid., p. 224.
9. *The Phyllis Schlafly Report* 14, no. 7 (February 1981), sec. 1, p. 4.
10. *Schlafly Report*, March 1980, p. 1.
11. *Schlafly Report*, February 1981, p. 3.
12. Henry Schipper, "Some Girls," *Rolling Stone*, no. 357 (November 26, 1981), p. 23. For a longer version of this interview, see Henry Schipper, "The Truth Will Out: An Interview with Phyllis Schlafly," *Ms. Magazine* 10, no. 7 (January 1982): 88–92. See also Sydney Weisman, "Just an Ordinary Housewife," *In These Times*, May 20–26, 1981, pp. 12–13, and Felsenthal, *Sweetheart of the Silent Majority*, p. 50.
13. Felsenthal, *Sweetheart of the Silent Majority*, p. 26.
14. *Schlafly Report*, March 1980, p. 1.
15. Schlafly, *Positive Woman*, p. 31.
16. *Schlafly Report*, March 1980, p. 2.
17. Ibid.
18. Schlafly, *Positive Woman*, pp. 24–25.
19. Eagle Forum flyer, Box 618, Alton, Ill. 62002.

20. Schlafly, *Positive Woman*, p. 26.
21. Ibid., p. 41.
22. Ibid.
23. Ibid.
24. Ibid., p. 170.
25. For a discussion of the concept of preferential treatment see Elizabeth H. Wolgast, *Equality and the Rights of Women* (Ithaca, N.Y.: Cornell University Press, 1980).
26. Quoted in Felsenthal, *Sweetheart of the Silent Majority*, p. 58.
27. Quoted in ibid., p. 55.
28. Quoted in ibid., p. 134.
29. Schlafly, *Positive Woman*, p. 50.
30. Ibid., p. 63.
31. Ibid.
32. Ibid., p. 142.
33. Rosalyn Yalow, "Men and Women Are Not the Same," *New York Times*, January 31, 1982, p. E21.
34. See Seymour Martin Lipset and Earl Rabb, *The Politics of Unreason: Right Wing Extremism in America, 1790–1977* (Chicago: University of Chicago Press, 1970).
35. Schlafly, *Positive Woman*, p. 42.
36. Emma Rothschild, "Reagan and the Real America," *New York Review of Books*, February 5, 1981, pp. 12–18. Also see Harry Braverman, *Labor and Monopoly Capital* (New York: Monthly Review Press, 1978), for a discussion of the changed nature of the working class, particularly in terms of blue-collar and white-collar work.
37. Schlafly, *Positive Woman*, p. 150.
38. Ibid., p. 145.

8. Revisionist Liberal Feminism: Freedom of Choice vs. Equality

Betty Friedan, who emerged as the spokesperson for liberal feminism in the late 1960s and early 1970s, has now rejected her earlier vision of women's equality as a "feminist mystique." Friedan has always rejected the radical implications of feminism.[1] However, her rejection of the radical implications of liberal feminism in the 1980s must be understood as part of the neoconservative rejection of egalitarianism and the so-called excesses of the seventies. As such, she is an ex-liberal feminist turned neoconservative—in reaction against the so-called excesses of feminism.

The similarities between Betty Friedan's revisionist liberal feminism and the neoconservative analysis of the crisis of liberalism are disturbing. Although Friedan is not a part of neoconservative circles nor does she accept their antiaffirmative action position, her rejection of the notion of equality meaning sameness, her concern with directing the focus of feminism away from questions of sexual freedom and freedom of sexual preference, her commitment to reembracing motherhood and the family although she subscribes to a pluralist (but heterosexual) notion of family life, her anger at feminism and the feminist mystique, her embrace of liberal individualism and rejection of the notion that women are limited by sexual and economic class and racist structures, tie her intimately to the neoconservative context that predominates in the country today.

Friedan fundamentally is revising liberal feminism away from its radical potential to demand real sexual equality, which at least means that women and men should be treated the same. Given that the differentiation of woman from man is what constitutes patriarchy, this tendency—toward sameness—is in fact *potentially* revolutionary. To the extent that neoconservatives are revisionist liberals, and to the extent that Friedan is attempting to revise (conservatize) liberal feminism, she can be termed a revisionist or a neoconservative feminist. It is important to note, however, that there is a difference between neoconservatism and its position on women and neoconservative *feminism*. The latter, from liberal feminist moorings, seeks to conservatize feminism. This is not the same as the neoconservative attempt to de-radicalize feminism from patriarchal liberal moorings.

From Liberal to Neoconservative Feminist

Friedan attempts to revise liberal feminism by rejecting the notion of sexual egalitarianism in favor of sexual difference. She does this by distinguishing between sexual equality of opportunity and freedom of choice for the sexes and sexual egalitarianism. Sexual equality of opportunity assumes that women should be free to choose to be different—from men. For Friedan, freedom to be different means freedom to choose motherhood. When women compete with men, they try to be like men, and this has straitjacketed them into rejecting their womanhood, that is, motherhood. The next stage of feminism must reject the reactionary aspects of feminism, which have negated the positive side of motherhood and family.

According to revisionist liberal feminists like Friedan, sexual equality of conditions, or egalitarianism, wrongly assumes that women and men are the same and not "different." This particularly means that women, thinking that they are the same as men, no longer feel free to have children. Friedan argues instead that women should embrace their difference, that is, feel free to have children. To the extent that Friedan blames feminism for being antimotherhood and antifamily, she wants to protect women from feminism. Feminism and its excesses have become the enemy.

The hierarchical relations of equality of opportunity (rather than sexual egalitarianism) necessitated by the competitive race of life are renewed and reinforced by revisionist liberal feminism. By differentiating women from men in the name of biological and hence "natural" difference, the hierarchical relations of society are defended against the greatest "excess" of liberalism, namely, feminism. It is this very hierarchical notion that the patriarchal relations between men and women simultaneously constructs, justifies, and mystifies that is used to draw the line between equality of opportunity, which allows people to compete, and equality of conditions, which presumes equality of social conditions.

One might wonder at this point what the revisionist aspects of the "neo" in neoconservative feminist represents. After all, there is little new about differentiating women from men; it lies at the heart of patriarchal relations themselves. However, the neoconservative discussion of woman's sexual difference from man in the 1980s reflects a rejection of the feminism of the 1970s. Interestingly enough, feminism has become the main enemy for the revisionist and neoconservative feminist because feminism supposedly demanded that men and women be the same.

More particularly, revisionist liberal feminism is a rejection of the radical impulse of feminism itself; a denial of the reality that woman *as a member of a sexual class* is differentiated from man. As (liberal) feminism has demanded rights for women as individuals, thereby extending the ideology of liberalism—the individual's freedom of choice, equality before the law, and equality of opportunity—to women, it has uncovered the fact that the sexual differentiation of woman from man has made her unequal in the race of life. As such, equality of opportunity to compete is not sufficient because of the ascribed sexual status of women within the race. In order for women to "achieve" in the race, affirmative action, the Equal Rights Amendment, reproductive rights, are needed. As feminists have demanded policy changes that begin to uncover the need for real sexual equality and not only sexual equality of opportunity, liberalism has been pushed to its outer boundaries. Hence the crisis of liberalism. (Liberal) feminism and the women's movement have played a vital role in creating the crisis of liberalism by uncovering the contradictory *reality* between the sexual class system and the ideology of sexual equality of opportunity. Revisionist liberal feminism is a response to the way feminism has heightened the contradictions contained within liberalism itself. Feminism moves beyond liberalism and its promises to the need for sexually egalitarian relations. This is exactly what the neoconservative feminist rejects: the sexually egalitarian impulse of (liberal) feminism that they believe will treat men and women as though they were the same.

The preceding discussion is a partial explanation of why the distinction between equality of opportunity and sexual egalitarianism is so central to Friedan. It is because (liberal) feminism has gone too far. This is why I argue that we must be very cautious about discussions of "sexual difference" that are used to explain and justify why the race of life should be different for men and women. We cannot forget the fact that sexual difference has been used both to define and to justify the patriarchal relations between men and women. If we now choose to rethink this issue—as Friedan demands we do—we must do so with a keen sense of political history. After all, what can it mean to be different but equal?

One last point of clarification on this term "revisionist liberal feminism." It applies not only to the set of substantive specific ideas about sexual difference but to the *reactionary* position these ideas hold in their relation to feminism and liberalism. Revisionist liberal feminism is not an abstract theory concerning motherhood, family life, or sexual difference. Friedan's concern to integrate "love and work," for example, is very similar to the ideas of earlier feminists like Elizabeth Cady Stanton and Charlotte Perkins Gilman. However, these early feminists sought to open up the conception of sexual equality, whereas Friedan wants to set limits on it.

What is extremely important to understand about Friedan is that she has always distinguished herself from what she calls radical feminism—the notion that women are oppressed as a sexual class by men. Despite this disclaimer, her early liberal feminism implicitly accepted the notion of sexual class:

> Friedan's politics is contradictory in its very nature. She accepts a liberal individualistic analysis of woman's problem alongside an implicit understanding of the social nature of woman's common condition, an implicit notion of woman's sex-class identity alongside the explicit rejection of a sex-class theory of power, and a liberal-individualist theory of power alongside the implicit conception of sex-class power.[2]

Friedan is now reacting against the very radical potential contained within her own earlier feminism even though, and maybe more significantly because, she never recognized it.

In 1963 Friedan rejected the "feminine mystique" and asked women to question and reject the way they were relegated to childrearing and housewifery; in 1983, she rejects the "feminist mystique." She now believes that women have gone too far in rejecting the feminine mystique—to the point where women no longer feel free to choose motherhood. Without for the moment asking whether this is an accurate description of a majority of women today or what freedom of choice means in relationship to motherhood, we need to examine how Friedan's assessment of the "feminist mystique" leads her to articulate a revisionist liberal feminist position.

Educated at Smith College, Friedan was a housewife and mother of three at the time she wrote *The Feminine Mystique*.[3] Later, she became a founding member of the National Organization for Women (NOW) and is often credited with being a major leader of the women's liberation movement. When Betty Friedan wrote *The Feminine Mystique*, more than one-third of the labor force was women. Fifty-four percent of these women were married, and 33 percent were mothers. As early as 1956, 70 percent of all families earning between $7,000 and $15,000 had two wage-earners.[4] Despite this social reality, Friedan wrote about the middle-class housewife and criticized the housewife role when it was already under assault by the needs of the capitalist marketplace. If she had looked at the lives of wage-earning women alongside that of the housewife, she would have understood that it is not enough for women to reject the role of housewife and enter the world of work because the household responsibilities remain theirs and their burden only doubles. As in *The Feminine Mystique*, in *The Second Stage* Friedan sees only a piece of the problem.[5] This time she focuses on the pressures that exist for the professional woman without analyzing why so few women can "make it" into this realm or why "freedom of choice" about motherhood cannot fully exist for a woman in capitalist patriarchal society.

What one needs to understand is how Friedan and Schlafly have come to share the same enemy. Originally, Friedan was responsible for a scathing critique of the housewife's life, whereas Schlafly was and remains a champion of this life. Although they still disagree on this issue, the lines of the argument have changed. Friedan now wishes to reembrace some of the traditional life of womanhood, and Schlafly has publicly welcomed her into the fold. Friedan has shifted her target from the feminine mystique to the feminist mystique, and she now tries to redirect the women's liberation movement back to family life and the choice of motherhood. We need to study this journey more fully if we are to understand the complicated relationship between neoconservatism and revisionist feminism.

Family Life and Revisionist Liberal Feminism

There have been significant changes in family forms in the past twenty years. As discussed in Chapter 5, the so-called typical American family of a working father and homemaker mother with two dependent children accounts for only a small percentage of husband-wife families.[6] Forty-five percent of mothers with children under six are at present working out of economic necessity. By 1990 it is expected that only one out of four mothers will be at home full time.[7] The "working mother" has replaced the housewife.

Friedan has focused on professional women rather than the majority of wage-earning women in defining the problem of what she terms "the second stage" of feminism—a questionable concept to begin with. She worries that professional women do not feel free to choose motherhood because of what it might mean for their careers. And she worries about the young women who focus on these career women as their models. Friedan wants to create options and alternatives that will allow the professional woman to compete in the market without rejecting family life and children.

In 1963, during what she calls the first stage of feminism, Friedan advised women to reject the straitjacket of housewifery and the rearing of children and instead to opt for a place in the market. She thought women could be like men or at least do the same things that men did. This vision of equality, which assumes that women should be like men, is a view Friedan now rejects. Schlafly has always rejected it. (Radical and third world feminists have also always rejected this vision, but for different reasons.) Friedan now believes that this vision merely engenders the feminist mystique: when women compete with men, they try to be like men, and this has straitjacketed them into rejecting their womanhood, namely, motherhood. The next stage of feminism must reject the reactionary aspects of feminism, which have negated the positive side of motherhood and family. Friedan assumes it is up to individual women (and men) to reject the feminist mystique. Friedan asks in *The Feminine Mystique*, "Why, with the removal of all the legal, political, economic, and educational barriers that once kept woman from being man's equal, a person in her own right, an individual free to develop her own potential, should she accept this new image?"[8] And in *It Changed My Life* Friedan again states, "Our own self-denigration of ourselves as women and perhaps our own fears are the main problem."[9]

While Friedan uses liberal individualism to reject woman's ascribed sexual status, Schlafly's liberal individualism exists contradictorily alongside her view of such an ascribed status. Both, however, deny that patriarchy, capitalism, and racism impose constraints on individual freedom. Therefore, neither Friedan nor Schlafly sees the institutions of patriarchal society, marriage, and the "institution of motherhood" as antithetical to woman's equality. Friedan argues that equality for women "never meant destruction of the family, repudiation of marriage and motherhood, or implacable sexual war against men."[10] Friedan thus disassociates herself from what she understands to be radical feminism. In so doing, she limits herself to a liberal individualist conception of power that obscures the institutional constraints of capitalist patriarchy. She also oversimplifies and misrepresents early radical feminism, which centered its critique specifically on the traditional patriarchal family, not on family life in general, and which today rejects only the institution of motherhood that links childbearing and childrearing, not biological motherhood itself. Her criticism of feminism as simply antifamily and antimotherhood distorts present-day radical feminism. Friedan and Schlafly nevertheless continue to criticize the women's liberation movement for being antifamily and antimotherhood.[11] According to Schlafly, feminists have a negative view of their own nature: "Most oppressive [to the feminist] is the cruel fact that women have babies and men do not."[12] This rejection of women's biological nature aptly describes Shulamith Firestone's writing in 1970 and some (disputed) aspects of radical feminism.[13] However, it hardly expresses the full spectrum of more recent feminist writing that focuses on the social "institution of motherhood" or criticizes the economic dependency of motherhood in marriage.[14]

Friedan argues that the feminist movement must move beyond the reactionary stance she imputes to it, which rejects motherhood and family. It is time, she says, to reembrace the parts of our femininity that will allow us to be whole again: the traditional role of woman still remains a source of purpose and self-worth. She urges women to experience "a familiar place from a different vantage point."[15] The new vantage point requires that men and women alike reject the split between home and work. They must seek alternatives such as flextime at work, paternity leave, and so on. If women and men can share the parenting, women will be free to choose motherhood. This is why "the second stage may not even be a women's movement. Men may be at the cutting edge of the second stage."[16]

Friedan completely denies that women are a sexual class within a system of patriarchal hierarchy. Her argument ignores the relations of the capitalist market to the family, the separation of public and private life, the constraints of one's job, or one's options. She therefore argues that the second stage of the feminist revolution is not about women's separate personhood but rather involves women's coming to terms with the family. Women must integrate love and work; they need to let men share in the joys of family life. Women must transcend the battle for equal power and instead transform the institutions and the nature of power itself. This requires "the restructuring of our institutions on a basis of real equality for women and men so we can give a new 'yes' to life and love, and can choose to have children."[17] Although she insists that we must challenge the feminist denial of the importance of family and children, Friedan does not discuss the role capitalist patriarchy plays in this denial.[18]

The Feminist Mystique vs. the Choice of Motherhood

When Friedan argues that women must reject the feminist mystique in order to be free to choose motherhood, she implies that women *have denied themselves* the freedom of choice because of the pressure they feel as professionals. The small minority of women who are caught up in the problems of careerism may find it difficult to have a child.[19] Is this because they think they are not free to choose otherwise or are there real constraints preventing them from making the choice and penalties to pay if they do? These constraints of time, energy, money, and so on, operate for any woman who must earn her living, even if she has no upward mobility. Friedan, in rare moments, acknowledges this herself: "How can a woman fully 'choose' to have a child when her paycheck is needed for the rent or mortgage, when her job isn't geared to taking care of a child, when there is no assurance that her job will be waiting for her if she takes off to have a child?"[20] What remains unclear is *how* the freedom to choose motherhood is to be created within a capitalist patriarchal society. If one has to be in the labor force and one "chooses" to have a child, how does one escape the inequities of the institution of motherhood: unequal pay, the lack of day care facilities, the lack of paternity leave, and so on?

Friedan does not recognize or understand how the institution of motherhood politically structures patriarchal relations between men and women in the home and in the market. In arguing that political considerations shape the form of motherhood and family, I do not mean to reduce motherhood to its political meaning. Nor do I regard motherhood as the same as all other political institutions. I merely wish to argue that the activity of motherhood reflects the nature of political relations in society at large, which are relations of power. One must recognize that society has linked its definition of motherhood to the subordinate position of women as a sexual class. Biological motherhood must be distinguished from the political institution of motherhood, but this cannot happen unless one acknowledges the political dimension of motherhood. Only after the problem of sexual inequality has been resolved can the freedom to choose motherhood have any meaning.

Neither Friedan nor Schlafly can help out here. Schalfly cannot because she presumes the sexual difference of woman from man, and Friedan assumes the difference does not need to create serious inequities of power. Friedan never really says women *should be* mothers but rather that they should have the freedom to choose motherhood; they should have the freedom to be different (from men). However, if Friedan means to create a real freedom of choice about motherhood, she has to be committed to structuring a sexually egalitarian society, not a society that merely promises sexual equality of opportunity within a system of political inequality based on sexual difference.

It is motherhood that Friedan wants women to be free to embrace. The second stage will not be complete "until our daughters can freely, joyously choose to have children . . . because the cycle we broke, and have to embrace again, is basic to life."[21] Schlafly would agree with this. She would also add that motherhood is the greatest accomplishment that exists for most women. Friedan is less enthusiastic about motherhood but warns that women should not be taken in by the glorification of work alone.[22] Schlafly believes that women were/are better off as housewives, while Friedan argues that women must reestablish their freedom of choice.

Friedan argues that "the great challenge we face in the 1980s is to frame a new agenda that makes it possible for women to be able to work and love in equality with men—and choose, if they so desire, to have children."[23] Friedan embraces the neoconservative view of equality of opportunity rather than (sexual) egalitarianism. She differentiates woman from man as a potential childbearer not by relegating woman to an ascribed sexual status, as Schlafly does, but by presenting motherhood as an individual's freedom of choice. As such, although her neoconservative feminist ideology promises woman freedom of individual choice, it does not challenge the structural relations of patriarchy that restrict that choice. What is it, therefore, that a woman is free to choose? If she recognizes patriarchy as a political reality, she realizes that her choices exist within a framework of sexual inequality; if, like Friedan, she denies the reality of patriarchy, she may think that equality of opportunity can lead to social equality. Friedan's position is not the same as Schlafly's because Friedan does not defend the natural God-given view of sexual hierarchy justified by antifeminism, nor does she believe that women should be economically dependent on men. However, she does defend the kind of inequality that results from a belief in abstract equality of opportunity, which does not also assure equality of conditions for all participants. Unlike sexual egalitarianism, such equality provides only the opportunity to achieve within the framework of unequally defined sexual differences. In contrast to equality of opportunity (and hence sexual equality of opportunity), which is what liberalism is supposed to be about according to Friedan, the feminist mystique supposedly represents the egalitarian excesses of liberalism: too much equality, which assumes that women are like (or the same as) men. Instead, Friedan argues that women need the freedom to choose to be different from men. Schlafly argues that women *are* different from men.

Friedan's commitment to the freedom to choose motherhood leads us away from the radical potential of feminism and toward neoconservative feminism because she has no understanding of how to create equality between the realms of love (family) and work (market). So long as home and work do not have the same value in society, the choice of motherhood will be a choice of inferior status. Women cannot be equal to men if the institutional structures of their lives are not of equal value and importance to society. Friedan nevertheless believes that individual women can bring about the union between love and work. Friedan argues that women must reunite love and work even though it was not women who divorced the two realms in the first place. This is the ultimate proof that she does not understand the nature of patriarchal power.

Since she does not acknowledge the reality of patriarchy as a structural system connected to capitalism, Friedan says nothing about the constraints that patriarchy imposes on feminism. According to her, no system of patriarchal power oppresses women by defining them as a sexual class; rather, each individual suffers from lack of choice. In *The Feminine Mystique* Friedan argued for women's right freely to reject housewifery (and motherhood) and to enter the market. In *The Second Stage* she argues that women should have the right to be in the market and to choose motherhood as well. The theme—the individual's freedom of choice—remains the same. The preferred choices have changed, but she offers no new analysis of how to create the real possibility of choice. Friedan has not figured out *how* one creates sexual equality of opportunity between men and women, or what choosing motherhood has to do with creating and/or negating the possibility of equality, or why being free to choose motherhood is essential to woman's personhood.

Friedan's position on motherhood is not new to feminism.

Many feminists, such as Elizabeth Cady Stanton, Mary Woll-stonecraft, Charlotte Perkins Gilman, and even Emma Goldman, believed motherhood was an important aspect of a woman's life. Sounding very like Friedan, Charlotte P. Gilman wrote in 1899: "A woman should be able to have marriage and motherhood and do her work in the world also."[24] Friedan's position on mother-hood, however, has a different meaning in 1983 because Friedan's defense of motherhood is a reaction *against feminism itself and its radical potential to transform society.*

If Friedan meant to create a sexually egalitarian relationship between men and women while at the same time asserting the importance of motherhood, she would have to propose the kind of sexual, political, and economic relations that would guarantee that bearing children would not be a liability in terms of a woman's work, freedom, and so on. Her demands would have to focus on how to guarantee woman her equality (her sameness) with man, not merely allow her to compete with him as different (unequal). Woman, as sexually different from man, can compete with him but is no longer his equal once she is classified as *differ-ent.* In order for women really to have the freedom to choose to be mothers, a system committed to sexual egalitarianism would have to be devised in which sexual difference would be politically irrelevant. Anything less would merely reaffirm sexual difference as a political inequality. For Friedan, however, freedom of choice is in conflict with sexual egalitarianism because egalitarianism supposedly recognizes only the sameness of man and woman.

Feminism as Evolutionary, Not Revolutionary

Friedan believes that feminism is an evolutionary movement that can achieve its goals within capitalist society. Instead of as-suming that American capitalism can accommodate the union of work (market) and love (family), Friedan needs to understand why policies on child care and flexible working hours have had so little governmental support. The Child and Family Services Act of 1975 (which was an extension of the 1971 Economic Opportunity Amendments) was initially rejected by Presidents Nixon and Ford because it supposedly represented the Sovietization of the American family.[25] In 1979, under President Carter, Arabella Martinez, assistant secretary for human development services in the Department of Health, Education, and Welfare, vetoed Senator Cranston's child care bill because she believed that government should not be involved in child care legislation. Presidents Reagan and Carter, like Nixon and Ford, adopted the position that child care was "purely family business," and government involvement in family issues would further weaken the American family. President Nixon specifically argued this position: "For the Federal Government to plunge headlong financially into supporting child development would commit the vast moral authority of the National Government to the side of communal approaches to child rearing over against the family-centered approach."[26] As a matter of fact, throughout the 1970s the government became less involved in providing child and family services, and this is even more true under the Reagan administration.

With the present downturn in the economy, rising unemployment, and increased inflation, it is less likely than Friedan believes that working conditions will become more flexible. Employers seem to have more freedom today to deny workers their rights to sick leave, flexible working hours, and paternity leave than before. This flexibility, however, is essential to Friedan's view of unifying work and family.

Members of the New Right understand more than Friedan does the economic reasons why capitalist business cannot abide her definition of family life or the union of work and home. They argue that Friedan's feminist conception of the family, defined as "two or more persons who share resources, share responsibilities for decisions, share values and goals, and have commitment to one another over time," would cost business millions of dollars and would also be a bureaucratic nightmare.[27] "The business implications of this [definition of family life] are staggering. Consider, for example, just the inhouse mechanics of maintaining the records on health care benefits if the law should be changed to recognize as a family any group that calls itself a family for any period of duration."[28] The New Right just as strongly believes that Friedan's notion of family stands counter to the patriarchal needs of society. Jerry Falwell and George Gilder, alongside Phyllis Schlafly, argue for the biological, heterosexual, nuclear family because they believe it is a prerequisite for a healthy capitalist economy. As such, they understand better than Friedan does that capitalist patriarchal America cannot accommodate her vision of family, home, and work.

Given the government's lack of commitment to child care, the rise of teenage pregnancies, the increasing number of woman-headed single-parent families, and the dismantling of social welfare programs, what does Friedan think freedom of choice means? And how can she assume that the present patriarchally organized capitalist market will accommodate the reorganization of family life in line with the freedom of choice for women? Interestingly enough, her political focus has been on the Equal Rights Amendment and its concern with economic equity for women in the marketplace, which does not directly attack woman's place in the sexual ghetto in the economic market or support a policy of full employment. These latter concerns would be necessary to create some of the economic equality women need to experience freely chosen motherhood. Nor does she focus her attention on the sexual policies that could begin to create a meaningful freedom of choice about motherhood: reproductive freedom and abortion rights, day care programs, freedom of sexual preference and sexual expression, and so on. Friedan instead denies a place to questions of sexual freedom and sexuality in the feminist agenda. She tries to separate feminism from issues of sexuality, to restrict the meaning of sexual equality to equality before the law. She does not extend her concerns to establishing sexual equality within the domain of sexuality and sexual relations themselves. After all, if woman does not control her sexuality, then what does sexual equality mean? Usually, for Friedan, sexual equality is reduced to a notion of economic equality of opportunity. In the end, as a revisionist liberal feminist, she rejects the radical feminist notion of sexual politics and reduces feminism to the struggle for legal equality, which is equated with political equality of opportunity.

Rejecting Sexual Politics

Friedan believes that the feminist movement should focus on the ERA and not be diverted by so-called sexual politics.[29] This narrowing of feminist concerns to the ERA is distinctive of the revisionism taking place within feminism. Although Friedan has always held this narrow substantive view of feminism in part, the position of her argument has changed within the political spectrum. Whereas liberal feminist politics has broadened its scope through the 1970s—as with NOW's forceful campaign to challenge the New Right on issues related to abortion and related issues of sexual freedom—Friedan argues for a narrowing of scope.[30] Her arguments in defense of focusing on the ERA and issues in the public sphere used to be directed to radical and lesbian feminists. Now she is making this argument to liberal feminists in the hopes of redirecting their focus away from its radical potential. Liberal feminists know, as I argued in the previous chapter, that although equality can be formulated in legislation, it cannot be created by it. Hence their more varied politics. If feminists were to narrow their scope away from the struggles for reproductive freedom, economic and racial equality, freedom of sexual preference, sexual freedom, and international peace, and center their politics in the ERA, the state would get exactly what it and Friedan want—a deradicalized women's movement.

In Friedan's mind, the ERA has nothing to do with abortion or homosexuality, which issues she thinks therefore should be kept separate. She considers questions of sex and sexuality a private matter. That is why she has always argued against connecting gay and/or lesbian politics with feminism: "It [lesbianism] twists the focus to sexual politics . . . it gets mixed up with the reaction against the female role, and threatens people who feel sex should be private and are mixed up about it themselves."[31]

Sexual issues and sexuality do have a political context, however. When Friedan states, "I am for life and for family. . . . I am not for abortion—I am for the choice to have children," she sounds like Schlafly.[32] Unlike Schlafly, Friedan is not against the legal right to abortion, but she is not for abortion either, because she believes that "being for 'abortion' is like being 'for mastectomy.'"[33] However, if she believed that sexual egalitarianism required that women ultimately be as free of childbirth as a man (like a man) before she can be truly free to choose motherhood, would not the right to choose abortion be a necessary prerequisite for a woman's assertion of personhood? In that case, abortion would be different from mastectomy.

In trying to save feminism from itself—to prevent the politicization of sexuality and the private realm—Friedan also seeks to save liberalism from its patriarchal crisis. She views the issue of economic equality, not sexual freedom, as central to the women's movement. This focus limits the feminist vision of equality of opportunity to the world of work and the market. She accepts the very split between love and work, family and economy, private and public, that she says must be destroyed. She reasserts the division between public and private life (a division used to restrict women's choices) in order supposedly to create freedom of choice for women—the freedom to choose motherhood. Her version of neoconservative feminism reaffirms the patriarchal division between family and economy by dichotomizing personal (sexual) and political (economic) life. Feminists should stay out of private matters and restrict themselves to fighting for equal rights before the law, defined as equality of opportunity.

Friedan never proposes a positive, egalitarian vision of the relations between men and women. Instead, she criticizes feminism for what she views as its egalitarian impulse: the view that men and women are the same and hence equal. She argues that this vision denies the difference between men and women and hence denies woman the freedom to recognize her difference and choose motherhood. Feminism defined as egalitarianism becomes the enemy for Friedan and for Schlafly as well. But Friedan rejects egalitarianism between men and women on liberal grounds, in the name of individual "freedom of choice." Schlafly rejects it on conservative grounds, in the name of the "natural order of things."

The difference between Friedan and Schlafly, and in this sense the difference between neoconservative or revisionist liberal feminism and New Right (conservative) antifeminism, is that Friedan argues that women should have the freedom to choose to be different—to be mothers—whereas Schlafly argues that women are different and are mothers. They are extremely similar positions and yet they are not the same. And because these similar theoretical positions give way to different politics, one cannot merely write these differences off as merely ideological.

Revisionist liberal feminism seeks to limit the excesses of sexual equality while still defending women's freedom of choice and equality of opportunity with men. This issue of equality is the crux of the problem. What can sexual equality mean in the neoconservative context, which differentiates women from men with the intent of rejecting egalitarianism? Nothing more than the equality of opportunity to remain unequal. And this is exactly how neoconservative feminism provides an answer to the "crisis of liberalism" today. It uses sexual difference to clarify the distinction between equality of opportunity and egalitarianism. The task of liberalism is to provide the first; the second, however, is an excess of feminism, which is in and of itself an excess of liberal democracy.

The Problem of Equality for Feminism

Friedan makes the same mistake in her assessment of the second stage of feminism as she did in her arguments regarding the first stage. She was wrong when she argued that women could enter the capitalist marketplace as men's equal. She is just as wrong to think that capitalism will allow women (or men) to combine work and love. In neither analysis does Friedan recognize the structural impact of patriarchy. After all, women have been trying to bridge the gap between family and work for a century. The problem of the double day of work for wage-earning women existed for women in 1963 and has only increased in the 1970s and 1980s. The combination of motherhood and wage labor may not be chosen freely today, but it is still the lot of a majority of women. In the first stage, Friedan rejected the home in favor of the market as the arena of women's fulfillment; in the second stage, she wants professional women to be free to choose both work and family. She does not recognize the need to move beyond the principle of equality of opportunity in the race of life toward achieving real egalitarianism, which would require the destruction of the separateness of family and work and of public and private life. Capitalism cannot tolerate equality in the marketplace, either among men or between men and women, nor can it tolerate equality between men and women in the home. In her neoconservative posture, Friedan rejects sexual egalitarianism in favor of the freedom to choose difference.

Friedan as a neoconservative feminist and Schlafly as an antifeminist focus on the relationship between sexual equality and feminism. They both reject a vision of sexual equality that negates the differences between men and women. Schlafly opts for the conservative notion of justice, while Friedan argues for freedom of choice premised on equality of opportunity. Schlafly assumes woman's sexual difference from men, and Friedan argues that women should be free to be different. Neither argues for sexual egalitarianism between men and women. Therefore, both believe that women can come to terms with motherhood and family life without its creating a problem for sexual equality.

Because Schlafly and Friedan equate egalitarianism with sexual sameness, treating women and men as though they were alike, the important feminist question is never asked: What does sexual equality mean and how does one try to create truly egalitarian relations while recognizing the biological difference constituted by women's ability to bear children? Because the question of sexual equality has been associated by radical and socialist feminists with liberal feminism, we have not adequately addressed this question either. We have argued that we do not want equality with men but liberation instead. What exactly can liberation mean, however, if it does not at least assume such equality? Of course, equality within capitalist patriarchy is not the same as liberation because its entire system is based on inequality and on relations of hierarchy. However, the meaning of equality in a noncapitalist, feminist society still poses the problem of *sexual* equality: how is a woman to be allowed her difference (her particular capacity to bear children) *and* her sameness (political and economic equality)? Her biological aptitude for childbearing must first be made politically inconsequential. This will happen when men and women enjoy truly equal political power stemming from conditions of economic, sexual, and racial equality. Unlike capitalist patriarchal society, such a society will not be organized hierarchically around the biological difference that exists between men and women. Under such circumstances, women would be free to explore their sexual difference or particularity, because it would have no consequence in terms of the amount of control and freedom they would have over their lives.

As a feminist one fights to guarantee sexually egalitarian relations between men and women, meaning not that men and women are presumed to be the same sexually but rather that it is assumed they are politically the same by guaranteeing that sexual difference has nothing to do with how much sexual freedom, economic independence, racial equality, intellectual opportunity, and so on, one has. Instead of reacting *against* the radical impulse of feminism, we need to utilize this radical potential for defining a radically feminist conception of sexual equality. This vision does not assume that men and women are sexually the same because sexual egalitarianism can exist despite the reality of sexual difference. But we must discover how real sexual equality is possible. If sexual difference, specifically women's capacity for childbearing, is not to be used to restrict woman's freedom of choice, then bearing children will have to be differentiated from the institution of motherhood, from women's economic dependence on man, from her secondary wage-earner status, from the system of heterosexual controls, from restrictive notions of sexuality. Only when woman's sexual difference is no longer the basis of her secondary political status can we begin to explore the meaning of sexual egalitarianism, which requires not merely economic and racial equality but equality in the sexual relations between men and women and in the relations of sexual reproduction.

Feminists must face the problematic relationship between the meaning of real sexual equality and the fact that only women can bear children. The relationship between motherhood, family life, and feminism is not an issue that is new to the women's movement, but it has particular political significance in view of New Right and neoconservative politics. These groups are using the issue of sexual difference epitomized by woman's capacity for childbearing to justify their attacks on feminist gains, particularly in terms of reproductive rights and questions of sexual preference. They argue that society suffers from an excess of equality, and hence they promote motherhood as a way to reestablish freedom of choice within a system of patriarchal controls.

If we do not think equality needs to be premised on the assumption that women are exactly the same as men and if we reject the notion of sexual equality of opportunity because it uses sexual difference as an inequality, then we must articulate a theory of sexual egalitarianism that does not deny our sexual particularity (childbearing) or our shared human qualities with men. The real answer to the crisis of liberalism is not antifeminism or neocon-servative feminism but sexual egalitarianism. In order to be free *and* equal as individuals, women cannot be defined in terms of their difference from men but rather they need the freedom and sexual equality to explore their particular and universal qualities. This freedom is highly dependent on, but not determined by, the social relations of society: the degree of sexual, economic, and racial equality, and the freedom of sexual preference. This vision of sexual egalitarianism, however, is not rejected by revisionist liberal feminists alone. Feminists of the Left reject it as well.

NOTES

1. Friedan's brand of liberal feminism has always rejected the radical potential embodied within it. Therefore, her movement toward an explicit revision of (liberal) feminism does not negate the fact that this radical potential exists; it rather documents that it does. It should also remind one that the potential for radicalism is never inevitable; it must always be fought for politically. See Zillah Eisenstein, *The Radical Future of Liberal Feminism* (New York: Longman, 1981), chap. 8.
2. Ibid., p. 179.
3. Betty Friedan, *The Feminine Mystique* (New York: Dell Books, 1963).
4. Sara Evans, *Personal Politics: The Roots of Women's Liberation in the Civil Rights Movement and the New Right* (New York: Alfred A. Knopf, 1979), p. 9.
5. Betty Friedan, *The Second Stage* (New York: Summit Books, 1981). Also see Friedan's "Twenty Years After the Feminine Mystique," *New York Times Magazine*, February 27, 1983, pp. 35–57. For other examples of revisionist liberal feminism see Suzanne Gordon, "The New Corporate Feminism," *The Nation* 236, no. 5 (February 5, 1983): 1, 143–47; and Susan Bolotin, "Voices from the Past-Feminist Generation," *New York Times Magazine*, October 17, 1982, pp. 28–116.
6. See U.S. Department of Labor, Bureau of Labor Statistics, "Employment in Perspective: Working Women," Report 531 (April 1978), p. 1.
7. Friedan, *Second Stage*, p. 23.
8. Friedan, *Feminine Mystique*, p. 61.
9. Betty Friedan, *It Changed My Life* (New York: Dell, 1977), p. 103.
10. Friedan, *Second Stage*, p. 47.
11. Friedan, *It Changed My Life*, p. 316.
12. Phyllis Schlafly, *The Power of the Positive Woman*, (New York: Jove/HBJ Books, 1977), p. 10.
13. Specifically I have in mind so-called cultural feminism, as an aspect of radical feminism that focuses on the importance of developing a women's "culture" to counter existing patriarchal culture. Some original founders of the radical feminist group "Red Stockings," such as Ellen Willis, argue that cultural feminism is a denial or a revision of the initial revolutionary concerns of radical

feminism and should not be considered a part of radical feminism. See Red
Stockings, eds., *Feminist Revolution* (New Paltz, N.Y.: Red Stockings, 1975).
Also see Alice Echols, "The New Feminism of Yin and Yang," in Ann Snitow
et al., *Powers of Desire: The Politics of Sexuality* (New York: Monthly Review
Press, 1983).

14. See Adrienne Rich, *Of Woman Born: Motherhood as Experience and Institution* (New York: Norton, 1976); and Christine Delphy, *A Materialist Analysis
   of Women's Oppression* (London: Women's Research and Resources Centre,
   1977). Also see Christine Delphy and Daniele Leger, "Debate on Capitalism,
   Patriarchy and the Women's Struggle," and Christine Delphy, "For a Materialist Feminism," *Feminist Issues* 1, no. 1 (Summer 1980): 41–50.
15. Friedan, *Second Stage*, p. 81.
16. Ibid., p. 28.
17. Ibid., p. 41.
18. Ibid., p. 23.
19. Most women occupy low-level service sector jobs rather than professional
   ones. In 1979, the median earnings of all working wives was $6,336. Among all
   working wives, with or without children, only 9.1 percent made more than
   $15,000 in 1979. See *Money Income of Families and Persons*, U.S. Bureau of
   the Census, P-60, no. 129, November 1981; and *Money Income and Poverty
   Status of Families and Persons*, U.S. Bureau of the Census, Current Population
   Reports, P-60, no. 127, U.S. Government Printing Office, August 1981.
20. Friedan, *Second Stage*, p. 23.
21. Ibid., p. 36.
22. Betty Friedan, "Feminism Takes a New Turn," *New York Times Magazine*,
   November 18, 1979, p. 98.
23. Ibid., p. 40.
24. Charlotte Perkins Gilman, *The Yellow Wallpaper* (New York: Feminist Press,
   1972), p. 45.
25. Gilbert Y. Steiner, *The Futility of Family Policy* (Washington, D.C.: The Brook-
   ings Institution, 1981), p. 93.
26. Quoted in ibid., p. 91.
27. "Militant Feminists Demand Restructuring of Family Values," excerpted from
   Persuasion at Work, no. 1, published by Rockford College Institute, 5050 East
   State Street, Rockford, Ill. 61101, in *Conservative Digest* 8, no. 5 (May 1982):
   16.
28. Ibid.
29. Friedan, *Second Stage*, p. 203.
30. NOW has been criticized by "feminist sex radicals" for denying its support of
   pederasty, pornography, sadomasochism, and public sex while trying to distinguish between the importance of sexual preference (which it supports) and
   sexual license (which it does not support). NOW adopted the position that
   lesbian rights issues needed to be delineated from nonlesbian (sex) rights
   issues. See "News Flash: People Organize to Protect Recent NOW Resolution
   on Lesbian and Gay Rights," *Heresies*, "Sex Issue," vol. 3, no. 4, issue 12
   (1981): 92–93. Also see Pat Califia, "Feminism vs. Sex, a New Conservative
   Wave?" *The Advocate*, February 21, 1980, pp. 13–15; and "The New Puri-
   tans," *The Advocate*, April 17, 1980, pp. 14–18.
31. Friedan, *Second Stage*, p. 319.
32. Ibid., p. 107.
33. Ibid., p. 209.

9. Revisionist Left Feminism:
Sexual Difference vs. Equality

Revisionist left feminism is anticapitalist. "Left" in this case applies to a variety of revisionist feminists who may be Marxist, socialist, and/or radical in terms of their stance on the economy. They are reactionary, however, in terms of their critique of family life and feminism. Revisionist left feminists have much in common with neoconservatives and so-called left-radicals such as Christopher Lasch in their defense of certain traditional notions of family life.

The revisionist stance of Jean Elshtain is defined particularly in terms of her (1) defense of sexual difference and criticism of androgyny; (2) rejection of sexual politics in terms of the personal *not* being political; and (3) reactionary positioning of this argument against feminism and radical feminism in particular. It is the *combination* of these three facts that constitutes the revisionism in Elshtain's work. One can believe that sexual difference between women and men exists and think that this must be incorporated into a theory of sexual equality and not necessarily be a revisionist. However, when the defense of sexual difference is used to contain and reject the radical aspects of feminism, it constitutes revisionism. Feminist revisionism contains both the substantive defense of sex difference within traditional instititutions and the indictment and revision of feminism on this basis. By doing so it rejects the notion that the "personal is political," or that there is a "politics to sex."

Like the Marxist revisionists of the early twentieth century who wanted to take revolution out of Marxism, these feminists seek to moderate the more radical demands of the women's movement. Feminist revisionists never falter in their commitment to sexual equality. But they believe that one can use traditional institutions, or traditional forms, to seek radical transformations of society. They therefore argue that sexual equality can exist alongside "sexual difference." Their view of how to achieve sexual equality, and exactly what equality means, thus remains open to serious question.

Defending Patriarchal Privacy

Elshtain is a left feminist, unlike Friedan; she therefore rejects the liberal paradigm of the "race of life," but contradictorily seeks to protect the distinctness of male and female life that is used to support the patriarchal aspects of liberal society. Elshtain presents the interesting case of a feminist revisionist who adopts a radical critique of the inequities of the capitalist economy and a reactionary position on the family and "sexual difference"; she delivers a critique of capitalism and a defense of the patriarchal institutions that protect and maintain it. Elshtain's defense of sexual difference is in the end a defense of the patriarchal relations necessitated by liberalism and ends up inadvertently defending sexual inequality by utilizing the ideology of liberalism to reject the radical contours of feminism. Without discussing how sexual difference is part of the patriarchal sexual differentiation of man from woman, Elshtain addresses the present crisis of liberalism by reformulating (liberalizing?) its patriarchal underpinnings.

Elshtain characterizes feminism as antifamily and antimotherhood, as does Friedan. She argues: "My concern is with that antifamilial feminist ideology that has become linked up in the popular mind with efforts to erode or destroy the meaning and relations of family life in the absence of any workable alternative."[1] Elshtain's attack centers on the radical potential of feminism to transform the differentiation of man from woman, public from private life. In doing so she characterizes feminism as "mean spirited denunciations of all relations between men and women and in expressions of contempt for the female body, for pregnancy, childbirth and childrearing."[2] She argues that feminists have chosen a public identity over a private one, which involves suppressing traditional female social worlds. Public identity supposedly overrides and has precedence over private lives and concerns.[3] She attacks feminism for echoing female helplessness and victimization: "I suffer therefore I have moral purity and none can question what I say."[4] Elshtain also accuses feminists of having "a silencing effect over free and open debate on a whole range of issues having to do with female sexuality, pregnancy, childbirth and childrearing, and family life, even as it provides no alternative vision of a revitalized concept of 'citizenship.' "[5] The problem for women, according to Elshtain, seems to be feminism rather than family life, or the split between private and public life, or the institution of motherhood.

Elshtain, like Friedan, rejects the radical feminist notion of patriarchy, particularly the conception of a sexual politics and the idea that the personal is political, and by doing so attempts to depoliticize the meaning of sexual difference. Elshtain's depiction of radical feminism—that it demands that women become like men by rejecting motherhood and family life—is wrong. Although there is much variation among radical feminists, when they argue that one must abolish women's oppression they do not mean that intimacy or family life or childbearing must be destroyed. "What is argued is that proprietary rights to appropriate women and children must be abolished."[6] It is the artificial relations of public/private life that feminists argue must be destroyed, not the essential meeting of human needs within these spheres.

Contradicting Elshtain's view, most radical feminists argue that to recognize woman's oppression does not mean that oppression defines all that they are. "The social system is contradictory since, despite the oppression which it exercises, it permits us to be feminist, to decode the mechanisms of oppression."[7] Moreover, many radical feminists argue that the main enemy is "a hierarchical type of social relationship, where men are involved as historically constructed, not as biological beings: as 'men' precisely, not as males."[8] And radical feminist Adrienne Rich makes clear from the start of *Of Woman Born*, "This book is not an attack on the family or on mothering, *except as defined and restricted under patriarchy*. Nor is it a call for a mass system of state-controlled child care."[9] She continues: "To destroy the institution is not to abolish motherhood. It is to release the creation and sustenance of life into the same realm of decision, struggle, surprise, imagination and conscious intelligence, as any other difficult, not fully chosen work."[10] Various forms of feminism can, and do, reject the biological family while fighting to reclaim family life.[11] Although one can find antifamily, antimotherhood statements within radical feminist writing (Shulamith Firestone's *The Dialectics of Sex*, for example), the question is why feminist revisionists choose to focus on this one aspect of radical feminism. A possible answer is that such a description depicts feminism as narcissistic, as a celebration of the self rather than the family. This depiction of feminism requires a basic revision of feminism, which Elshtain supplies in her discussion of the family and sexual difference.

Revisionist Left Feminism and the Family

Nathan Glazer, reviewing Christopher Lasch's *Haven in a Heartless World*, states: "A funny thing happened on the way to developing a radical critique of the American family: it has turned out that the old model was not so bad after all."[12] This statement reflects the fact that it is possible to be considered a radical while being a traditionalist on the family. Although Elshtain rejects what she terms Lasch's view of family retrenchment, that is, the reestablishment of the traditional patriarchal family, she argues that "some form of familial ties and mode of child-rearing is essential to attain the minimal bedrock of human social existence."[13] Her argument is functionalist: the family as a biological unit reproduces and cares for children and creates a needed continuity through generations. "Familial existence is [therefore] a presuppositional feature of social existence."[14] The family or family life, neither of which is defined, becomes a human necessity. "Tradition does have claims on us; history does limit us."[15] The family, as tradition, binds us. The family's status derives from "universal pan-cultural existence in all known past and present societies," and familial ties are what have always made us "minimally human."[16] The family has always been—therefore it must always be. Elshtain sounds very similar to Lasch on questions of family life and tradition. He is bothered with "a devaluation of the past" that leaves us with a "narcissistic preoccupation with the self."[17] Lasch, like Elshtain, criticizes feminism for its supposed commitment to androgyny, its flight from feeling, its endless selfishness.[18]

Elshtain recognizes that "the family is a contradictory institution; it serves several masters."[19] Yet she focuses on its positive, nurturing aspects to the exclusion of its oppressive qualities.[20] She ends up protecting the family, structured by marriage and heterosexuality, with its so-called privacy. Elshtain believes that by identifying with the private sphere and its positive functions— loving, caring, nurturing—women can resist the state and the competitiveness of the public world. She simply ignores the way Nazi Germany and fascist Italy have used women's identification with the family to defend the state. And she never questions the way the ideology of privacy and family life obfuscates the political relations of family life. Elshtain uses the ideology of private life as distinguished from public life, and equates public with political life, instead of questioning its ideological (liberal and patriarchal) content. She argues that we must preserve the private sphere where women have developed a distinct and moral language. "We must take care to preserve the sphere that makes such a morality of responsibility possible and must extend its imperatives to men as well."[21]

The "Personal Is Not Political"

Elshtain argues for preserving the private sphere, or family life, because she rejects what she terms the equation of personal and political life made by radical feminists. The family is not a political institution of oppression for her. Her rejection of the "personal as political" stems partially from her equation of public life with political life; if political life is the public sphere, then private life cannot be political. She would have to question her equation of public and political life before she could take seriously the radical feminist conception that the personal is political.

In fact, Elshtain does not believe that the personal is political, that sexual intimacy, love, parenting cannot escape political definition. She believes feminists erode "private life by construing it as a power-riddled battleground, thus encouraging a crudely politicized approach toward coitus, marriage, childrearing, even one's relationship to one's own body.[22] Once again, feminism for Elshtain is defined as a force that erodes private life. Her major concern is with protecting the differentiation of personal and political life, because if one is reduced to the other both are lost in the end. "For if politics is power and power is everywhere, politics is in fact nowhere and a vision of public life as the touchstone of a revitalized ideal of citizenship is lost."[23] If the distinction between public and private life is eliminated, "no politics can exist by definition."[24] But this is not necessarily true. Politics can and has existed without the division of public and private life as it exists at present. After all, if politics exists everywhere, it merely exists everywhere, not nowhere.

Elshtain creates a false argument. Radical feminists do not wish to collapse personal and political life. Rather, they argue that personal (sexual) and political life are interrelated. Feminists do not argue that politics should be based on family life.[25] They argue that the relations of the family *are* political and *should not be*. The intent of the feminist argument is to depoliticize the family—or to depoliticize its patriarchal aspects—not to conflate it with the state realm. Radical feminists want to destroy the *ideology of public and private life in order to uncover the reality of the sexual politics of the family and the state,* whereas Elshtain accepts and uses the ideology that masks the politics of sex. One must first question the ideological distinction of personal vs. political or public vs. private before one can conceptualize the meaning of sexual politics, and Elshtain does not do this. As a construct, sexual politics requires the deconstruction of the language public/private, personal/political.

Revisionist Left Feminism and "Sexual Difference"

Examining the question of sexual difference, Elshtain states: "A *sexual difference* is neither an affront, nor an outrage, nor a narcissistic injury."[26] However, she never specifies what her vision of society based on sexual difference might look like, stating only that the sexual distinction between male and female is "constitutive of a way of life."[27] She rejects androgyny because she presumes that sexual distinctiveness between male and female would be eliminated. She rather believes that human sexual differences are essential to individual identity and uniqueness— "that bodily identity is a necessary feature of personal identity and that personal identity is necessarily a sexual or sexed identity."[28] Differentiation on the basis of sex constitutes the basis of social life. "A child can neither physically negate nor conceptually transcend the manner in which his or her body 'registers itself,' and that body must be understood within the terms of each successive stage of psychosexual maturation."[29]

Elshtain believes that a sexed identity need not embody the unequal relations of the sexes. She agrees with Richard Wollheim that "to live in a sexed, social universe is not, necessarily, to inhabit a world in which differential evaluations are placed on 'maleness' or 'femaleness.' "[30] But one wonders what the relationship between sex (as biological) and gender (as social, cultural, political) is for Elshtain, because she also argues that "children locate themselves in that world on the basis of gender."[31] Is the body merely a sexual biological category or a gendered body? And how can we disassociate sexual inequality from sexual difference within the sex-gender system itself? Elshtain does not answer these questions but merely asserts that "the sex distinctions of a biological or psychological nature which have been linked historically to inequality between the sexes are not necessarily thus linked."[32]

Elshtain rejects the notion that people are blank slates, totally molded by external pressures, without some sort of "nature" that can be fully understood by social forces themselves.[33] But all the serious problems are avoided here by creating simple dualities. If we deny that people are merely a reflection of social forces, and yet also believe that bodily identity is both a biological, material reality and simultaneously a part of a sex-gendered system, then how do we think about "sex differences"?

Woman's Different Voice as Maternal Thinker

Not all feminists who at present are concerned with the question of sexual difference are revisionist; however, Elshtain uses their arguments for her own purposes. This should not make the work of these feminists suspect, but rather should caution us about the way Elshtain interprets and manipulates arguments about sexual difference. The work of Sara Ruddick and Carol Gilligan, which tries to construct a notion of woman's reality (as different from man's), elucidates many of the cultural differences that exist between men and women but does not reject feminism for challenging the social and political arrangements that have (partially) created these differences, as Elshtain does.[34]

Elshtain defends a female identity she identifies with the private world of the family. Women, as mothers, have not been totally victimized and oppressed, but have been able to construct a positive reality within the sex-gender system. She adopts Sara Ruddick's notion of "maternal thinking" because it "refuses to see women principally or simply as victims, for it recognizes that much good has emerged from maternal practices and could not if the world of the mother were totally destructive."[35] Ruddick uses the concept toward clarifying woman's reality. She identifies maternal thinking as a residual power accruing from woman's capacity to bear and nurse infants: "Although maternal thinking arises out of actual child-caring practices, biological parenting is neither necessary nor sufficient."[36] The biological body, which Ruddick thinks is partly a cultural artifact, "may foster certain features of maternal practice, sensibility, and thought."[37]

Ruddick believes that although there is no a priori reason, such as "a woman's essence," to explain it, women have a cognitive style that is more moral than men's; women are more peaceable than men because they are involved in maternal care, which teaches them preservative love. "Preservative love is a caring for or treasuring of creatures whose well-being is at risk . . . priority is given to keeping over acquiring, to reconciling differences, to conserving the fragile, to maintaining the minimal harmony and material conditions necessary to a child's life."[38] This peaceableness is transmitted to women as daughters in maternal practice: "Women are daughters who learn from their mothers the activity of preservative love and the maternal thinking that arises from it."[39] But Ruddick, unlike Elshtain, stresses the importance of feminism in the process of trying to bring "a *transformed* maternal thought into the public realm, to make the preservation and growth of *all* children a work of public conscience and legislation."[40] She argues that woman's distinctive peaceableness (which is defined by her positioning in relation to the care of children) must be "transformed by a critical feminist consciousness" for it to become a reliable resource for peace, and further states that we need "to free traditional 'womanliness' from the crippling institutions in which it grew" and "link a feminist transformation of sexuality and gender with an ancient preservative love."[41] Feminism is hardly the enemy here.

Carol Gilligan, in much the same vein, argues that women have a "different moral voice." Gilligan goes out of her way to state that she is not generalizing about either sex because the sexual differences she discusses arise within a social context "in which factors of power combine with reproductive biology to shape male and female life."[42] Nevertheless, Gilligan's findings show that women do center on affiliative relationships of care rather than on individual achievement.[43] As a result, women perceive social reality differently from the way in which men do. They appear to focus on relationships of caring and responsibility whereas men focus on achievement and their work.

Alice Rossi has also raised the issue of the maternal aspects of woman's identity, but from a revisionist liberal perspective. Her earlier feminism equated equality with the identity of the sexes and their inequality with diversity. She now argues that diversity is a biological fact and equality is a political precept.[44] In 1964 Rossi was committed to a conception of sexual equality "meaning a socially androgynous conception of the roles of men and women."[45] She rejected traditional conceptions of masculine and feminine life: "By far the majority of the differences between the sexes which have been noted in social research are socially rather than physiologically determined."[46] She left to "speculative discourse and future physiological research the question of what constitutes irreducible differences between the sexes."[47] Today she adopts a biological perspective that "suggests that the biological conventions shape what is learned and that there are differences in the ease with which the sexes can learn certain things."[48] Rossi rejects egalitarian ideology that denies the reality of innate sex differences.

Elshtain, in arguing that women as a group experience their social worlds differently from the way in which men as a group do, merely sidesteps the issue of whether the "difference" is natural, inevitable, or preferable. Her attempt to clarify her definition of "difference" remains inadequate: "This locus is not some solid rock, not an ontological, definition of female 'being,' rather it is a series of overlapping intimations of a subject in the process of defining herself both with and against the available identities, public and private, of her epoch."[49] The female subject is an identity-in-becoming grounded in tradition. And the traditions of familial life supposedly ground women in the relations that allow them to stand in criticism of the state and public world. The question can be raised of how the welfare mother is free to stand against the state or where the privacy of her family life begins and ends.

Elshtain also argues that feminist theory must move away from sentimentalizing ourselves and idealizing our specialness and rather recognize the way such activity relates to our oppression.[50] She criticizes the early suffragists for assuming that woman's moral superiority could be transferred to the public level.[51] Nevertheless, she makes a similar argument herself: she seeks to protect the familial realm in the hope that maternal thinking can have an impact on public morality. She asks "for women to affirm the protection of fragile and vulnerable human existence as the basis of a mode of political discourse."[52]

Elshtain adopts Ruddick's argument that we must use transformed maternal thought in the public realm. But what does transformed maternal thought mean for Elshtain? or for Ruddick? Does maternal thought remain the province of women? Would Margaret Thatcher's dealings with the Falkland Islands qualify as maternal thought? And how does one transform maternal thinking and the social relations of childrearing while defending the traditional institutions—marriage, heterosexuality, and sexual difference? Elshtain seems more interested in protecting maternal thinking than in transforming it. Her belief that the biological body is a natural construct that necessitates the biological family, heterosexuality, public as distinguished from private life, and masculine and feminine gender defines her revisionist priorities. Instead of showing how sexual difference can be transformed by feminism, she chooses to use sexual difference to reject feminism.

Feminists need to rethink how to view biology and nature itself and how they affect the sex and gender system. It is not merely biology that makes women a sexual class. It is because women's biology is as political (unnatural) as it is natural that women are defined as a sexual class apart from men. Some radical feminists argue that as anatomical women they seek to destroy themselves as sociological women; "we have to abolish the social classes of sex."[53] Whereas Elshtain argues that radical feminists deny their biological selves, they more often reject the patriarchal politics of biology and wish to construct a feminist politics that recognizes their bodily selves as part of who they are. All feminists are left with the question of how one can think about the abolition of the gender system while recognizing sexual particularity between men and women. And the significant sexual difference on which all other discussions of sex difference depends is that of child-bearing.

Radical Feminism and the Problem of Sexual Difference

Elshtain does not recognize the similarity that exists between her concerns and much of radical feminism and therefore presents her discussion of "sexual difference" as a corrective to radical feminism's denial of biological distinctness and "sex difference." Shulamith Firestone argued in her now decade-old *The Dialectic of Sex* that woman's biology (sexual difference) in and of itself was oppressive to women. In some more recent radical feminist analyses the problem of women's oppression is located in the political manipulation and use of women's biology and therefore it does not call for an end to biological (sex) difference. However, the biological determinist frame out of which Firestone wrote is still to be found in radical feminist conceptions of "woman's essence." Whereas Firestone rejected the biological female as sexually different in order to destroy the oppression of politicized woman, radical feminists such as Mary Daly, Susan Griffin, and Andrea Dworkin affirm woman's sexual difference.[54]

Some radical feminist writers, notably Adrienne Rich, believe we can retain the female (biological childbearing) while rejecting the political institution of motherhood. Rich has stated: "We need to explore and understand our biological grounding, the miracle and paradox of the female body and its spiritual and political meanings."[55] She believes women need neither to become their bodies nor to try to exist in spite of them. Rather, we need to connect our mental capacities, our tactile sense and our multi-pleasured physicality.[56] Although radical feminist analysis reflects the unresolved tension between a celebration of women (neofemininity and the traditional female, maternal values) and a commitment to androgyny, Elshtain depicts it as only the latter.

Radical feminism reveals the related problem, which has existed within feminism from its earliest beginnings: the fact that in order to become a woman one must first be a female and all females are politically defined as women. Although the two—being female and being a woman—are not one and the same, they are always intertwined, never completely separable. The problem is how one can reject being a woman without completely rejecting being female. Or how one transforms the political (woman) while not negating the biological (female) that is constituted in the woman. The real truth is that women's lives do not allow a neat separation between the rejection and celebration of their lives because there is a biological component that connects femaleness with womanliness, sex with gender. And the exact contours of this relationship remain unknown.

The particular problem with much of radical and revisionist feminism is that there is confusion about what "neofemininity" or woman's essence means. When I stated earlier that radical feminists reject the patriarchal politics of biology but want to recognize their bodily selves this was not meant to oversimplify a complicated issue. It rather is meant to highlight the fact that Elshtain misrepresents the radical feminist position on sexual difference, however varied and inconsistent it may be. Elshtain helps nothing by ignoring the fact that the problem of sexual difference exists within radical feminism and that radical feminism recognizes and identifies with many of the issues she raises about the celebration of womanhood. She merely reproduces many of the same problems that already exist in radical feminism on this issue, while she argues against the feminist quest for equality. Let us therefore look briefly at the radical feminist discussion of woman's essence or sexual difference.

Female Essentialism and Radical Feminism

Factions within radical feminism assume that there is such a "thing" as a female essence, although they have varied definitions and conceptions of what that might mean. The female, as a biological thing unto herself, constitutes a particular and "sexually different" reality. Often this vision of woman's essence (as fundamentally biologically constructed) takes on a spiritualist dimension. Susan Griffin in *Woman and Nature* elicits such a vision: "and listen as we speak to each other of what we know: the light is in us."[57] In Griffin's radical feminist view it is the biological female (more than the politicized woman) who is the mother: "When we awaken there is a child given to us. We are mothers. We feel a pain where the vulva has been cut. We are mothers. We feel that the skin of the child is soft. The face to us in sleep is beautiful. The small body lying against our body is vulnerable. The cries move us. . . . We love this body, because we are part of the body. We are mothers."[58] Woman, as female, is close(r) to nature (than man): "And yes we are close to animals."[59]

Elshtain seems to ignore the fact that woman is very much understood in terms of her bodily distinctness in radical feminism. "Her body. Her body holds. Her body has seized what had to be seized, what had to be learned, her body is a fortress, her body is an old warrior . . . her body living its secret life, her body sheltering wounds, her body sequestering scars, her body a body of rage."[60] The body is an expression of nature for Griffin: "We know this earth is made from our bodies. For we see ourselves. And we are nature. We are nature seeing nature. We are nature with a concept of nature. Nature weeping. Nature speaking of nature to nature."[61] Radical feminism differentiates woman from man and argues that she is superior. If there is an androgynous view of human life in radical feminism it is that men should become like women, not women like men.

Mary Daly argues in this vein that feminism is the struggle to deny patriarchy, which has denied woman her essence. Woman must find her reality. Daly's book *Gyn/Ecology* is an attempt to do just that.

> That is, it is about dis-covering, de-veloping the complex web of living/loving relationships *of our own kind*. It is about women living, loving, creating, our selves, our cosmos. It *is* dis-possessing our selves, enspiriting our selves, hearing the call of the wild, naming our wisdom, spinning and weaving world tapestries out of genesis and demise.[62]

Daly believes that female energy has a significant biological content to it, much as does Susan Griffin. "Since female energy is essentially biophilic, the female spirit/body is the primary target in this perpetual war of aggression against life. Gyn/ecology is the re-claiming of life-loving female energy."[63] The spiritualist nature of this notion of woman's essence is explicit in Daly's writing: "The proximity that she feels is not merely geographic/spatial. It is psychic, spiritual, in the realm of inner life-time. She senses gynaesthetically that there is a convergence of personal histories, of wavelengths."[64] Radical feminism for Daly is the process of women's reaffirming their own original birth and integrity. It is the process of breaking through the silence that patriarchy has created about woman's essence.

This issue of (biological) essentialism—that woman is different from man in that she is more spiritual, loving, caring and that these differences are located (in some significant sense) in her biological self—is an important aspect of much radical feminism. This vision of woman defined by her biological self has also been at the heart of much patriarchal theory. Aspects of biological essentialism are in fact found in conservative theory: human and social relations are merely a mirror for the God-given natural (biological) order of things. Although radical feminism does not justify the existing political order on the basis of woman's (biological) difference from man, and instead uses biological essentialism to challenge the existing patriarchal order, it is troublesome to find this conservative epistemological stance within radical feminism. The woman's "essence" and her "difference" appear predetermined and in some sense apolitical. Although this vision of sexual difference within radical feminism is not revisionist in and of itself, there is a problem with its static-biological view of woman. Sex and its relation to gender seem to collapse; woman becomes the female. The presence of this stance within radical feminism lends it credibility in revisionist feminism and even forms of antifeminism. More problematically, it restricts the possibilities of radical feminism within a conservative epistemology that is significantly biologically determinist.

Radical feminist Andrea Dworkin shows that the view of woman as more moral and better than man has been used by men all along the political spectrum.

Being good or moral is viewed as a particular biological capacity of women and as a result women are the natural guardians of morality:

> a moral vanguard as it were. . . . Motherhood is especially invoked as
> biological proof that women have a special relationship to life, a
> special, intuitive knowledge of what is right . . . women all along the
> male-defined political spectrum give special credence to this view of
> a female biological nature that is morally good.[65]

Dworkin argues that the notion of a biologically based morality,
which she terms the "woman superior" model of antifeminism, is
in the end used to keep women down. "To stay worshiped, the
woman must stay a symbol and she must stay good."[66]

It is interesting that Dworkin does not recognize the presence of
the woman superior model within radical feminism. Her own
vision of women alludes to such a model in terms of her discussions about pornography: good women do not like it, bad women
do. She also has a biological view of woman's oppression and a
biologically determinist view of patriarchy: sex-class warfare in
Dworkin's view is more between males and females than between
men and women. One cannot help but wonder if some of the same
dynamic that Dworkin attributes to right-wing women is not true
of radical feminism. "Being worshiped (for most women) is preferable to being defiled, and being looked up to is better than being
walked on. It is hard for women to refuse the worship of what
otherwise is despised: being female."[67] Where Dworkin clearly
differentiates herself and radical feminism from the antifeminist
position on sex difference is that she does not believe that women
are treated as a sex congruent with what they are or can be. She
rejects the relationship between men and women as it presently
exists as necessary or inevitable.

Elshtain says she rejects a vision that posits a natural essence
for women, yet in the end she defends a view that is quite similar.
It is true that the notion of maternal thinking that she adopts from
Ruddick is not a vision that is limited to woman's biological nature, but rather reflects the particular social and political positioning of woman in terms of childbearing and childrearing.
Nevertheless, Elshtain argues in defense of present institutions
like the family, on the basis that sexual distinctness necessitates
them. In actuality, she ends up defending the essentialist position,
even inadvertently: women are sexually distinct from men and
the difference is to be valued and protected. The radical feminists
argue in defense of woman's essence but simultaneously demand

the destruction of patriarchal privilege; Elshtain argues in defense of maternal thinking and the existing (patriarchal) institutions.

The Problem of the Body in Radical Feminism

Adrienne Rich, more hesitantly than Daly or Griffin, embraces a notion of woman's essence that is not solely rooted in the body. She does not assume that the body is simply a biological construct. "The body has been made so problematic for women that it has often seemed easier to shrug it off and travel as a disembodied spirit."[68] She rejects the biologically determined view and the view that denies the importance of biology in constructing women's lives. "We have tended either to become our bodies—blindly, slavishly, in obedience to male theories about us—or to try to exist in spite of them."[69] Rich argues that there is a female biology that needs to be taken into account as a resource instead of as a destiny.

> That female biology—the diffuse, intense, sensuality radiating out from clitoris, breasts, uterus, vagina; the lunar cycles of menstruation; the gestation and fruition of life which can take place in the female body—has far more radical implications than we have yet come to appreciate. Patriarchal thought has limited female biology to its own narrow specifications. The feminist vision has recoiled from female biology for these reasons.[70]

But there are still overtones of a biological essence and a predetermined destiny here: "We must touch the unity and resonance of our physicality, our bond with the natural order, the corporeal ground of our intelligence."[71]

Rich recognizes that a woman's body contains a series of contradictions. It is a "space invested with power, and an acute vulnerability; a numinous figure and the incarnation of evil; a hoard of ambivalences, most of which have worked to disqualify women from the collective act of defining culture."[72] Rich also believes that the maternal or nurturant spirit of women can "prove a liability so long as it remains a lever by which women can be controlled through what is most generous and sensitive in us."[73] She argues that feminists must deal with the ambiguities that exist when they choose to construct theories of female power of female ascendancy.

Unlike Elshtain, Rich does not merely glorify the nurturing aspects of women: "We learn, often through painful self-discipline and self-cauterization those qualities which are supposed to be 'innate' in us: patience, self-sacrifice, the willingness to repeat endlessly the small, routine chores of socializing a human being."[74] But this does not mean that Rich brings closure to the question of the role of biology in defining woman's essence, or that she entirely rejects the neofemininity argument.

> From brain to clitoris through vagina to uterus, from tongue to nipples to clitoris, from fingertips to clitoris to brain, from nipples to brain and into the uterus, we are strung with invisible messages of an urgency and restlessness which indeed cannot be appeased, and of a cognitive potentiality that we are only beginning to guess at.[75]

Exactly what, then, does this notion of "woman's essence" mean? Sometimes it assumes a biological definition, that women are sexually different from men. Most often this blurs into a view of gendered differences as well. Sex (nature) and gender (culture) are intertwined in most notions of essence. The differences on this issue arise in terms of whether one wants to say it is a natural or a cultural phenomenon or a mix of both.

The antifeminist stance of Schlafly argues that the differences between men and women are natural and biological. Radical feminists Daly and Griffin also lean in this direction and construct a notion of woman's essence from it. Radical feminist Adrienne Rich thinks that both nature and culture play a part in defining woman's body; revisionist Elshtain takes this same position but denies the ambiguity involved. Friedan adopts the notion of sexual difference particularly in terms of motherhood.

The politics drawn from the above are more varied than one might expect, given the similar positions on sex difference. Antifeminists and neoconservatives argue against androgyny and sexual equality and for protection of sexual difference. Radical feminists argue against the politics of sexual inequality while celebrating women's essence and sometimes defend the notion of androgyny if it means extending woman's culture throughout society. Revisionist feminists, such as Friedan and Elshtain, argue to protect sexual distinctness and celebrate the nurturing maternal aspects of womanhood while challenging sexual inequality.

Biological essentialism can be used by the feminist, the anti-feminist, or the revisionist feminist; by the neoconservative or New Rightist. And it can take on somewhat different meanings depending on how much woman's "essence" or "difference" is being defined by biology, culture, and politics, or some combination of the three. However one chooses to think about woman's difference from man, or rather how men and women are different from each other, it becomes imperative to clarify the role of patriarchal relations in defining those differences. Whether one wants to say this difference or essence is natural (biologically determined) or culturally defined (by social, political, economic relations that construct women's lives particularly in terms of childrearing), the notion of woman's difference from man is completely implicated in the politics and political theories of patriarchy.

Feminism, to the extent it directs itself to the dismantling of patriarchal relations, is faced with the "problem of sexual difference." Given the way woman's capacity for childbirth has been institutionalized within the series of patriarchal controls, and "maternal thinking" and woman's "essence" are tied up with this fact, it becomes very difficult to distinguish sex and gender or the female from the woman. Different forms of feminism reflect this problem. Nineteenth-century American feminists assumed the difference of woman from man and argued for women's right to the vote on the basis that they would purify politics. Anarchist-feminist Emma Goldman, who rejected this particular line of argument, believed motherhood distinguished women emotionally from men. Actually the full break with this line of argument does not happen in the United States until the 1970s, when liberal feminists such as Friedan and Rossi put forth an androgynous model of equality and some early radical feminists such as Firestone rejected the difference argument. Interestingly enough, the second half of the decade saw revisions away from this notion of sexual equality back toward a notion of difference.

To the extent that revisionist feminists highlight the problem of sexual difference for feminist theory they help direct us to a realm that needs further clarification. But to the degree that they choose to see feminism rather than patriarchal social relations as the problem, one cannot look to them to answer the question of how sexual equality can encompass sexual difference or sexual particularity. In order to do this we must retain the feminist understanding that the personal is political; that there is a politics not only to gender but also to sex.

NOTES

1. Jean Bethke Elshtain, "Feminists Against the Family," *The Nation*, November 17, 1979, p. 499. For an interesting critique of Elshtain see Arlie Hochschild, "Is the Left Sick of Feminism," *Mother Jones* 8, no. 5 (June 1983): 56–58.
2. Ibid., p. 481.
3. Jean Bethke Elshtain, "Antigone's Daughters," *Democracy* 2, no. 2 (April 1982): 46–48.
4. Jean Bethke Elshtain, "Feminist Discourse and Its Discontents: Language, Power, and Meaning," *Signs* 7, no. 3 (Spring 1982): 612.
5. Elshtain, "Feminists Against the Family," p. 499.
6. Mary O'Brien, *The Politics of Reproduction* (Boston: Routledge & Kegan Paul, 1981), p. 193.
7. Editors of *Questions Feministes*, "Variations on Some Common Themes," *Feminist Issues* 1, no. 1 (Summer 1980): 6.
8. Ibid.
9. Adrienne Rich, *Of Woman Born: Motherhood as Experience and Institution* (New York: Norton, 1976), p. 14.
10. Ibid., p. 180.
11. See Barrie Thorne and Marilyn Yalom, eds., *Rethinking the Family: Some Feminist Questions* (New York: Longman, 1982).
12. Nathan Glazer, "The Rediscovery of the Family," *Commentary* 65, no. 3 (March 1978): 49. For a discussion of the "left" and family issues, see Greg Calvert, "Why Are Leftists Leaping to the Family's Defense?" *In These Times*, September 30–October 6, 1981, pp. 13–14; Dialog, "The Family and Defense of Gay Rights," *In These Times*, March 10–16, 1982, pp. 12–15; Barbara Ehrenreich, "Family Feud on the Left," *The Nation* 234, no. 10 (March 13, 1982): 303–6; Barbara Epstein, "Family Politics and the New Left," *Socialist Review* 12, no. 3–4 (May–August 1982): 141–61; Andrew Hacker, "Farewell to the Family," *New York Review of Books* 29, no. 4 (March 18, 1982): 37–44; Michael Lerner, "Recapturing the 'Family Issue,'" *The Nation* 234, no. 5 (February 6, 1982): 141–43.
13. Jean Bethke Elshtain, "Family Reconstruction," *Commonweal* 1 (August 1980): 431.
14. Jean Bethke Elshtain, *Public Man, Private Woman: Women in Social and Political Thought* (Princeton: Princeton University Press, 1981), p. 323.
15. Ibid., p. 321.
16. Ibid., p. 327.
17. Christopher Lasch, *The Culture of Narcissism* (New York: Warner Books, 1979), pp. 25 and 21.

18. Ibid., p. 349.
19. Jean Bethke Elshtain, "Thank Heaven for Little Girls—The Dialectics of Development," in Elshtain, ed., *The Family in Political Thought* (Amherst: University of Massachusetts Press, 1982), p. 297.
20. See Jane Collier, Michelle Rosaldo, and Sylvia Yanagisako, "Is There a Family? New Anthropological Views," in Thorne and Yalom, *Rethinking the Family*, pp. 25–39, an interesting discussion of the contradictory nature of family life. Also see Mary Jo Bane, *Here to Stay: American Families in the Twentieth Century* (New York: Basic Books, 1976); Michele Barrett and Mary McIntosh, *The Anti-Social Family* (London: Verso, 1982); and Lynne Segal, *What Is To Be Done About the Family* (Harmondsworth: Penguin, 1983).
21. Elshtain, "Feminist Discourse," pp. 620–21.
22. Elshtain, "Feminists Against the Family," p. 500.
23. Ibid., p. 497.
24. Elshtain, *Public Man, Private Woman*, p. 201.
25. For this reason, Elshtain's paralleling of Filmer's patriarchal arguments with feminists' analysis of family and political life is faulty. See her *Public Man, Private Woman*.
26. Jean Elshtain, "Against Androgyny," *Telos* 47 (Spring 1981): 20.
27. Ibid., p. 13. For feminist discussions of androgyny see Ann Ferguson, "Androgyny as an Ideal for Human Development," in Mary Braggin, Frederick Elliston, and Jane English, *Feminism and Philosophy* (New Jersey: Littlefield, Adam, 1977), pp. 45–69; Kathleen Grady, "Androgyny Reconsidered," in Juanita Williams, ed., *Psychology of Women: Selected Readings* (New York: Norton, 1979), pp. 172–77; and Carolyn Heilbrun, *Toward a Recognition of Androgyny* (New York: Alfred A. Knopf, 1973).
28. Ibid.
29. Ibid., p. 15. The heterosexual bias of Elshtain's support of sexual distinctness becomes clearest in her discussion of psychosexual maturation.
30. Ibid.
31. Ibid.
32. Ibid., p. 18.
33. Ibid., pp. 10, 11. In this discussion, Elshtain unselfconsciously adopts the liberal theory of human nature.
34. Sara Ruddick, "Maternal Thinking," *Feminist Studies* 6, no. 2 (Summer 1980): 342–67, and "Pacifying the Forces: Drafting Women in the Interests of Peace," *Signs* 8, no. 3 (Spring 1983): 471–89; Carol Gilligan, *In a Different Voice: Psychological Theory and Women's Development* (Cambridge: Harvard University Press, 1982). Also see Nancy Chodorow, *The Reproduction of Mothering: Psychoanalysis and the Sociology of Gender* (Berkeley: University of California Press, 1978).
35. Elshtain, "Antigone's Daughters," p. 59.
36. Ruddick, "Maternal Thinking," p. 346.
37. Ibid.
38. Ruddick, "Pacifying the Forces," p. 479.
39. Ibid.
40. Ruddick, "Maternal Thinking," p. 361.
41. Ruddick, "Pacifying the Forces," pp. 479, 489.
42. Gilligan, *In a Different Voice*, p. 2.
43. Ibid., p. 170.
44. Alice Rossi, "A Biosocial Perspective on Parenting," *Daedalus* 106, no. 2 (Spring 1977): 2. Also see "Viewpoint: Considering 'A Biosocial Perspective on Parenting,'" *Signs* 4, no. 4 (Summer 1979): 695–717; and Rossi, "Maternal-

ism, Sexuality, and the New Feminism," in Joseph Zubin and John Money, eds., *Contemporary Sexual Behavior: Critical Issues in the 1970's* (Baltimore: Johns Hopkins University Press, 1973), pp. 145–74.

45. Alice Rossi, "Equality Between the Sexes: An Immodest Proposal," *Daedalus* 93, no. 2 (Spring 1964): 608.

46. Ibid., p. 609.

47. Ibid.

48. Rossi, "A Biosocial Perspective," p. 4.

49. Elshtain, "Antigone's Daughters," p. 52.

50. Elshtain, "Thank Heaven for Little Girls," pp. 301–2.

51. Jean Bethke Elshtain, "Aristotle, The Public-Private Split, and the Case of the Suffragists," in Elshtain, *The Family in Political Thought*, p. 63.

52. Elshtain, *Public Man, Private Woman*, p. 336.

53. *Questions Feministes*, "Variations," p. 19.

54. Mary Daly, *Gyn/Ecology: The Metaethics of Radical Feminism* (Boston: Beacon Press, 1978); Andrea Dworkin, *Pornography: Men Possessing Women* (New York: Perigree Books/Putnam, 1979); Susan Griffin, *Pornography and Silence: Culture's Revenge Against Nature* (New York: Harper & Row, 1981). Neoconservative Rachel Flick in "The New Feminism and the World of Work," *Public Interest*, no. 71, Spring 1983, notes the fact that radical feminists have always recognized the importance of sexual difference. "Although radical feminism has always had its finger on this truth—radical feminists have maintained a bitter and unshaken conviction of the differences between men and women—the women's movement of the 1960s and 1970s in the professional and middle classes was primarily intepreted in establishing the similarities between the sexes, so that employment opportunities once denied to women could be made available" (p. 35).

55. Rich, *Of Woman Born*, p. 284.

56. Ibid.

57. Susan Griffin, *Woman and Nature: The Roaring Inside Her* (New York: Harper & Row, 1978), p. 227. Also see Charlene Spretnak, *The Politics of Women's Spirituality: Essays on the Rise of Spiritual Power Within the Feminist Movement* (New York: Anchor Books, 1982).

58. Griffin, *Woman and Nature*, p. 73.

59. Ibid., p. 180.

60. Ibid., p. 207.

61. Ibid., p. 226.

62. Daly, *Gyn/Ecology*, p. 11.

63. Ibid., p. 355.

64. Ibid., p. 371.

65. Andrea Dworkin, *Right-Wing Women* (New York: Perigree Books/Putnam, 1983), p. 205.

66. Ibid., p. 206.

67. Ibid., p. 207.

68. Rich, *Of Woman Born*, p. 40.

69. Ibid., p. 295.

70. Ibid., p. 39.

71. Ibid.

72. Ibid., p. 102.

73. Ibid., p. 283.

74. Ibid., p. 37.

75. Ibid., p. 284.

10. Developing Feminist Theory: Sexually Particular, Equal, and Free

The issue of sexual difference has posed a problem for a feminist theory of sexual equality since the beginning of the mid-nineteenth-century American feminist movement. One may grant that the only significant sexual particularity between men and women that has an impact on the organization of society is child-bearing. One may grant also that there is nothing natural about women's nurturing and caring self, and that this self does not exclude intellectual capacity. Still one is left with the problem of constructing a notion of sexual equality given the way these differences presently exist and the way they have been implicated in patriarchal relations.

Right-wing forces and revisionist feminists in this country have focused on this problem and have used it to argue against the quest for sexual equality in the 1980s. The conservative political context in which the issue of sexual difference is presently embedded makes it all the more difficult for feminists to deal with sexual difference on their own terms. Nevertheless, it is important for feminists to confront the issue of sexual difference, or our sexual particularity, from a political standpoint that remains committed to sexual equality. The revisionist attempts to deal with this issue are unacceptable because of their rejection of the notion of sexual equality, their wrongheaded notions about the biological imperatives of sexual distinctness, and their oversimplified conception of the relationship between sex and gender.

The purpose of this final chapter is to examine how the notion of sexual difference both operates ideologically to distort and misrepresent woman's particular individuality and describes real biological difference as well as cultural gendered particularities between men and women. These three levels of analysis—patriarchal ideology, biological sex, and culturalized gender—are not always easily distinguishable within the concept of sexual difference. Yet one needs to attempt to clarify them in order to evaluate and define the possibilities for sexual equality. Because the issue of sexual difference has been used to embrace the notion of woman's "protection" and reject her need for freedom, it becomes necessary to explore how sexual difference in the end denies the possibility of sexual freedom and with it equality between the sexes. Given that society is so much better at protecting us from equality and freedom—let alone privilege and reward—than from danger and discrimination we must be very careful to understand how sexual difference is used to deny us our freedom, and with it sexual equality.

The argument and analysis in this chapter is not always neat. I argue that while biology never exists solely outside its cultural, political definition, it is nevertheless a reality to be contended with. Moreover, while the concept of sexual difference operates as a part of patriarchal ideology and distorts woman's reality as such, there are particular differences that exist between the sexes, both biologically and culturally, which need to be taken into account when constructing a theory of sexual equality for the here and now, rather than the distant future. It is to the exploration of the relationship between sex and gender, biology and culture, sexual difference and sexual equality, and sexual protection and sexual freedom that we now turn.

The Politics of Sex and Gender

The radical feminist position on "woman's essence" suffers from some of the same problems that revisionism does: it often assumes a predetermined biological essence and therefore has a limited understanding of the politics of sex that defines woman's essence. This is true even though radical feminists first elucidated the idea that the personal is political, that there is a politics to sex. They nevertheless collapse sex, as biology, and gender, as its cultural expression, which leads to oversimplified visions of the relationship between the two. Patriarchy becomes male bodies. Feminism becomes the fulfilled body of a woman. Neither the revisionists nor the radical feminists have a sufficient understanding of the relationship between sex and gender to develop a theory of sexual equality.

What feminists need to do is to rethink the relationship between nature and culture, sex and gender, in order to better understand the meaning of sexual politics. Women are both biological sexual selves and simultaneously a politicized gender. This is what it means to think of women as a sexual class: they are at one and the same time an assemblage of individuals defined by their biology within a set of political relations that particularize their bodies. A woman has a body and her body is significant in defining her as a woman within the relations of patriarchy. The *meaning* of her body outside patriarchy does not exist and yet there is such a "thing" as the body. Monique Wittig is somewhat uneasy about this position. Distinguishing between the body and history assumes that there is a biological explanation of the division of women and men that stands outside the social facts.[1] But the fact that we cannot deny that there is such a thing as the body *may* have a meaning that cannot be fully reduced to its social context. While (patriarchal) history has defined the body, one must wonder how the biological body has defined history. This is not to suggest that the body should determine feminist politics, but that feminist politics cannot ignore the body. Neither can feminism afford to ignore how patriarchal politics has used woman's body.

If sex and gender define each other simultaneously, how does one separate the female from the woman? the woman from the female? sex from gender? gender from sex? nature from culture? culture from nature? Gayle Rubin has distinguished the realms of sex and gender in helpful ways:

> Sex is sex, but what counts as sex is equally culturally determined and obtained. Every society also has a sex/gender system—a set of arrangements by which the biological raw material of human sex and procreation is shaped by human, social intervention and satisfied in a conventional manner, no matter how bizarre some of the conventions might be.[2]

Sex is the realm of biological raw material and gender reflects human, social intervention. But even what is thought of as sex is culturally determined. Sex and gender, though different realms, are not separate. Catharine MacKinnon rejects Rubin's view and reduces gender to the realm of (biological) sex and sexuality by setting up a causal relationship between them that assumes that sexuality determines gender. "Sex as gender and sex as sexuality are thus defined in terms of each other, but it is sexuality that determines gender, not the other way around."[3] How does one determine where sexuality ends and gender begins? Or how sex and sexuality are not one and the same? And if, as MacKinnon argues, gender as socially constructed embodies sexuality, and not the reverse, then what can one say about the possibilities for changing gender?

Only when the interrelation between sex and gender is understood can one deal with the problematic aspect of "sexual difference" for feminism. The interrelation reveals the problem of distinguishing between what women want to retain and what they want to reject about themselves, given the complicated history of the patriarchal definition of sexual difference. This ambiguous reality can be seen in the difficulty of distinguishing between the institution of motherhood and biological motherhood; between sexual oppression and sexual desire; between woman's difference and woman's particularity; between woman's inequality and woman's difference. Let us therefore explore the issue of (biological) sex and politics and the way this impacts on the problem of sexual difference for a theory of sexual equality.

The Politics of Biology as Nature

The terms of discourse used in discussing the issues of sexual difference need to be rethought because they are premised on the false dichotomy of nature vs. politics, or nature vs. society. Instead, one needs to ask how the natural or the biological is political and how the political is biological. After all, as Ruth Hubbard has argued: "Women's biology not only is not destiny, but is often not even biology."[4] Biology defined as nature is assumed to be static and unchanging and hence unchangeable. It therefore is assumed to set the constraints in which human experience can operate. But biology as nature is not static and inevitable. One can modify nature. Evelyne Sullerot argues that "given the present state of science and civilization, *it seems to be much easier to change natural than cultural facts.* It was much easier to relieve women from obligatory breastfeeding than to make fathers give babies their bottles. . . . It is inertia built into cultural phenomena that seems to slow down our control over natural phenomena."[5]

Simone de Beauvoir points to the way that cultural determinants have more to do with defining woman than does biology. "Biology is not enough to give an answer to the question that is before us: why is woman the Other?"[6] History intervenes to define humanity: "Human society is never abandoned wholly to nature."[7] This understanding leads to de Beauvoir's now famous statement: "One is not born, but rather becomes a woman. No biological, psychological, or economic fate determines the figure that the human female presents in society: it is civilization as a whole that produces this creature, intermediate between male and eunuch."[8] Yet de Beauvoir also distinguishes between women and the proletariat in that women, unlike the proletariat, have *always* existed. "They are women in virtue of their anatomy and physiology. Throughout history they have always been subordinated to men and hence their dependency is not the result of a historical event or a social change—it was not something that occurred."[9] For de Beauvoir, one is not born a woman, but one is born a female, and being female, one becomes a woman. It is a biological and a historical process.

Although cultural notions of femaleness and femininity reflect aspects of woman's biological characteristics, "biology becomes important largely as it is interpreted by the norms and expectations of human culture and society."[10] Feminists in trying to understand the politics of sex may have overstated the irrelevance of biology. But is is also true that there is no such thing as mere biology. "It is the social construction of biology, not biology itself, that determines women's destiny."[11] As Sherry Ortner has argued, gender in this sense does not "simply reflect or elaborate upon biological 'givens,' but is largely the product of social and cultural processes."[12] On this basis, Nancy Chodorow rejects Rossi's biological argument about women and maternal behavior: "Whatever the hormonal input to human maternal behavior, it is clear that such hormones are neither necessary nor sufficient for it."[13]

Ortner argues that gender is *largely* a product of social and cultural processes; biology plays a part. It is the distance between *largely* and *completely* that remains for feminists to delineate. If there is anything that people conceptualize as an atomized "thing," as an entity unto itself, it is the biological self and biological processes such as reproduction. However, sexual meanings such as male, female, sex, and reproduction cannot really be understood outside the larger context of interrelated meanings established in any given culture.[14] If biology plays a part in defining how gender is constructed and gender plays a part in constructing the meaning of biology, then biology is not static and yet it sets up the confines in which human choices are made. It is therefore never irrelevant that women can bear children, and yet in a sexually egalitarian society a woman should be both equal and free to say that her (individual) capacity for childbearing should not determine her social, political, and economic options. The devaluation of woman, and her "sexual differentiation" from man, is what patriarchal relations of power are primarily about. In demystifying patriarchy—uncovering the politics of sex—we must not reproduce biological arguments that are really as much a part of the politics of patriarchy as they are about biology.

In political theory the body is not dealt with as such. The female body—which is distinguished by its capacity for childbearing—must become central to feminist political theory if a sexual equality is to be constructed that neither denies sexual particularity nor uses it to constrain women. In recognizing the female body, one recognizes the capacity for childbearing. It is a capacity that distinguishes women from men and it is a biological capacity. But it is a biological capacity that will always have political significance because through childbearing a new generation is born and society is in and of itself kept alive. Because childbearing, in this sense, can never be unimportant to any society, it will always be of political interest. In spite of its political significance, sexual reproduction has been relegated by ideology to the realm of biology and nature, as have been woman's life and the gender system. This realization has political usefulness. If woman's sexual difference can be said to be biological, or natural, and not political, then her vital role in the (sexual) reproduction and sustenance of society can be obfuscated. And that is what patriarchal relations are in and of themselves: the political relations that mystify sexual politics in the name of biology.

Woman clearly is not inferior to man biologically but merely different. She has the ability to bear children, which he does not. The inequality is constructed economically, politically, emotionally—in the name of biology. As Sara Ruddick states: "In most societies, however, women are socially powerless in respect to the very reproductive capacities that might make them powerful."[15] Margaret Mead argued early on that men sought to find meaning and prestige in their lives to compensate for the fact that they could not bear children. Men's achievement is defined in terms of doing something a woman cannot do, or does not do, "so that the male may in the course of his life reach a solid sense of irreversible achievement, of which his childhood knowledge of the satisfactions of childbearing have given him a glimpse."[16]

This discussion sets up a clear difference between men and women. Women can bear children, men cannot. But this is a biological reality that has never been only that. The politics of sexual difference has been used to define women's biological particularity as a biological *and* political inequality. One must recognize this political history when discussing sexual difference. There is a politics to sex; the personal structures the political.

Thinking About the Problem of "Sexual Difference" for Feminism

What does it mean to argue that women are sexually different from men? The argument accepts men as the known referent and as such accepts women in a dependent relation to men.[17] Emmanuele de Lesseps reiterates this point when she argues that "man is the reference, woman is the difference."[18] Woman becomes the "other." Monique Wittig has also argued that "men are not different, whites are not different, nor are the masters."[19] It is women who are "different." In this sense, the concept of "sexual difference" reflects an unequal political relation between men and women. Sexual difference, as such, has a political history. Guillaumin, de Lesseps, and Wittig's criticism of the concept "difference" leads them to reject the essentialist argument that presumes the existence of a woman's essence, different from and preferred to man's essence. Although my discussion of sexual difference is limited to the capacity for childbearing, the criticisms raised by Wittig et al. still apply. The sexual difference of childbearing that exists *between* men and women has been used to politically differentiate women *from* men. This political differentiation has constructed women's oppression at the same time as, and possibly because, it reflects women's unique capacity for childbearing.[20] We must be alert to both realities: how childbearing and the institution of motherhood have been used to oppress women and how childbearing can encompass an important, particular, dimension of one's identity. The complicated relationship between sex and gender, and biology and politics, is what defines the problem of sexual difference.

Men and women are sexually different from each other, but this statement obscures more than it clarifies because we are not necessarily as different as we are said to be or different in the ways that we are described. "We are in fact different. But we are not as different FROM men (as false consciousness claims) *as we are different* FROM THAT WHICH men *claim that we are.*"[21] One must wonder how much of what is termed "difference" is biological sex and how much is gender-related, reflecting society and politics. The creation of gender defines biological differences. As such, biology itself does not remain separate from social forces in defining sexual difference. The body is then never merely biology and yet it is at least that.

I therefore cannot accept Elshtain's argument that the sexual distinctness of female from male is necessary to the development of children and the moral ordering of society.[22] I rather agree with Rubin that "far from being an expression of natural differences, exclusive gender identity is the suppression of natural similarities."[23] Before Elshtain can argue for the necessity of sexual distinctness, she must clarify the distinction between sex and gender. What is it, after all is said and done, that necessitates sexual distinctness? And whose interests is it in? This is not to argue, as Elshtain says feminists do, that our sexual identities are unimportant or that sexual differences between men and women, or for that matter among women or among men, are not interesting and exciting. But it is to say that woman's sexual difference from man is not what makes her unique and/or interesting. It is our capacity to partially shape our sexual selves, rather than be wholly determined by them, that makes us human—creative and interesting. When we allow sexual difference to determine the relations between men and women, we allow ourselves to become less interesting, less individual, and, in the end, less human. "Isn't the multiplicity of individual varieties richer than the in-electability of *two* types?"[24]

If one is not born a woman but becomes one by being born female and entering the realm of "femininity" then not "every female human being is necessarily a woman."[25] A woman then is not predetermined by her hormones or by the structure of the female brain but is shaped by her social situation.[26] De Beauvoir rejects biological determinism whether it is used to deny or defend a notion of the "eternal feminine": "A priori, a woman has no special virtue because she is a woman. That would be the most retrograde 'biologism,' in total contradiction with everything I think."[27] Recently, in an interview in *Ms.* magazine, de Beauvoir reiterated her hostility to the notion that woman has a natural essence or is *naturally* more peaceable than man.

> That's absurd. Absurd—because women should desire peace as human beings, not as women! That whole line is completely irrational. After all, men are also fathers. Pacifist women, like pacifist men, can simply say they don't want any more young generations sacrificed. Certainly the point isn't that it's my child, born of my womb, or that it's worse for him to die than the neighbor's son. . . . So women should absolutely let go of that baggage. And if they're being encouraged to be pacifists in the name of motherhood, that's just a ruse by men who are trying to lead women back to the womb. Besides, it's quite obvious that once they're in power, women are exactly like men. You have only to look at Indira Gandhi, Golda Meir, Mrs. Thatcher, and so on. They're not the least bit angels of compassion and pardon or of pacifism.[28]

Nature plays a part in the development of the human being. But the female part of what is considered to be feminine is not the most interesting thing about us. "The fact that we are human beings is infinitely more important than all the peculiarities that distinguish human beings from one another."[29] This does not mean that the emancipation of women requires they be denied their particularity, but it does mean that they should not be confined to it. The distinctiveness of human existence is to be found in the differences that exist between individuals as individuals, not sexual types. *Individual distinction is not to be found in our sexual difference—it actually can develop only when sexual difference becomes politically irrelevant, which is different from saying that it becomes uninteresting.* Woman's sexual difference, her capacity to bear children, can only contribute to her individuality once she is not defined by it.

In this sense, one can argue that the reality of two dichotomous genders involves the exaggeration of sexual difference and the suppression of similarities between men and women.[30] This statement requires that we clarify the relationship between sexual difference and gender difference so that the political usage of biological sex is deciphered. As the editors of *Questions Feministes* have put it: "I will not be a woman nor a man in the contemporary historical sense. I will be a Person in a woman's body."[31] However, this should not mean that the biological component be entirely denied: "The social existence of men and women does not depend at all on their nature as male and female, i.e., on the shape of their anatomical sexual organs."[32] After all, the biological body is a reality even if it is never merely or purely a biological entity devoid of history and society. If the biological is used as an ideology rationalizing the political, then the way that the biological is political and how the political is biological must also be dealt with. As we now entertain the question of the role of biology in politics we must not forget that this relation structures patriarchal relations themselves.

This leads to another set of questions about the nature of feminism and its relationship to the question of sexual difference. Monique Wittig asks whether the feminist is one who struggles to destroy the sexual-class system on behalf of the sexual class of women or whether the feminist is one who fights for women and in their defense.[33] One must wonder how feminism can embrace the concept of sexual difference and not relegate woman to significant aspects of her present oppression. Wittig thinks it is impossible: "It puts us in a position of fighting within the class 'women' not as the other classes do, for the disappearance of our class, but for the defense of 'woman' and its reinforcement."[34]

It is true that many women have developed qualities within the present system of sexual and political differentiation—such as loving, caring, supporting—that it is hard to imagine not wanting in a sexually egalitarian society. But we need to remember that the other side of many of these qualities is the dependence, anxiety, fear, and insecurity that also exist within many women. As Wittig points out, "What the concept of 'woman is wonderful' accomplishes is that it retains for defining women the best features [best according to whom?] which oppression has granted us, and it does not radically question the categories 'man' and 'woman' which are political categories and not natural givens."[35]

In the end, feminists must figure out how we understand the relationship between sexual difference and sexual equality. The two need not be mutually exclusive, although the political past does not speak well for their union. Nevertheless, I think it would be a mistake to choose either in favor of "difference" or in favor of an equality that requires sexual sameness. Because "the idea of the equality of the sexes often stirs up a fear of losing bodily identity," we must think politically about how sexual difference can be embodied within a theory of sexual egalitarianism.[36] When we speak of wanting to preserve altruism, nonviolence, and the love of children, we need to make sure that we do not try to have these qualities remain as differences."Equality supposes simply that everyone has a right to the socially possible. To want a difference to remain a difference is to establish a prohibition."[37]

Feminism and the "Problem" of Sexual Difference

The present renewal of the discussion of sexual difference is a reaction against feminism. It is worth remembering that "biological explanations of behavior characterize conservative eras."[38] Although one need not reject feminism in order to believe sexual difference exists, one can, like Friedan or Elshtain, use the discussion of sexual difference to indict feminism and sexual egalitarianism with it. Woman's difference from man has structured her oppression, and in reconsidering how difference can be used to dismember the relations of patriarchy feminists must be careful to clarify a commitment to sexual egalitarianism. Unlike capitalist patriarchal society, a sexually egalitarian society will not be organized around the sexual differentiation of woman from man but rather around the characteristics they share in common, while recognizing sexual particularity.

This means that men and women will be politically the same by virtue of the fact that sexual difference has nothing to do with how much sexual freedom, economic independence, racial equality, intellectual opportunity, and so on, anyone has. Instead of reacting *against* the radical impulse of feminism, one needs to utilize this radical potential for defining a radically feminist conception of sexual equality. If sexual difference, specifically woman's capacity for childbearing, is not to be used to restrict woman's freedom of choice, then bearing children will have to be differentiated from the institution of motherhood, from women's economic dependence on men, from her secondary wage-earner status, from the system of heterosexual controls, from notions of patriarichal sexuality. Only when woman's sexual difference is no longer the basis of woman's secondary political status can one begin to explore the meaning of sexual egalitarianism, which requires not only economic and racial equality and freedom of sexual preference but equality in the (hetero)sexual relations between men and women and their relation to sexual reproduction.

Feminism must develop a sexual theory of equality—one that does not desexualize women and that deals responsibly with the reality of the "politics of sex." Interestingly enough, the New Right, neoconservatives, and revisionist feminists, in their rejection of the radical impulse of feminism as part of the crisis of liberalism, have pinpointed the need for such a theory. Conservative forces not only have sought to replace the commitment to sexual equality with sexual difference but have done so while arguing for sexual protection rather than sexual freedom for women. Woman's difference is said to require her protection rather than her freedom or equality. I would therefore argue that in order to develop a theory of sexual equality, feminists not only have to redirect the discussions of sexual difference toward a commitment to equality but also have to establish the importance of sexual freedom for a theory of sexual equality. But first we need to examine the "politics of sex," which is embodied in the struggle toward sexual equality.

The Politics of Sex in Sexual Equality

Existing theories about sexual equality have problems because they most often assume sexual equality means economic or political equality.[39] A theory of sexual equality that focuses on the sex in sexual equality, meaning the biological reality of the female with the capacity of childbearing, has not been formulated. Clearly men and women are not the same in terms of their sexual selves (most importantly in terms of childbearing) so a simple economic or political egalitarianism assuming the sameness between men and women will not work. This does not mean, however, that the commonalities between men and women are less important than their differences. It just means that sexual particularity must be taken into account. And this is exactly what the New Right antifeminists, neoconservatives, and revisionist feminists are so eager to point out.

Can women be recognized as sexually different and yet sexually politically equal? This can happen only when the social relations of society are organized to create woman's equality while recognizing her particularity. Equality does not mean merely sameness as it does for Schlafly and Friedan. And it does not mean being equivalent to or similar to men as they are now without equality.[40] Sexual equality rather means that men and women would share in the power relations of society with no regard to their (biological) sex or sexual preference. This would not mean that men and women would have identical access to the systems of power but rather that their access to power would equalize the different sexual relations they have to the activity of childbearing. Central to establishing such equality is the right to abortion and reproductive freedom, freedom of sexual preference, adequate day care facilities, new visions of child care, paternity leave, and so on. Health care, economic independence, racial equality, and sexual freedom also become requisites of such a notion of sexual equality.

Sexual equality necessitates the destruction of the sexual-class system. This does not mean the denial of male and female life but does mean the redefinition of "man" and "woman" as we know them. It means the destruction of gender while retaining our sexual selves, and organizing society to recognize childbearing and rearing as integral to the reproduction of society rather than as an economic, psychological, and cultural liability. Instead of struggling to preserve the caring and loving aspects that have developed within the present system of mothering, as Elshtain argues, we must dismantle the institutions—sexual division of labor, sexual ghetto in the labor force, enforced heterosexual marriage—in which mothering presently takes place and then try to redefine these loving qualities in new ways.

There is a real problem in imagining what it might look like to dismantle the institution of motherhood while retaining biological motherhood because it would require an entire reorganization of the sexual, economic, political, and cultural arrangements of society. In essence it would mean the destruction of the linchpin of patriarchal relations. And American society is nowhere near this revolutionary moment in history. Instead, we are at the point of demanding shared parenting, pluralistic models of family life, flextime, equity in the labor force, affirmative action programs, and so on. These demands do begin to erode the institution of motherhood, however, and are therefore a necessary step toward establishing sexual equality.

The contradictory aspect of the institution of motherhood—that it is both creative and oppressive—has intensified today as a majority of married women have needed to enter the labor force. The institution embodies the unequal sexual, economic, political, cultural aspects that are tied up with relegating women to a secondary status in the private sphere where childbearing and rearing are performed. Biological motherhood (the bearing of children) becomes further differentiated within the institution of motherhood as women leave the private sphere for the market. They have less time to be mothers and therefore need a series of supports that are becoming less, not more, available. Women's entry into the labor force is redefining the institution of motherhood in ways that intensify the contradictory aspects of capitalist patriarchy. Woman is to be both mother and wage-earner. Most women's options in the labor force are seriously limited by the patriarchal organization of society, family, and market, and their options in performing their duties as mothers are tied up with this patriarchal status. Yet at the same time that women as gendered selves are constrained in and by the institution of motherhood, they also recognize and value the positive aspects of biological mother-hood.

This is what Schlafly alludes to when she argues that given the present options of most women, they are better off cuddling a baby than a typewriter. Although this is not a fully accurate read-ing, and most women do not have a real choice in the matter of whether they must earn a living, the fact that women's relation to childbearing and rearing can be a source of joy and creativity is true. Although patriarchal motherhood has been a major source of women's oppression, it also contains the possibility of creativity and pleasure in women's lives. It is hard to think about giving up (biological) motherhood, which is a source of at least partial joy, while other relations of patriarchal privilege that limit and curtail women's lives are left intact. This dilemma reflects the contradic-tory nature of motherhood within patriarchal society. It simulta-neously embodies creativity and alienation, potential power and oppression, and is therefore not easily given up. Recent de-velopments in child custody cases having to do with "fathers' rights" are a case in point of women's ambiguous situation in the institution of motherhood, which defines her as childbearer.

The "tender years doctrine"—the belief that the early years of a child are best spent with the mother—reflects an aspect of the patriarchal institution of motherhood that assigns early childrear-ing to women.[41] The present challenge to this doctrine made by fathers seeking custody catches women in their unprivileged posi-tion as mothers. In most cases the tender years doctrine is the mother's only protection in a custody battle because the father/husband will most often be better off financially, more established professionally, and so on. Without the tender years doctrine, which favors the woman as the "mother," she has little protection in a custody battle. Although the challenging of the tender years doctrine can be seen as a rejection of the patriarchal notion of motherhood, it is something women still need, given their am-biguous position as mothers: childbearing has relegated women to a secondary status and yet it is one of the more creative options allowed a majority of women.

Annamay Sheppard, discussing the unspoken premises in cus-tody litigation, states that "it is understandable if some feminists see erosion of the doctrinal preference for maternal custody as a premature, even punitive, response to women's equality claims and continue to invoke the tender years presumption."[42] This position creates problems for the demands for gender neutrality, however. So Sheppard argues that we need a custody theory that recognizes the principle of equal parental rights, "but, like racial equality advocacy, takes into realistic account and adequately compensates for the starting gate inequalities that female parents have inherited from the Victorian past."[43]

Patriarchal institutions protect women within their relations of dependence *at the same time that the system of protection based on the notion of "women's difference" is part of their oppression.* To give up the limited protection in the hopes of dismantling the relations of patriarchy is a frightening proposition. The antifeminists choose protection for women over equality and do not see this protection as part of the relations of patriarchy. The dilemma is that the relations of protection justified on the basis of women's difference from men are part of patriarchal privilege but can also be used for women, in their *partial* interests, while patriarchal relations continue to be challenged. The problem is delineating a politics that grasps this dilemma but does not support the patriarchal politics implied by it. A politics that attempts to create sexual equality must recognize this problem: that the politics of sex necessitates women's protection in and from patriarchal relations at the same time that it must move beyond protection and the notion of "difference" toward equality.

Protection, Sexual Freedom, and Sexual Equality

The issue of women's protection looms as a significant problem for feminists. Antifeminists such as Schlafly and Gilder have an easy time pointing out that women are in need of "protection." What often masquerades as protection, however, is a dynamic central to woman's oppression, or to what is used to differentiate woman from man as being less capable of taking care of herself either sexually or economically. Given present economic inequalities in society, it is often true that women are less capable of being independent. As a feminist one hardly wants to protect women in this dependence, and yet one does not want to punish women either. In this same way, the feminist wants to protect women from sexual exploitation and abuse and yet does not want to deny women the expression of their sexuality. This particular concern with (sexual) protection lies at the heart of both feminist and antifeminist politics. Until feminists can figure out a better way to deal with the contradictory aspects of woman's sexuality— that we need freedom and equality as much as or more than we need protection—a full notion of sexual equality cannot be explored.

Conservative forces have most often denied woman equality on the basis of her need for sexual protection. After all, if woman needs protection, she is different from man and hence not equal, not the same. The concern with protection sets women apart from men with a different set of needs. It is also argued by conservatives that because woman is different (weaker, more passive), she needs protection from sexual abuse. They construct the argument both ways. We must step outside this traditional conservative framework, which adopts sexual difference and protection as its key concerns regulating women's lives, and demand a sexual equality based on sexual freedom. Sexual equality requires equality in sexual matters; it recognizes the particularity of sex while not denying the necessity of freedom.

The relationship between sexual equality and sexual freedom is different from the relationship between economic equality and freedom in the marketplace. Whereas freedom in the marketplace can often negate the possibility of economic equality, sexual freedom is a prerequisite for sexual equality; without freedom one is left being "protected."

We are not free to deny the need for protection given our present patriarchal society. By protecting women from forms of abuse, society in fact gives women a certain freedom. But we also need to recognize that women, in actual fact, are not adequately protected from sexual abuse or economic inequality, or wife-battering, and that we never will be sufficiently protected in these realms. By arguing for particular forms of protection, given specific historical relations—such as the tender years doctrine, pregnancy disability payments, or protective labor laws—one formulates the beginnings of a sexual equality that recognizes difference between men and women as it presently exists. And present laws also must recognize woman's vulnerability in the realm of sexual abuse such as in rape. But we must move beyond the ideology of protection while recognizing the actual need for protection in order to really free women. The purpose of the law and the social relations of society matter: is the purpose to curtail and constrain women within the relations of capitalist patriarchal society or to expand sexual equality?

The concern with protection is always problematic for feminism because it operates within the constraints of patriarchal privilege. Fighting for the protection of women as a political strategy reflects the problem of limiting women to the need for protection, which makes them less than men, in need of protection both from men and by men. It is therefore important that as we argue for the protection of women in custody struggles, or labor law, or comparable worth, or antipornography rulings, we do not reproduce the patriarchal motive in protection legislation. Rather, we must move beyond this position and imagine the possibilities of a sexual equality that no longer is limited to protection and instead explores the potential for freedom.

The meaning of the term "sexual" is not limited to the realm of sexual reproduction although my discussion has been largely limited to that realm. In the end a full discussion of sexual equality will have to entertain the realm of sexuality itself. Although the realm of sexuality or woman's biological self should not be reduced to her reproductive capacity, this capacity is never irrelevant and becomes a necessary focus for a theory of hetero(sexual) equality. (Hetero)sexuality for women is almost always tied up with the possibility of sexual reproduction and poses the problem of needed sexual protection. But once feminists establish the necessity of woman's sexual freedom, they need no longer limit women to protection, difference, inequality. However, we are still left with the problem that protection remains necessary. The problem is that *while* one attempts to establish woman's sexual freedom (and equality), her present difference and certain protections must be taken into account.

An interesting example of the feminist dilemma resulting from a focus on (sexual) protection rather than on freedom can be seen in the <u>antipornography movement</u> in the United States, led by radical feminists. The radical feminist antipornography stance has similarities with that of evangelical Jerry Falwell and anti-feminist Phyllis Schlafly. Thus biological essentialist epistemology, which assumes a conservative vision of human existence, is not the only area of similarity between radical feminists and the New Right. This in no way is meant to say that radical feminists are basically the same as the New Right. It rather is meant to highlight the fact that despite the *completely different politics* of radical feminists and New Rightists in terms of what they believe women's life choices should be, they still agree in profound ways that woman must be sexually protected from man; that too much sexual freedom is a dangerous thing. The antipornography movement poses a dilemma for feminism and also reflects the dilemma inherent in feminism in that it addresses the important issue of trying to protect women from sexual objectification and abuse, and it also denies women a certain exploratory sexual freedom.

Given the contradictory nature of our sexual selves defined within the relations of patriarchy one must wonder what it means to be antipornography. Defining pornography is a problem in and of itself; it is most often distinguished from erotica. Erotica is defined in the dictionary as sexual love that tends to excite sexual pleasure or desire. The dictionary defines pornography as a description of prostitutes or whores or a portrayal of erotic behavior designed to cause sexual excitement. The problem is that erotica can be pornographic and pornography can be erotic. The distinction depends on the social and political relations involved, just as it does for intercourse as an act of love or rape. The problem becomes how to be antipornography when pornography depends on unequal relations, without becoming antierotica.

When one looks at prevailing radical feminist definitions of pornography, distinctions between erotica and pornography, sex and violence, violence and pornography, sex and pornography, merge. As a result it becomes very difficult to think about the issue of sex in any other than protective terms. Gloria Steinem defines pornography as follows: "Its message is violence, dominance, and conquest. It is sex being used to reinforce some inequality, or to create one, or to tell us that pain and humiliation . . . are really the same as pleasure."[44] Robin Morgan views "pornography as the theory, and rape as the practice."[45] Susan Griffin argues that sexuality, in pornography, becomes woman's humiliation.[46] Catharine MacKinnon regards sexual harassment, rape, and ordinary heterosexual intercourse as not all that different.[47] And Adrienne Rich somewhat similarly states: "Pornography does not simply create a climate in which sex and violence are interchangeable, it widens the range of behavior considered acceptable from men in heterosexual intercourse."[48]

Most of the antipornography movement writing links sex and violence, heterosexual sex and rape. Feminism has given up too much here. Although patriarchal relations do define the context in which sex is experienced, not all sex is violent nor is heterosexual intercourse when consented to the same as rape. If we collapse the contradictory reality that all sex has the potential for the erotic and the capacity to be pornographically objectified the only thing we can focus on is the need for protection. And, unless one wants to argue that all sexually active women are victims of false consciousness, one must deal with the contradictory mechanism by which, in spite of the patriarchal contours, heterosexual women desire sexual pleasure with men, women are aroused by pornography, lesbians desire sex in a patriarchal society, and so on. Women seem to operate while taking risks all the time. Feminist theory has yet to grapple with this reality sufficiently. The antiporn movement says that it is not against sex, or erotica, but against pornography. Given their view of sex as violence, however, there is no erotica, and women are left needing protection, not freedom.[49]

It is also important to recognize that at the same time that pornography objectifies and degrades women as sexual objects, it is subversive to patriarchal culture, which defines woman as an asexual mother. Although one might want to reject both visions as forms of patriarchal sexuality, the asexual notion of woman is no more realistic than the (sexual) pornographic one. Pornography does present women as sexual, however deformed a representation this may be. One is left to wonder whether women draped in the chador in Iran and Afghanistan (which hides their bodies) present any more or less a pornographic image, if pornography is depicted as the objectification or misrepresentation of sexuality. One reacts differently to the naked Playboy bunny and the Iranian woman hidden in cloth. Does the latter seem more protected? more free? more equal?

As a feminist, one is always caught in the dilemma of living simultaneously in and against the society as it exists. To the extent that we are in the society we have internalized values about sexuality that we may not want to hold, or even worse, we may not be self-conscious about holding. To the extent that women feel violated by pornography this is in part because we are in the society and have adopted the (liberal patriarchal) values that sex is private, belongs in the privacy of one's home, is potentially dangerous (unwanted pregnancies or forceful rape). Our bodies make us feel vulnerable and we feel more protected when clothed and hidden. Our sexuality, which has been used against us in limiting our ability to determine full and meaningful lives, leaves us feeling ambiguous about our sexual selves. These values, these feelings residing in us, that elicit our antipornographic stance have been used as much against women as they have been used to protect women. The notion that sex is private has relegated it to the sphere of the natural and necessary, rather than the political realm of which it is a part. Although radical feminists themselves uncovered the important reality that sex is political, an aspect of the antipornography movement attempts to reprivatize sex. Privacy and protection have both been a part of the dynamic of the sexual oppression of women.

The notion that the personal is political demystifies the idea that sex and sexuality, or private life, or family life are disconnected from public and political life. The way that sex is practiced, thought about, and acted out is defined in and through the relations of power in society. The notion that sex is private—which is contradicted by the laws about sex in any state—or that sexual life is apolitical (natural) has been as damaging for women in their struggle for equality as any public depiction of sex has been. So why focus on pornography as the central underpinning of male domination? And what happens to the possibility of constructing a notion of sexual freedom and equality as one does this? If sex is represented by pornography and feminists equate sex with violence, we lose the ability to construct a notion of feminist erotica, and with it a notion of sexual freedom. If sexual freedom, as opposed to protection, is a prerequisite for sexual equality, feminists must remain committed to this exploration. This point is not meant to ignore the fact that protection in some circumstances may also be a condition of freedom, however.

Feminists must argue against the misrepresentation of people's bodies, their feelings, their desires, thoughts, and yearnings. We must fight the objectification, the exploitation, and the denial of women's lives. But we must be very careful how we construct a politics out of this, particularly given the reactionary political climate today. As New Right antifeminism stresses the violence of sex and the promiscuous aspects of sexual freedom, and Betty Friedan asks feminists to stay centered in a politics about the ERA and to stay away from questions related to sexuality, feminists who remain committed to equality must commit themselves to exploring the realm of sexual freedom. Ellen Willis has argued this well:

> In short, it is a losing proposition for feminists to compete with the right in trying to soothe women's fears of sexual anarchy. We must of course acknowledge those fears and the legitimate reasons for them, but our interest as feminists is to demonstrate that a law-and-order approach to sex can only result in a drastic curtailment of our freedom. In the long run, we can win only if women [and men] want freedom [and love] more than they fear its consequences.[50]

The antiporn movement is a necessary radical feminist indictment of patriarchal society and privilege. But no radical movement is solely autonomous and free to control and represent itself. This is true for the antiporn movement. One therefore must wonder how the antiporn movement is useful to patriarchal society in terms of asserting certain controls on the expression of sexuality itself. It is both these things at the same time: a radical indictment of patriarchal sexuality and a controlling and limiting force on sexual freedom. It is a movement that is both *in* and *against* society.

What do we do with these contradictory realities? We must protest pornography that explicitly depicts violence while rejecting the antiporn movement's conflation of sex and violence. We must demand erotica and the sexual freedom to explore it even if this means possible danger. The danger already exists, feminist explorations are not what create it, although the conservative forces today say that they do. Better to have a suspect erotica and sensuality that one can argue and fight about than to be denied one's sexuality and sense of it all. Let feminists not replace the discussion of sex with the equation of sexual violence; or the concern for freedom with protection; or the commitment to equality with difference. We, as feminists, will lose too much. We will lose the ability to define our sexuality and will be given protection once again, because it is on the basis of sexual protection that sexual equality has so often been denied.

Sexual freedom, however this remains to be defined, must underlie a theory of sexual equality.[51] In the most general meaning, sexual freedom must recognize the need for protection of women in patriarchal society, but we must not relegate feminist politics to its desire for safety. Sexual freedom will have to encompass freedom of sexual preference, a nonpatriarchal sexuality, and reproductive freedom. It will also be predicated on a nonracist and noneconomic class hierarchy. These commitments will allow the reformulation of a sexual equality that can encompass woman's particularity as a childbearer. Equality in this sense means individuals' having equal value as human beings. In this vision equality does not mean to be like men, as they are today, or to have equality with one's oppressor. But this notion of equality does not fear the sameness of the sexes, because we are as much alike as we are particular.

Given the crisis of liberalism and the rejection of the notion of equality today, it is imperative that feminists continue to demand equality particularly in the realm of sex and as females who have the capacity for childbearing. Feminists will have to map out this notion of sexual equality and figure out how we can get from a society in which the state is dismantling affirmative action programs to a society organized at its core as sexually egalitarian and sexually free. We can draw from liberalism its commitment to freedom; from socialism its commitment to egalitarianism; and from feminism its demand that these notions of equality and freedom apply to the realm of sexuality and personal life. In this sense we need a theory of sexual equality that deals straightforwardly with the fact that at this point in history we are both in and against society; female and woman; sexed and gendered.

It is no accident that so much of the New Right, neoconservative, and revisionist feminist argument against equality and particularly sexual equality is tied up with the fear of sexual freedom. The narcissistic society is supposedly feminist, homosexual, and sexually promiscuous. Sexual controls are needed to reorder society toward less equality and more (patriarchal) order. Amidst the promiscuity antifeminists call for the protection of women, and revisionists speak of how difference makes equality impossible. Feminists, as frightened as we might be, must reject the choice of protection over freedom and difference over equality, and struggle to achieve a sexually egalitarian society, which is also nonracist and economically just. Sexual equality, in this sense, will truly mean an extraordinarily different society from that we know. It is what the conservative forces fear. It is what feminists must recommit ourselves to.

NOTES

1. Monique Wittig, "One Is Not Born a Woman," *Feminist Issues* 1, no. 2 (Winter 1981): 48.
2. Gayle Rubin, "The Traffic in Women: Notes on the 'Political Economy' of Sex," in Rayna Reiter, ed., *Toward an Anthropology of Women* (New York: Monthly Review Press, 1975), p. 165.
3. Catharine MacKinnon, "Feminism, Marxism, Method, and the State: An Agenda for Theory," *Signs* 7, no. 3 (Spring 1982): 531.
4. Ruth Hubbard, Mary Sue Henifin, Barbara Fried, eds., *Women Look at Biology Looking at Women* (Cambridge: Schenkman, 1979), p. xiii. Also see Ruth Hubbard, Mary Sue Henifin, and Barbara Fried, eds., *Biological Woman—The Convenient Myth* (Cambridge: Schenkman, 1982).
5. Evelyne Sullerot, "The Feminine (Matter of) Fact," trans. Yvonne Rochette-Ozzello, in Elaine Marks and Isabelle de Courtivron, eds., *New French Feminism* (Amherst: University of Massachusetts Press, 1980), p. 158.
6. Simone de Beauvoir, *The Second Sex* (New York: Bantam, 1949), p. 33.
7. Ibid., p. 456.
8. Ibid., p. 249.
9. Ibid., p. xviii.
10. Michelle Zimbalist Rosaldo and Louise Lamphere, eds., *Woman, Culture and Society* (Stanford: Stanford University Press, 1974), p. 4.
11. Janet Sayers, *Biological Politics: Feminist and Antifeminist Perspectives* (New York: Tavistock, 1982), p. 105.
12. Sherry Ortner, "Accounting for Sexual Meanings," in Sherry Ortner and Harriet Whitehead, eds., *Sexual Meanings: The Cultural Construction of Gender and Sexuality* (Cambridge: Cambridge University Press, 1981), p. 10.
13. Nancy Chodorow, *The Reproduction of Mothering: Psychoanalysis and the Sociology of Gender* (Berkeley: University of California Press, 1978), p. 28.
14. Ortner, "Accounting for Sexual Meanings," p. 2.

15. Sara Ruddick, "Maternal Thinking," *Feminist Studies* 6, no. 2 (Summer 1980): 343.
16. Margaret Mead, *Male and Female: A Study of the Sexes in a Changing World* (New York: Morrow Quill, 1949), p. 160.
17. Collette Guillaumin, "The Questions of Difference," *Feminist Issues* 2, no. 1 (Spring 1982): 45.
18. Emmanuele de Lesseps, "Female Reality: Biology or Society?" *Feminist Issues* 1, no. 2 (Winter 1981): 101.
19. Monique Wittig, "The Straight Mind," *Feminist Issues* 1, no. 1 (Summer 1980): 109.
20. See Mary O'Brien, *The Politics of Reproduction* (London: Routledge & Kegan Paul, 1981).
21. Guillaumin, "Questions of Difference" p. 43.
22. Jean Bethke Elshtain, "Against Androgeny," *Telos* 47 (Spring 1981): 16–17.
23. Rubin, "The Traffic in Women," p. 180.
24. de Lesseps, "Female Reality," p. 100.
25. de Beauvoir, *The Second Sex*, p. xiii.
26. Ibid., p. 362.
27. Simone de Beauvoir, "From an Interview," trans. Elaine Marks, in *New French Feminism*, p. 153. Also see the proceedings from "The Second Sex—Thirty Years Later," Conference on Feminist Theory, September 27–29, 1979, New York University.
28. Quoted in Alice Schwarzer, "Simone de Beauvoir Tells About Sartre," *Ms. Magazine* 12, no. 2 (August 1983): 90.
29. de Beauvoir, *The Second Sex*, p. 685. For further discussion of the cultural aspects of sexuality and sexual difference see Michel Foucault, *The History of Sexuality* (New York: Pantheon, 1978); *Radical History Review*, "Sexuality in History," 20 (Spring/Summer 1979); Martha Vacinus, "Sexuality and Power: A Review of Current Work in the History of Sexuality," *Feminist Studies* 8, no. 1 (Spring 1982): 133–56; Jeffrey Weeks, *Sex, Politics and Society: The Regulation of Sexuality Since 1800* (New York: Longman, 1981).
30. Barrie Thorne, "Feminist Rethinking of the Family: An Overview," in Barrie Thorne and Marilyn Yalom, eds. *Rethinking the Family: Some Feminist Questions* (New York: Longman, 1982), p. 9.
31. Editors of Questions Feministes, "Variations of Some Common Themes," *Feminist Issues* 1, no. 1 (Summer 1980): 16.
32. Ibid., p. 5.
33. Wittig, "One Is Not Born a Woman," p. 50.
34. Ibid.
35. Ibid.
36. de Lesseps, "Female Reality," p. 100.
37. Ibid., p. 101.
38. Pauline Bart, "Biological Determinism and Sexism: Is It All in the Ovaries?" in Ann Arbor Science for the People, ed., *Biology as a Social Weapon* (Minneapolis: Burgess, 1977), p. 69.
39. See Philip Green, *The Pursuit of Inequality* (New York: Pantheon, 1981); and Michael Walzer, *Radical Principles: Reflections of an Unreconstructed Democrat* (New York: Basic Books, 1980). Also see Maxine Molyneux, "Socialist Societies Old and New: Program Towards Women's Emancipation," *Feminist Review* 8 (Summer 1981): 1–34.
40. Editors of Questions Feministes, "Variations," p. 13.
41. Annamay Sheppard, "Unspoken Premises in Custody Litigation," *Women's*

Rights Law Reporter 7, no. 3 (Spring 1982): 229–34; and Wendy Williams, "The Equality Crisis: Some Reflections on Culture, Courts and Feminism," ibid., pp. 175–200.

42. Sheppard, "Unspoken Premises," p. 233.

43. Ibid., p. 234.

44. Gloria Steinem, "Erotica and Pornography: A Clear and Present Difference," in Laura Lederer, ed., Take Back the Night (New York: William Morrow, 1980), p. 37. For an interesting discussion of pornography see Angela Carter, The Sadeian Woman and the Ideology of Pornography (New York: Harper Colophon, 1980), and Irene Diamond, "Pornography and Repression: A Reconsideration," Signs, Journal of Women in Culture and Society, Special Issue "Women, Sex, and Sexuality," 5, no. 4 (Summer 1980): 686–701.

45. Robin Morgan, "Theory and Practice: Pornography and Rape," in Lederer, ed., Take Back the Night, p. 139.

46. Susan Griffin, Pornography and Silence: Culture's Revenge Against Nature (New York: Harper & Row, 1981), p. 39.

47. See MacKinnon, "Feminism, Marxism, Method, and the State."

48. Adrienne Rich, "Compulsory Heterosexuality and Lesbian Experience," in Catharine Stimpson and Ethel Spector Person, eds., Women, Sex, and Sexuality (Chicago: University of Chicago Press, 1980), p. 72.

49. See Andrea Dworkin, Pornography: Men Possessing Women (New York: Perigree Books Putnam, 1979). Also see Robin Linden et al., Against Sadomasochism: A Radical Feminist Analysis (California: Frog in the Well Press, 1982). For feminist critiques of the antipornography film "Not a Love Story," see Martha Aspler-Burnett, " 'Not a Love Story' . . . Notes on the Film," Cine-Tracts 4, no. 4 (Winter 1982): 1–3; see the rest of this same issue for other critiques as well; Susan Barrowclough, "Not a Love Story," Screen 23, no. 5 (November–December 1982): 22–34.

50. Ellen Willis, "Toward a Feminist Sexual Revolution," Social Text 2, no. 3 (Fall 1982): 210.

51. This issue of what a theory of sexual freedom should look like has been discussed in terms of a libertarian viewpoint. Although I think this view is both problematic and insufficient for a feminist theory of sexual freedom, it raises important issues. See Pat Califia, The Book of Lesbian Sexuality (California: Naiad Press, 1980); Samois, Coming to Power, Writings and Graphics in Lesbian S/M (California: Up Press, 1981). For an interesting critique of these books see Ann Jones, "Fit to Be Tied," The Nation 236, no. 21 (May 28, 1983): 667–72. For other feminist-related discussions of a theory of sexual freedom see Deirdre English, Amber Hollibaugh, and Gayle Rubin, "Talking Sex: A Conversation on Sexuality and Feminism," Socialist Review 2, no. 4 (July–August 1981): 43–62; Diary of a Conference on Sexuality, the proceedings of "The Scholar and the Feminist Conference," Barnard College, April 24, 1982; Linda Gordon and Ellen Dubois, "Seeking Ecstasy on the Battlefield: Danger and Pleasure in Nineteenth Century Feminist Sexual Thought," Feminist Studies 9, no. 1 (Spring 1983): 7–26; M/F: A Feminist Journal, "Double Issue— Sexuality," nos. 5 and 6, 1981; Amber Hollibaugh and Cherríe Moraga, "What We're Rollin Around in Bed With," Heresies 3, no. 4, issue 12 (1981): 58–62.

Index

Kirkpatrick, Jeane, 62, 134
Kristol, Irving, 62, 63, 65, 68, 69–70, 71–72

Labor/capital conflict, 100–1
Labor force, 51. *See also* Women in labor force
Labor laws, 247, 248
Laclau, Ernesto, 91
Lasch, Christopher, 105–7, 210; *Haven in a Heartless World*, 59n4, 214
Laski, Harold, 91
Lautenberg, Frank, 145
Law, 99, 248; patriarchal, 97–100
Laxalt, Paul, 35–37, 42, 57, 180
Laxalt-Jepsen Family Protection Act, 131
Legal Services, 120
Legislation, reform, 180, 181
Lesbian feminism, 162
Lesbian rights, 25, 209n30
Lesbians(ism), 203, 250
Lesseps, Emmanuele de, 237
Levin, Michael, 72–73
Lewis, Drew, 57, 134
Liberal establishment, 59–60n7
Liberal feminism, 18, 139, 162, 164, 181, 186; and the state, 23–27
Liberalism, 71, 88, 127, 131, 166, 253; conflict within ideology of, 87, 89, 91, 96–97; excesses of, 74, 165, 179, 184, 190, 199; feminism subversive to, 12–13; as ideology, 41, 191; neoconservatives and, 57, 62–86; patriarchal bias in, 73–74, 78; and "race of life," 62–65; support for, by public, 30–31, 37. *See also* Crisis of liberalism; Welfare state liberalism
Liberty, 62–63, 68
Library Court, 43
Lipset, Seymour Martin, 77
Love/work integration, 192, 196, 198, 199, 200, 205

McClure, James, 42
McGovern, George, 20–21
MacKinnon, Catharine, 151, 233–34, 250
Male privilege, 17, 73, 75, 96, 155
Male role, 11, 12, 53, 54, 55, 56, 115–16
Man/male distinction, 109–10
Market(place), 41, 50–52, 75–76, 82–83;

conflict with institution of motherhood, 94, 96–97; patriarchal authority in, 115–16, 118
Marriage, 48, 75, 107, 152, 195; neoconservative view of, 78–79, 82
Married wage-earning women, 49–53, 128, 170. *See also* Women in labor force
Marshner, Connie, 43
Martinez, Arabella, 201
Marx, Karl, 151
Marxism, Marxists, 94, 147–49, 153
Marxist feminism, 210
Masculinity, 26, 54–55
"Maternal thinking," 216–18, 225, 227
Mead, Margaret, 237
Meany, George, 43
Medicaid, 63, 101, 109, 120, 122
Medicaid abortions, 25, 26
Medicare, 63
Meese, Edwin, III, 135
Meir, Golda, 182, 239
Men, 13, 30, 115. *See also* Black men
Meritocracy, 64–65
Meyer, Jack, 68, 69
Middle class, 43
Militarism, 30, 117, 156; and antifeminism, 32–35, 36
Military spending, 28, 122, 126
Mill, John Stuart, 182
Minorities, 117–18. *See also* Blacks
Model City Programs, 63
Moral Majority, 23, 37, 43, 163
"Moral mothers," 32, 34
Moral order, 79, 171, 174, 238
"Moral society," 34, 36
"Moral wars," 32
Morality, 54, 55, 127
Morgan, J. P., 171
Morgan, Robin, 249–50
Mother hatred, 107–9
Motherhood, 163, 189, 190, 227; freedom to choose, 95, 179, 193, 194–200, 202, 203, 204, 206, 207. *See also* Institution of motherhood; Working mothers
Moynihan, D. Patrick, 62, 71, 130
Mulhauser, Karen, 20, 21

Narcissism, 78, 79, 88, 212, 254
National Abortion Rights Action League, 43